Suicides and Jazzers

NOT ADDED BY
UNIVERSITY OF MICHIGAN LIBRARY

Poets on Poetry   **Donald Hall, General Editor**

DONALD HALL	*Goatfoot Milktongue Twinbird*
GALWAY KINNELL	*Walking Down the Stairs*
WILLIAM STAFFORD	*Writing the Australian Crawl*
DONALD DAVIE	*Trying to Explain*
MAXINE KUMIN	*To Make a Prairie*
DIANE WAKOSKI	*Toward a New Poetry*
ROBERT BLY	*Talking All Morning*
ROBERT FRANCIS	*Pot Shots at Poetry*
RICHARD KOSTELANETZ	*The Old Poetries and the New*
LOUIS SIMPSON	*A Company of Poets*
PHILIP LEVINE	*Don't Ask*
JOHN HAINES	*Living Off the Country*
MARGE PIERCY	*Parti-Colored Blocks for a Quilt*
DONALD HALL	*The Weather for Poetry*
JAMES WRIGHT	*Collected Prose*
ALICIA OSTRIKER	*Writing Like a Woman*
JOHN LOGAN	*A Ballet for the Ear*
HAYDEN CARRUTH	*Effluences from the Sacred Caves*
ROBERT HAYDEN	*Collected Prose*
JOHN FREDERICK NIMS	*A Local Habitation*
ANNE SEXTON	*No Evil Star*
CHARLES SIMIC	*The Uncertain Certainty*
LOUIS SIMPSON	*The Character of the Poet*
WILLIAM STAFFORD	*You Must Revise Your Life*
TESS GALLAGHER	*A Concert of Tenses*
WELDON KEES	*Reviews and Essays, 1936–55*
DONALD HALL	*Poetry and Ambition*
CHARLES WRIGHT	*Halflife*
WILLIAM MATTHEWS	*Curiosities*
CHARLES SIMIC	*Wonderful Words, Silent Truth*
TOM CLARK	*The Poetry Beat*
WILLIAM MEREDITH	*Poems Are Hard to Read*
PETER DAVISON	*One of the Dangerous Trades*
AMY CLAMPITT	*Predecessors, Et Cetera*
JANE MILLER	*Working Time*
DAVID LEHMAN	*The Line Forms Here*
HAYDEN CARRUTH	*Suicides and Jazzers*

Hayden Carruth

Suicides and Jazzers

Ann Arbor

THE UNIVERSITY OF MICHIGAN PRESS

Copyright © by the University of Michigan 1992
All rights reserved
Published in the United States of America by
The University of Michigan Press
Manufactured in the United States of America

1995   1994   1993   1992   4   3   2   1

A CIP catalogue record for this book is available from the British Library.

Library of Congress Cataloging-in-Publication Data

Carruth, Hayden, 1921–
    Suicides and jazzers / Hayden Carruth.
        p.   cm. — (Poets on poetry)
    ISBN 0-472-09419-X (alk. paper). — ISBN 0-472-06419-3
    (pbk. : alk. paper)
    I. Title.   II. Series.
PS3505.A77594S85   1992
814′.54—dc20   92-29114
                                                     CIP

Parts of this book originally appeared in *American Book Review, American Poetry Review, CEA Critic, Conjunctions, The Exquisite Corpse, Ironwood, Sewanee Review,* and *Southern Review.*
    "Essays for Wendell" was originally published in *Wendell Berry,* edited by Paul Merchant (Lewiston, Ind.: Confluence Press, 1991).

This book is for Joe-Anne

Preface

For years my friends have urged me to write my autobiography. They have been interested in how I overcame the psychiatric illness which incapacitated me for most of my life. I've made no secret of this illness in my poems and essays, but I haven't written about it as a historical and social happening either, and I don't intend to. I don't like autobiography, don't trust it, and seldom read the autobiographies—or for that matter biographies—of others. Beyond this my illness has been my life for seventy years and is far too complex to be explained in a casual memoir. Only clinical veracity could do it justice. Too many people have been intimately engaged in it, for one thing, the few who damaged me, the many who helped. All writers are custodians less of our own pasts than of others', and we must proceed with the nicest discretion and respect.

Nevertheless one has memories. From time to time I've felt like writing about a few of mine in brief essays which were filed away, never shown to anyone nor submitted for publication. Now I have taken some of them for this book. It's a very miscellaneous book, no doubt, yet no more than most of my others. My mind has always tended to go off in all directions at once.

The big essays, the one on my suicide, the one on Paul Goodman's poetry, were written more deliberately, of course, as were the assigned reviews and shorter essays which celebrate primarily fine writers and musicians who have been neglected by the establishment, I think often intentionally. Isn't the "establishment" really a conspiracy? Power cannot be amassed and organized democratically, not in the arts and apparently not in the polity either.

In the past objections have been raised to my typical strategy in writing essays. People have said that I ask questions, then assert the induracy of the questions before human mentality, and finally go on to offer personal thoughts and feelings anyway. It's true. What else can a writer do who unabashedly lacks faith—either a received faith or a more popular faith in psychoanalysis or history or some other desperate fantasy of the time? No, in the bar fight between the individual and the powers out of control, political and metaphysical, one arms oneself with ambivalence, indecision, and the resolute quest for discovery. And thus intellectual discourse, as opposed to ideological standoff, becomes possible.

So much for apology. I commend these pieces to anyone who will read them, but especially to young artists. The curse of America in my lifetime has been a lust for conformity, fed by our institutions everywhere, especially our universities. It is ruinous. We are so busy giving away the independence of mind, spirit, and practice for which we once were known that now we are pretty nearly hog-tied and throttled. It's time to recover the moxie of our great forebears.

—H.C.
20 November 1991

Contents

Suicide

Suicide

To be frank—and in the present case anything less would defeat the purpose, which is not poetic—no topic in fifty years of writing has blocked me as thoroughly and persistently as this one, my own suicide. For six months and more I have been unable to write anything that pleases me. Why not skip the suicide then and go on to something else? One needn't and can't turn every experience into a piece of writing. Sometimes in the past I've made this skipping maneuver and dropped a whole aspect of my life out of my literary consciousness, and then have been able in a short while to go on to other things. But that won't work now, and the reason why it won't is what I want to elucidate if I can, hoping to free myself and so return to the normal life, if there is such a thing, of a writer.

But this may not work either, because I do not wish to make public the circumstances, including peripheral actors, in which the event occurred; they are private and should remain private. Yet these circumstances may be precisely the factors that are causing my blockage, and what do I do then—give up being a writer? This would mean casting away the whole mental and emotional apparatus I have acquired, by luck and hard study, in a lifetime devoted to many kinds of writing. I'm sixty-seven years old. Obviously I'd be reluctant to take such a course, but I know I may have to and I'm not altogether unwilling.

Early in the morning of February 24, 1988, I intentionally and massively overdosed myself with every pill I possessed. Since I had been treated by doctors over many years for insomnia, anxiety, depression, cardiac irregularity, occasional spinal pain, and I don't remember what else—except that I'm by nature hypochondriacal and usually go to the doctor three or four times a year no matter what—and moreover since no one in the past, meaning primarily my doctors, had ever suspected me of suicidal propensities, I had a fair collection of partly used bottles of medication. I opened them one after another and washed the contents down with loathsome port wine which someone had sent me from California. I was surprised, not disagreeably, by the quickness of the effect. It seems to me still that I began to feel myself going under immediately and that the process itself lasted no more than a few seconds—though I know from what I was told afterward that this cannot be true—just long enough for me to experience a sense of relief amounting to euphoria and to tell myself that this was the first time I'd been happy in years. The next thing I knew I was flat on my back, too weak to stir, with nurses, doctors, relatives, and friends staring down at me. Again I was surprised, again not disagreeably. In fact I was astounded. How could this be? I thought to myself, this guy is invincible, he's like the soldier in battle who believes he can't be killed and consequently isn't, he's never going to die. Then right away: that's a myth, that's poetry. Even in the turbulence of awakening, my mind was literary.

I was in the intensive care unit of a hospital, of course, which is anything but poetic. I awoke fourteen or fifteen hours, I think, after I had lost consciousness, though to this day I have no clear notion of the sequence of events or the length of time they took. In fact for several months after I was discharged from the hospital I thought the whole episode had occurred a week later than it did, and I learned my error only when the bill from the hospital, giving the date of my admittance, finally reached me after its useless meandering in Medicare. For a while after I awoke—maybe a day, maybe longer—I drifted in and out of consciousness. I remember somebody saying, "This guy isn't going to make it." I remember a nurse saying, "Hayden, we have to give you a shot now, we have to paralyze you," followed by a dream–vision in which I saw my own body as a heap of jumbled bricks that all at once sprang into neatly ordered rigidity, a wall—not in the least painful. But I was indeed paralyzed, couldn't move a muscle. Afterward I was told this had been necessary because I was pulling the tubes from my mouth and nose with my hands. I remember bright lights and electronic noises. I remember someone remarking, "He can't weigh that much, he's got a pot belly but it's not as big as mine." I remember occasional sharp pains in my stomach or my hands and arms, pains that subsided almost instantly. Etc. But now I cannot put these sensations and scraps of language into any consecutive order.

Gradually but, everything considered, quite rapidly, I returned to full consciousness. I found myself with tubes in my mouth and nose, one of which passed between my vocal cords and prevented me from making a sound, IVs in my arms and hands, an arterial tap in one wrist, catheters in my heart and bladder, a respirator that wheezed rhythmically somewhere out of my line of vision and was apparently in control of my breathing, and numerous electronic monitoring devices attached to me here and there. I was not uncomfortable. Presumably I was being drenched with painkillers. I dozed a good deal. Once or twice I made panicky attempts to communicate, first by trying to speak or at least whisper or at least make intelligible mouth movements, all to no avail, and then by trying to write with a pencil and pad that were put in my hands; but I was unable to form a legible word. I had to give up and content myself with nods and smiles, which most of the time was easy.

After a while, perhaps a couple of days, some of the tubes were removed, and an oxygen mask (wet and ill-smelling) was attached to my face. After several more days the mask was replaced with a double tube running on either side of my head and ending in two little nozzles fitted into my nose. I came to despise the odor of oxygen, though I was told it has no odor, and then to understand that it was all in my head, that actually I had no remaining sense of taste or smell at all. They were gone. Would they come back? The nurses said probably. The food brought to me on trays tasted and smelled like oxygen or what I took to be oxygen, a chemical smell that could more accurately have been formaldehyde. Months later, I still smell it occasionally; it seems to exude from my fingers. I had no appetite, no taste for anything but ginger ale, though I tried to force something down at each mealtime. I was x-rayed several times a day and my blood was constantly tested for its content of gases— mostly oxygen, I presume. Finally, days later, the oxygen was turned off momentarily and I was permitted to disengage from the cardiac monitors long enough to go to the bathroom. I could sit in a chair from time to time. I was even taken for a wobbly stroll around the center of the ICU with a nurse holding me by the arm.

Twice I sneaked a cigarette from the pack I'd had in my dressing gown, along with matches, before I came to the hospital. Apparently no one had bothered to look in the pockets. I blew the smoke toward the ventilator, and never knew whether anyone detected the smell or not. The fact that I was using fire only a couple of feet from the apparatus controlling the oxygen and that this was dangerous, to say the least, did not occur to me. Then once late at night a nurse, a very likable, kindhearted nurse who was a smoker, took me to the murses' lounge, where we each smoked a cigarette. It made me cough, and later I found out that that cough had been recorded on my dossier as a bad sign. Otherwise I went without tobacco.

As I say, the pain was not bad. What I had expected to hurt me, such as the removal of catheters, really didn't, though when they pulled the catheter out of my heart I had a brief unpleasant sensation of being turned inside out. The worst was that the doctors would prescribe no aid for sleeping. When I asked my principal doctor for a sleeping pill, he spun on one foot and motioned outward with both hands, like an umpire signifying a foul ball: "I'll be damned if I'll give you a sleeping pill," and he stomped out. In the circumstances I couldn't blame him exactly, but I did wonder if he'd had any experience, personal or professional, with chronic insomnia. After I had recovered enough strength to stay awake, I think on the third night, I lay for five days and nights without a wink, 120 hours, which is a record for me. At one point I wrote a half-delirious "poem" in my head about sleep deprivation as a means of torture. I even wrote down parts of it I could remember the next morning. As poetry it was disjointed and sloppy. But it described accurately enough how I felt: weak, jittery, a little crazy. At night in the light of a small lamp that was part of the monitoring console I read crime fiction, books that people bought for me at the drugstore, and sometimes I played extended jam sessions in my head, hours and hours of blues, up-tempo, moderate, and draggy. At other times I felt enraptured for no reason I could ascertain. I watched the heart monitor on the console behind my right shoulder until my neck got sore from being twisted like that. That little green puppy leapt endlessly for the unreachable biscuit, each time falling back and springing up again. I experimented with controlling my pulse rate and discovered I could bring it down to about 75 by consciously relaxing myself, though most of the time it remained at 90 or higher. As their shifts changed, by day, evening, and night, I talked with the nurses when they were between chores, sweet-natured, intelligent women who came and sat by my bedside and seemed to enjoy being there; they told me their stories, often in detail, their hopes and disappointments. They told me about life in the hospital and complained about hours, assignments, and this supervisor or that. At last I began to sleep fitfully for two or three hours a night. Sleep deprivation is a torture all right, Amnesty International says it and so do I. But in fact it didn't have much to do one way or the other with my recovery, and of course in the hospital I had no work to do and it didn't matter whether I could think straight.

Eventually I learned from the nurses, chiefly by letting them talk and not asking questions, what had happened to me or at least some of it. They seemed eager to tell. For one thing, the doctors had loaded me with charcoal, which was supposed to absorb the toxins in the pills I'd taken. No doubt it did; but it also caused me to vomit, which in the nature of the case must have been intended, while at the same instant I aspirated a sizable amount of the stuff into my lungs, which presumably was not intended. Not until much later, after I had been discharged from the hospital, did I begin to think that those in charge ought to have foreseen this possibility, or even probability, and to have prevented it, which might have been easy. If someone had turned my head toward the side, I might not have breathed in all that junk. But I don't know when or where the charcoal was administered, in the emergency room or the ICU, or even in the ambulance on the way to the hospital. No doubt the people were working as hard as they could and events were occurring rapidly. I don't blame anyone. In effect, however, I ended up with suffocation and radical pneumonia, the latter continuing to be the chief problem after I regained consciousness, not the poisons I had given myself. I've said I suffered no pain, but there was a time—maybe more than once—when the doctor pushed a rod down into my lungs to make me cough. I don't know if this was a pain or not, but it was horrifying, the choking and gasping, the thumping of my heart. It was like being asphyxiated right there and then. I had an impression of the doctor, a stocky man, leaning over me, his knee on the bed, one hand holding down my shoulder, the other pushing this thing in and out of me. It was a rape, it was terrifying, one of the most awful things that ever happened to me. I remember Ray Carver telling me about the same procedure after his operation for lung cancer. He said it was the worst part of the whole ordeal. In my case it had the desired effect and some of the junk came up. But some stayed down, and until the day I left the hospital the doctors and nurses continued to hear sounds of pneumonia when they listened to me, as they did unrelentingly even after I felt okay and ready to go home.

One doesn't know, lying there, how weak one is. Or how awful one looks. On the seventh or eighth day, when I was first permitted to go to the bathroom, I saw my face in the mirror. To get shut of the urinals and bedpans was a break, a big one, but the shock of the vision, the apparition, in the mirror was a more than equal shove in the opposite direction. My beard, which I'd worn for more than twenty years, was gone, but I had known that because I'd felt the sharp stubble with my fingers; the nurses had told me it interfered with the tape needed to hold my tubes in the right positions. But what a face was revealed! I had lost weight precipitately, of course, twenty pounds or more; my cheeks were hollow, my eyes much larger than I'd ever seen them, like frogs' eyes, and my skin was dark and bruised, covered with tiny creases as if it were tanned cowhide. I looked eighty-five years old. In fact I looked like my mother when she was eighty-five, paralyzed by stroke and dying. I gaped in revulsion and dismay. Then I became fascinated and stared at myself until the nurse rapped on the door and said loudly, "Are you okay in there?" I flushed the john and walked out and went back to bed. But after that I always studied myself in the bathroom mirror when I could. It was like looking at myself as painted by Dürer or Ivan Allbright. It was as close to seeing myself dead as I expect to come.

What had I seen when I had been dead? Not myself, but not much else either. I remember what Carl Jung wrote in his memoirs about the vision that occurred to him when he was near death, how he had found himself in space near a floating castle, a place of serenity and happiness which would have been his destination if his recovery from whatever was wrong with him had not intervened. What trivial nonsense! At least it's trivial to me because, although I can't say for a fact that Jung was deceived or was lying, at the same time I can't see what relevance his vision has in the real world, which is the only world. At best it must be a kind of wishful dreaming or hallucinating. A good friend of mine has told me of a similar vision she saw when she was close to death, a vision so in keeping with her benevolent and sensitive character that I believe, myself, it was just an extension of that character. Indeed, if one is conscious at such a time of any perception at all, dream, fantasy, hallucination, or whatever, to my mind it means only that one is not sufficiently dead.

What I saw was blackness. It was neither underground nor in outer space. It was not the darkness of a closed room. It was neither a solid, a fluid, nor an atmosphere. I cannot think of any analogy or metaphor to explain or describe it. It was blackness, nothing else, and it was enclosing me—except that "I" was not there and no action, either of enclosing or any other, occurred. Yet somehow I was aware—aware of the blackness and that it was not quite entirely still. It was composed of indistinguishable particles, perhaps what the ancients meant by atoms, which were in flux, not going anywhere but moving in a slow dance backward and forward. Since I could not "see" this, even inwardly, I don't know how I "knew" it. But no doubt my perception of the movement meant that I was still technically alive, as of course I was, when I arrived at the hospital, even though I exhibited none of the ordinary "vital signs"—breath, pulse, pupillary reflex, etc. My brain was still generating electrical impulses, or doing whatever a brain does. If the motion of the blackness had ceased I would have ceased—entirely—and there would have been neither motion nor blackness nor anything else.

I "remembered" the blackness and its motion when I first became conscious in the ICU. In fact I think the "memory" existed before I became conscious, so that at the very first instant of awakening, or just before that instant, I was "in" the blackness. At any rate it was the first "impression" I was cognizant of after my going under, and it had the kind of "depth-beyond-time" that dream-reality often has when one remembers it just after waking up. That is, the blackness existed in another "state," which was literally timeless: it could have been a minute, a year, or a century; or it could have been faster than instantaneous, occupying no time at all. Is that eternity? I don't know; I am ignorant of this. Eternity means no more to me now—but certainly no less—than it did when I was five years old and gazed in fear and wonder at the stars. But whereas the idea of "eternity" has always made me unhappy, or at least uncomfortable (which behaviorists say is the same thing), my "memory" of the blackness was not at all uncomfortable but quite the contrary: it was happy. Not in the sense of *ecstatic* as we normally use the term now, meaning sexual or generally appetitive transport, being "out of this world," but rather in the sense of *blissful,* a replete contentedness. It was a state of mind I had never experienced before, and I mean that literally; but it was present in my mind clearly and strongly when I first came to, and it has been present ever since. It has become part of my being. I don't mean that after my suicide the fears, angers, weaknesses, and other obsessive responses of my prior mind did not return; they did, all of them, at times very powerfully. But the sense of strange, new, astounding happiness has remained with me as well.

I was not afraid. I felt no fear whatever. Emphatically. If no "scene" or "vision" appeared to me in the blackness, then nothing to frighten me could be in the blackness either, no conventional sense of the "void," the "beyond," the "mystery." I know this means giving up a notion so dear to even the most hylotheistic imaginations that it seems a stark necessity. The mystery of death has always in every time and place been the most constant element of human feeling, as we know from art and writing, even though it must always be evoked indirectly. Proust gives us a sense of it in the final volume of his huge novel when he writes about soldiers on leave in Paris during the First World War:

> It seemed almost that there was something cruel in these leaves granted to men at the front. When they first came on leave, one said to oneself: "They will refuse to go back, they will desert." And indeed they came not merely from places which seemed to us unreal, because we had only heard them spoken of in the newspapers and could not conceive how a man was able to take part in these titanic battles and emerge with nothing worse than a bruise on his shoulder; it was from the shores of death, whither they would soon return, that they came to spend a few moments in our midst, incomprehensible to us, filling us with tenderness and terror and a feeling of mystery, like phantoms whom we summon from the dead, who appear to us for a second, whom we dare not question, and who could, in any case, only reply: "You cannot possibly imagine."

From "the shores of death," exactly. Even as great a word-spinner as Marcel Proust must resort to cliché. These soldiers have been to those shores and have returned with nothing more than a bruise on the shoulder, meaning that they are men like the rest of us and cannot say anything about their experience of mystery with which we might assuage our tenderness and terror. There is no mystery. Or rather, the mysterious thing about death is that it is not mysterious. Our elemental sense of fitness is appalled by this—death ought to be mysterious—and we are beset by great romantic frustration because it isn't. Well, we are people of the world as it is this minute, the modern world, and as human beings who wish to wear our humanity with a certain grace—though what we really wish is to justify it—we acknowledge our frustration and go on with our lives. Above all we do not ask what we can know. In the ordinary sense of cognition we cannot *know* death any more than we know most other states of existence, such as the mind of a newborn infant or a dinosaur, or even the fullness of our own minds in their commonest moments, walking along a street of our home town, tying our shoes, etc.

This was how I felt in the hospital. And although my image in the mirror was shocking, repulsive, peculiarly fascinating, and took some time to adjust to, my happiness was not diminished. I was high—and not from the oxygen either. I was high on life, my recovered life, even though "life" for me at that time was thoroughly elemental. I couldn't go anywhere or do anything. I could hardly think. I don't remember any mental activity that wasn't involuntary. But the animal in me was responding to this remarkable turn of events like the rabbit that is dropped unaccountably from the eagle's talons. I was alive. I had been happy when I was dead and now I was happy when I was alive. It had nothing to do with thought, but only with sensory experience, touching my own arm or belly, swallowing, excreting, being touched by the nurses, listening to the music in my head, etc. I carried on presumably intelligent conversations with nurses and eventually with visitors, but only in a kind of academic autonomia, my tongue still running—like a cartoon character running in the air above a chasm—from the impetus of the classroom; or maybe I was talking nonsense, babbling uncontrollably, and the nurses and visitors were too kind to tell me so. I talked to everyone, doctors, nurses, aides and technicians, the young woman who mopped the floor of my room and told me about her 1965 Mustang and gave me copies of *Road and Track* to read, without the least discomposure. I was manic, I suppose, though I don't care for clinical language. "Carruth," I said to myself, "you are experiencing exactly the conditions you have all your life and in all your acute and chronic psychopathology feared *more* than death, being in a hospital, locked up, among total strangers, no way to escape, nothing to quell the scream bubbling in your throat, etc." Yet I felt none of the anxiety that had destroyed large parts of my life during the sixty-six years before I ended up in the ICU.

A lot of people are talking about rebirth nowadays. It's the fundamentalist fad in these last years of the old millennium. Apocalyptic behavior is to be expected, we are told. And all of us are sometimes fundamentalists, all of us who take the trouble—and trouble is what it is—to face "ultimate reality" from time to time. I don't know about being reborn in the exuberance of an evangelical camp meeting, but if it's anything like being reborn in an ICU, it's wonderful. And it lasts a long time. Not that such a course as mine can be recommended; it obviously can't. Nor can it be faked; near suicides and theatrical suicides, perhaps compulsive suicides of any kind, won't work. One has to have a clear and resolute intent to die, which apparently everyone agrees—medical doctors, psychiatrists, etc.—was the case with me.

Of course everyone agreed I was crazy too. Doctors are by profession devoted to life and to saving life; for them to believe that suicide can be anything but insanity, at least in ordinary American middle-class life, would require them to be crazy themselves. And of all people who are not crazy the most not crazy are doctors. In their world this is axiomatic. So there I was, surrounded by doctors, under the control of doctors, my life and being regulated by doctors, and though they were kind enough to pretend they thought I was rational, especially after friends pointed out to them that I was a "professor"—I dislike the word myself—and a somewhat well-known writer, it was understood by everyone that I really was crazy and that my friends were as well. Consequently, when it came time for me to be discharged from the ICU, the doctors would let me go only with the proviso that I pass immediately into the laughing academy, the hatchery, the local asylum. I had no choice; I was still too weak to dress myself and walk out the way heroes do in the movies. But even then, when I had agreed to their condition, two days more were required—at better than $1,000 a day—to negotiate the terms and methods of transfer from one hospital to another, so that both hospitals could have in writing, certified and attested, exactly the point at which one hospital's responsibility ended and the other's began. Perhaps this was partly impelled by fear of legal liability, which we know has become a grave enough problem for medical people in recent years; but I believe the doctors would have behaved the same even if no question of legal liability had been posed. I was a suicide and I was crazy, and that was the end of it. The result was that eventually I was taken from one hospital to the other, a journey of about an hour and a half between two cities, in a locked ambulance with two burly young men to attend me and with impressive receipts and delivery invoices signed by both parties when I was handed—which is the precise word—from the locked vehicle to the door of the locked loony bin.

I could have protested. If I had done it vigorously enough, I could have succeeded. Legally, I was not a certifiable nut, was still responsible for myself. But in such circumstances who has the strength for that? Not only the doctors but friends and family, having been "counseled" by the doctors, all believed I must go to the psychiatric hospital. I had made phone calls to friends who were shrinks, and they said the same thing. Everyone said the same thing, so what was I to do? I was the only one who knew that the hatch was the wrong place for me. But though I knew this—partly because I had spent a long time in the hatch thirty-five years earlier in a vain attempt to deal with the psychoneurotic anxiety—and knew also that what I really needed was to go home and relax, the truth was that I didn't have a home, and I knew this too, knew it well, with the consequence that I didn't protest and found myself in a locked ward with a number of people who were hollering or banging the walls or walking around full of Haldol, stiff, jerky, headed for tardive dyskinesia, God help them. On the other hand this was not a hospital that treated violent mental illness, I got out of the locked ward and onto an open ward after about three days, and I remained in the hospital only two weeks altogether. Not a bad hitch compared to the fifteen months I had served thirty-five years earlier.

And I was happy the whole time. Happy as a clam, and for the same reasons: I was alive, more or less comfortable, protected. But the chief reason was being alive. Again, as in the

ICU, I talked to everyone, made friends with nearly all the other patients on the ward, about forty people, plus scores of staff workers of every description. I said little about myself but listened to account after account of personal miseries, including the complaints of injustice at the hands of the hospital administration heard again and again from nurses, aides, and technicians, I attended scores of "group therapy" sessions, which were a farce when they weren't a persecution, making people cry, etc., especially the women, young and old, and one noted that nearly all the group leaders were men, even the leaders of the special "women's group"—what could be more ridiculous?—though when I asked one of the women if she wasn't affronted by this, she said, "No." Also it's worth noting that of the forty-odd people on the ward, only two of us were men, and even if for unknown reasons these numbers were extreme at that particular time, I can't believe the disparity isn't significant. Etc., etc. Everyone has heard about these places.

At the same time many changes for the better had been introduced since the last time I'd been an inmate. For one, the hospital had no shock room; the few patients for whom electroshock was prescribed were taken to another hospital, and no one ever suggested it for me. (I had had a series of ten shocks in 1954, which were no help at all.) For another, all of us had ready access to the phone. Our outgoing mail was not read by doctors. Two days after I was admitted a person from an independent legal organization came and informed me of my rights, including the right to dispute and I think interdict any medications I thought were wrongly prescribed, and he gave me a printed leaflet confirming my legal status. All this was markedly different from my earlier immurement, when one could not make free contact with anybody outside the institution, certainly not a lawyer. Moreover I was not now subjected to any of the foolish treatments I had had to undergo formerly, "hydrotherapy" (in which one stood naked in a tiled stall while being battered by two cold and high-powered jets of water), "occupational therapy" (making belts and neckties) or "physical therapy" (though I could volunteer for exercise classes if I wished—I did—and a weight-lifting

15

room was provided for younger people). But the greatest change is in the length of time one is expected to stay. Earlier I had spent a year and a quarter in the hospital and had known others who had been confined for many years, but now of the forty-odd people on the ward only three or four had been in the hospital for more than a month and most were discharged in two or three weeks. On other wards, such as those for people addicted to drugs or alcohol or with eating disorders, the expected time until discharge was longer, and there may have been wards I was unaware of. But I saw only one patient who was a chronic long-time loser, an elderly senile woman who was said to have been in psychiatric hospitals since she was seventeen. She spent her days in a reclining chair in the lounge, talking unintelligibly to herself and making strange angry noises. Nothing could be done for her. It struck me that she was there more to furnish an example—edifying without doubt—for the rest of us than for any benefit to herself.

This lounge, in fact, was the greatest discomfort in the hatch. It was the only place where smoking was permitted. It was also the only place where a television set was turned on from six in the morning until midnight. Dozens of times a day I was up against the choice of a cigarette with MTV or the smokeless quiet of my room. Not much of a discomfort. Even less, considering that most of the time I could find someone to talk with in the lounge, someone who would join me in facing away from the tube and ignoring its racket. We were not permitted to have lighters—the institute has not changed in this— but an electric lighter, similar to a car lighter but with a fine wire mesh across the front of it, was fixed on the wall and could be made to glow by pressing a button. Most of the patients were smokers—the opposite proportion to that outside; let the surgeon general make of it what he will—with the result that hundreds of times a day, perhaps thousands, someone would walk into the lounge with a cigarette ready, go up to the button and press it, then lean close to the lighter to get the smoke going. It was ritualistic. Kissing the wall is what we called it.

"Hey Jim, you going to kiss the wall?"

"Damn right."

Well, I was there two weeks, as I've said. I went to a fair

number of group therapy sessions, took many psychological tests, was interviewed by various doctors and other people, saw a psychiatrist who had been assigned to me for fifteen minutes each day, went out several times with groups in a big Dodge van to visit parks on the outskirts of the city, and toward the end went out with friends to dinner. I was mildly scared a couple of times when younger patients got into a fracas. I was irritated late at night when I couldn't sleep and the nurse in charge wouldn't authorize anyone to open the lounge (locked from midnight until six o'clock) and let me smoke, though sometimes, inconsistently, this was permitted. But mostly I was happy. Not only that, I was cheerful. This is confirmed in the "report" that was written on my case, which I was given to read after my discharge and which summarized the immense file that had accumulated in only two weeks, hundreds and hundreds of observations by doctors, nurses, technicians, aides, and who knows how many others, plus data from physical and psychological tests of many kinds. It was a file three inches thick—what an expense of paper! The report said I was outgoing, good-humored, etc.—not my usual self at all, not a pessimist, skeptic, and grump. I was a *new man.* Exactly.

Seeing my psychiatrist once a day in the hospital, incidentally was another change from earlier, when I had been lucky to see a doctor once a week. I can't say the psychiatrist assigned to me in Syracuse, Veena Kayastha, who is a wise and magnanimous woman from India, taught me anything I hadn't known before—after all my years in psychotherapy this would have been unlikely—but she changed the angle of vision from which I looked at myself, and this was indispensable. I have continued to see her, though less and less frequently, since being discharged from the hospital.

In many of the group sessions the question came up of the acute embarrassment most suicidal patients feel before friends and relatives afterward, and of the hindrance a history of suicide may be, once it gets on the record, to finding a job. Many patients on the ward were suicidals, I'd guess more than half, ranging from high-school girls, fresh and pretty and naïve, to people my age or older; some were long-time repeaters. When one of the group leaders asked me how I felt about this, I said, "Well, in my line of work it's more an advantage than a disadvantage." By this time nearly everyone knew I was a poet. So my remark got a laugh, and a laugh was by no means a bad thing in that place, though the group leaders often didn't think so: they'd look annoyed and then right away put on a false smile and get back to the serious business of making somebody squirm. I became annoyed with their implacable Rotarian optimism and formulism, their essentially authoritarian methods—they always knew best—and their moral impeccability. Once I tried to suggest that attitudes toward suicide are relative and derive from diverse cultural sources. Social, religious, and ethnic factors are variable. We all know about the spy who keeps a dose of cyanide in his ring so he can do away with himself when the going gets rough. A fictional stereotype; yet I have no doubt he exists in reality. Even in our Christian culture, which since the days of the early church has regarded suicide as a sin, most people would agree that someone facing extreme physical torture ought to have the choice of taking his or her own life. In Japan a politician who has failed in office is expected to retire, not to his estate in the country, but to the next room, where he sticks himself with a horrid big knife. This is the honorable thing to do. For centuries in India a new widow, even if she was still in her teens, was expected to commit suttee by casting herself on her husband's pyre. Again it was the honorable thing to do, no matter how sexist and stupid. I wonder if Christianity may not be the only prominent religion which proscribes suicide categorically as sinful, i.e., denies suicides a burial in the common, consecrated graveyard. At any rate attitudes toward suicide vary. Even in our ordinary American social cross section attitudes toward suicide are more variable than the doctors care to admit. For that matter, doctors themselves have a higher suicide rate than many other professions, perhaps—who knows?—right up there next to the priests.

I have had three close friends who died of the same kind of cancer within the past year. One of them lingered longer in the final stage than the others, and everyone agrees that the latter were the luckier. Death for them was a blessing. In fact this feeling has become so commonplace with respect to victims of cancer that we scarcely wince any more when we express it. The sooner one dies the better.

Some years ago I had a friend whose domestic life was in a shambles. Part of the trouble was not his doing, but he was so bound up, so repressed, that he could talk to no one, either psychiatrist or friend, about it. He was forty-five years old, had three minor children, was a success in his work, a liked and respected person. He went into the woods and shot himself. I had to go with the search party three days later; when we found him I had to identify him. It was awful. Anyone could have told him that what he should do was forget the whole mess and go to California, the common, effective American expedient. He was simply incapable of this. Incapable. In such a case can anyone say certainly that his suicide was wrong?

The idea of suicide makes everyone shudder, even those who have done it. It's the *frisson* we feel when we encounter the nonbeing we carry inside us, when somebody, as we say, walks over our grave. Perhaps this is why we make excuses for suicide, excusing ourselves in the potential future. John Donne, who was as rigorously devout in his later years as anyone could be, in his *Biathanatos* excuses religiously motivated suicides, against the teaching of the church. Indeed, almost every philosopher has discussed suicide in one work or another because the topic is obviously, almost conveniently, close to the heart of all moral problems. The most famous example in our time is Albert Camus in *The Myth of Sisyphus*.

I've always thought that if we must have capital punishment—and I don't accept the necessity—the Athenians invented the best, most humane method when they gave Socrates the cup of hemlock and let him administer it to himself. At that same time not far away the Macedonians, Spartans, Israelites, and others were hacking at people with axes or roasting them over fires or nailing them to crosses. For that matter who today would not, if allowed to do so, choose suicide over hanging, electrocution, or the gas chamber, no matter how "painless" these methods may be? Irrational, yes. But when an inevitability has been established, presuming philosophically that all inevitabilities are in themselves and of necessity unjust, at some point the human being then wishes to choose it, to make it his or her election, even in the case of the death sentence, as if to ratify not only the injustice but his or her own autonomy by acting in the semblance of freedom. Whether or not this makes good sense, it is good psychology.

Suicide has been chosen by many and all kinds of people, including many writers. Off the top of my head I think of Lindsay, Mayakovsky, Yesenin, Teasdale, Virginia Woolf, Crane, Hemingway, F. O. Matthiessen, Kees, Cesare Pavese (that most vigorous of poets), Berryman, Jarrell, Plath, Sexton . . . etc. And painters too: Van Gogh, Mark Rothko. Again and again they do it, many different people for many different reasons. And is anyone able to say that all these people are wrong?

Some say that suicide is against nature. This is the "faith" of the doctors, I think. All nature strives to live, is what they say, the survival of the fittest, *élan vital,* etc. But in the first place this is wrong. Among some species it is death to copulate, but they copulate anyway. Among others a parent will give up her own life for the sake of her young. Among still others individuals that are old or diseased cause their own deaths, or conspire in them. And in the second place it doesn't matter what nature does. What matters is the human mind and spirit, as I assume I need not argue.

My own mind and spirit became filled, during the time in question, with happiness, as I have said. It was a peculiar feeling, something like the high I experienced in the ICU during my all-night, internal jam sessions, and I can't say enough about the excitement of that. I've been playing the blues all my life, sometimes on musical instruments but, like most musicians, even more often in my head, yet I never knew another time when I felt the exhilaration I felt that night. I was flying; my whole body was buzzing and writhing; though I was too weak to walk, almost too weak to raise my head, I was incandescent with energy; and I believed—but who can tell?—that my musical imagination was soaring in extraordinary new inventions. I was drugged? Maybe. I don't know what was flowing into me through those tubes, except for the oxygen, and my experience of drugs otherwise (except for alcohol) has been limited. But I can't believe (1) that I could achieve so high a high or (2) that I could perceive and remember it so clearly if I were merely intoxicated. And this was the feeling, this happiness, that I felt, varying in intensity, all the time in both hospitals and continue to feel to this day. A feeling of frothiness in my head, of effervescence. It is like falling in love ten times, but not successively, simultaneously, and with no other person implicated. The happiness is generated entirely within myself and directed entirely back to myself.

Yet the knowledge of it is sharable.

Is this what St. Theresa felt? For pages I've been skirting the idea of mystical experience. I have used the word *spiritual* and I have alluded to rebirth. I suspect that in its sensational manifestation my happiness is indeed close to religious ecstasy. But at the same time I've been a backcountry Yankee pragmatist and cynic all my life, and I cling to this conviction still, not only because it seems to my mind, which has been drawn to the question since I was a child, to be right, but because it is one of the very few continuities in my life that can hold thought and experience and feeling, my personality, together. I do not believe at all that a contradiction exists between my happiness and my rationalism. I resist to the end—this is part of the clinging—my friends who smile and say, "Well, we knew you'd come round to god at last." God has nothing to do with it, if only because he or she is in my view functionally nonexistent, an abstraction with no power and no intelligence. And no mystery; the mystery is within oneself, at the bottommost pit of oneself, and to call *this* a god is to commit suicide in a more drastic and distraught way than I ever contemplated with my mere overdose. It is to give up one's humanity, which is precisely our being not godly, our incapacity.

Elsewhere I have argued for the notion that spiritual and mystical experience are different.[1] The mystic is someone

---

1. "The Act of Love: Poetry and Personality," *Working Papers* (Athens: University of Georgia Press, 1982), p. 219.

who has immediate knowledge of supernatural power. This has never happened to me; all the hallucinatory incidents in my life can be convincingly explained by rational means. (Of course, this does not at all preclude mystical knowledge in other minds; it does not even preclude the fact of this in my own mind. I have a friend who is a painter, for instance, and when she is stumped by a problem in her work, Picasso tells her what to do by means of messages transmitted through a pencil held in her left, nonwriting hand. I believe what she says. But nothing remotely like this has ever happened to me.) Spiritual, as distinct from mystical, knowledge is all knowledge of the human spirit in its surpassing of material cause in Aristotle's sense of the word. The human spirit is human, grounded in our bodies, but it is still spirit. Spirituality is an extension of materiality, in the same sense that love is a refinement of sex, but is no less spiritual for that. The differences between spiritual and esthetic experience, or between either of them and emotional experience, are too abstruse for discussion in this essay, but to my mind, briefly, these differences entail discriminations among states or levels of feeling and have more to do with the way the feelings are evoked or produced than with their intrinsic qualities.

Is this a cynical view? It is necessary to bear in mind that cynicism does not mean merely a sardonic attitude toward life, love, or any other value, although this is what the word most often signifies in ordinary discourse. My dictionary says: "The Cynics [in ancient philosophy] taught that virtue is the only good, and that its essence lies in self-control and independence." It is easy to put too much stock in self-control and independence, as some cynics have, which results in a kind of puritanism; but it is equally easy to dismiss them altogether, which results in quietism. For me virtue is indeed the only good. Self-control and independence are the states of being toward which I strive continually, acknowledging that I'm damned lucky to attain either of them for even a moment.

And luck has a good deal to do with virtue, and with self-control and independence too. Any artist knows this. A poet or painter must work in exceptional and solitary diligence to sustain technique and the required pliancy of imagination, that is, to keep the artistic apparatus in a state of readiness for the stroke of luck that alone can materialize a genuine work of art when it comes; more than this, the artist must not only work but *live* in a state of devotion to things greater than himself. But no dereliction from hard work and devotion is implied in deferring to luck. Deference is a recognition of reality, what Wallace Stevens called "the necessary angel," who must mediate the imaginative procedure. A work of art—a work of virtue—is luck welcomed and accepted, the success of chance. And happiness is the feeling that goes with it. What I mean to say is that happiness itself is not virtue, in spite of the official American philosophy to the contrary, but it is the feeling that accompanies virtue. Often it's the feeling of being lucky.

The example may seem crass to some, but not to realists: happiness is winning the lottery. Everyone knows this. The guy who goes to bed with a million dollars more than he had when he got up is happy without a doubt. (It's a fact that the words *happen* and *happiness* both come from the root *hap*, which means chance.) Money is not everything, and for those of us who are serious about virtue it is not even much; we would rather produce a fine poem or painting than a fat bank account. Some of us would even rather produce a good action in the world. And we believe that our feeling when we do these things is happier by far than the gambler's mere rapture. In my case the happiness I've been speculating about came from the luck of being alive. And what is being alive at all if it isn't luck, whether good or bad? At any moment in our lives we know we might never have existed; our conception, that obscure beginning, was the extreme fortuity—chance as the absolute foundation—and awareness of this stays with us always. My suicide was a reminder of it, as my recovery was a resumption. I don't believe I experienced rebirth, which can come only from an unimaginable reconception and in effect would be a second origin—a contradiction in terms. Each of us has only one origin, one fundamental piece of luck (good or bad). In my suicide I experienced a *renewal* of luck. And I believe that because I was an artist, a person who had lived in devotion and worked in discipline, I was ready for that renewal and for its reward in happiness.

Why worry it like this? What is this need to understand and explain? My luck was not a change of knowledge but of vision. My happiness was not a state of doing but of being. Why not accept what had been given to me and be grateful and let it alone? This is what many of my friends—and especially those who are artists—would recommend.

I can only say that acceptance without questioning is contrary to my nature. The urgency in me—in my mind, my soul—is precisely to understand and explain. When I am presented with a gift, my impulse is to examine it, to look it in the mouth. How else can one appreciate it? How else can one arrive at an estimation of value, of moral and esthetic quality? In sessions of group therapy at the hospital I was accused of being too intellectual; both the staff and my fellow patients thought my responses to questions were too abstract and buried the essential feeling or instinct in an array of complication. I've been used to this all my life. The only thing to do when it happens is shut up, which is what I pretty much did. But I felt violated. Everything I know as writer and critic, everything I know about poetry and life, tells me that the effort to analyze a feeling makes that feeling stronger, not weaker. At the same time any effort to suppress or circumvent one's own intelligence leads to self-rebuke and depression. As my friend Paul Goodman used to say, I can't be any stupider than I am. But I should add that for me analysis is rather close to what I think other people mean by meditation.

The *recognition* of these things—the *lucid* recognition, as Camus would say—is important to me. And this too has to do with vision.

Another way to look at happiness and luck is under the rubric of time—the way people always look at it. True luck is not money but time, additional time: ask any veteran of Vietnam. Not one of them would take a million dollars for the extraordinary luck that brought them through alive. Poets and theologians have insisted from the beginning that happiness is an escape from time, human time, either through a life after death or, before death, through an experience of spiritual communion or mystical or esthetic transport. But a third way, as mythology attests, is to die and come back to life. This is the meaning in Western culture of the descent to the underworld, from Inanna to Dante. If one dies, then one's life is ended, meaning that the human computation of time, which is imposed on us by death, has ended, has been, as people say, terminated or wiped out. If one comes back from death then one must either begin a new life, which is impossible because all the defining elements of one's personality have already been established, or one must live in a new, different computation of time. Can one die twice? Of course; no human being has ever returned to life without eventually dying again. (The gods were always jealous and hard-nosed on that score.) This seems to mean that one's new computation of time would be imposed by one's new forthcoming death, however near or remote, and that in consequence this new computation is not much different from the old one. This is the logic of it. But the psychology of it, the spirituality of it, is another matter. One's inner intuitive organ of cognizance knows that dead is dead; but it cannot know the distinction between all-but-dead and dead. That is to say, one's inner intuitive organ of cognizance cannot accommodate itself to the idea of dying twice. If one all-but-dies, then the awareness of time as a human computation dies too, and the new, regained time when one returns is uncomputed.

This is what people call "borrowed time" or even "stolen time," which are mere folkifications, a common irrational wish-fulfillment. From whom or what could one possibly borrow or steal it? No, uncomputed time is much closer to what is called "free time," in both the sense of time with which one may do what one chooses and of time that is given without the normal payment, which is death. It is time outside the ordinary understanding of succession. And what I mean by "the ordinary understanding of succession" is precisely the imposed computation of one's lifetime under the pressure of predictable death that I have pointed to in the last paragraph. Free time is what Proust was talking about when he said that a remembered sensation in its sensory immediacy but temporal remoteness gives one an experience outside of normal chronology. It is the time that Alice found when she popped down the rabbit hole. It is the time that old people find when they fall in love, a release or reprieve from the predicted progression of sexuality-to-impotence-to-senility-to-death; Ford Madox Ford gave us a wonderful picture of this in his poem called "Heaven," and it was no accident that he chose—or more likely acceded to—the metaphor of an afterlife to represent the state of erotic gratification in old age. But in all these cases—Proust's, Alice's, and Ford's—the free time was acquired through complicated procedures entailing extra-personal agents or events. My free time, on the other hand, has come essentially from the experience of death, which is as inward and personal as any experience can be. In this my experience is like the mystic's, though the mystic would probably say that his or her experience is on the contrary as outward and impersonal as any experience could be, thus raising the question, which is unanswerable, of whether the utterly inward and utterly outward may not be the same thing.

All of which seems to mean that the luckiest kind of luck is that which gives one free time or time-outside-of-time. Moreover it is that which occurs solely within consciousness and with no reference to any externality whatever. Hence it goes without saying, at least in the terms of this essay, that this is what gives one the greatest happiness. One could achieve it by catching Alzheimer's disease and then arresting it just at the stage before complete loss of self-consciousness; one could achieve it in ways I have never thought of and would be unlikely to imagine. But one way to achieve it is by all-but-dying, and probably, though I see no way to demonstrate it, the degree of happiness resulting will be in direct ratio to the nearness of one's approach to death. One of my doctors remarked that my attempt at suicide had been "lethal," and it was clear from the context that this was meant literally. (The dictionary: "*lethal* is applied to that which by its very nature is bound to cause death or which exists for the purpose of destroying life.") So my luck, my unintentional discovery of time-outside-time, has been great indeed, and, leaving aside questions of possible brain damage or other physical impairments, so has my happiness.

A further consideration arises under the heading of identity, which is, heaven knows, a hackneyed enough refrain in the literature of my time, both fictional and clinical. I won't pursue it here. But it's worth mentioning that during my whole life prior to my suicide I had never been able to identify any part of my ego that might be central to the rest or that functioned in a way beyond the mere response to external stimuli. Among writers this is called style or voice. When I was young and under the influence of W. B. Yeats, I believed I knew his "voice" so well that if a new poem turned up purporting to be by him, I could tell right away, simply by reading the lines aloud to myself, whether the claim was genuine. But I could never find so distinct a voice in my own work, which instead seemed a disconcerting concatenation of voices, other people's voices mimicked or faked, including in some poems the voice of Yeats himself. This is a matter of perception, of course, and other people tell me that no matter how many *personae* appear in my poems, they recognize in the language, the thought, and the feeling a consistent personality. I hope they're right, but I don't know if they are. What is important here is that I discovered in suicide a way to unify my sense of self, the sense which had formerly been so refracted and broken up. This will seem bizarre to many of my friends, including my students. The truth is, however, that the practice of writing poetry, to which I have given a lifetime, has always seemed to me suspect, not quite legitimate, while suicide is without doubt an action in the world, something that one has done or not done, really and objectifiably. This is what I am. This is my identity, whatever anyone may think of it. Suicide is not only what I did but what I was capable of doing. Elemental thought it may be, it still gives shape, integrity, and a certain fullness to the figure of myself—minuscule, of course—that I see out there in history. It isn't much, but it's more than I had before.

And this is a real and significant feeling in me, no matter how other people may recoil from it, as I myself would have recoiled if it had been presented to me in my ante-suicidal ignorance.

At any point in this discussion but particularly at this one the question is whether my suicide was a mistake. I see no way to answer in terms of what had happened before the suicide. I'd had a long run of bad luck, no doubt of that, precluding the possibility of virtue, at least in my private life. But exactly how bad was it? And how bad must it be to justify suicide? We have no measurement. The church is right, from its standpoint, in making a blanket rejection, because even if absolute objective criteria could be found, which they can't, they could never be applied reasonably in individual cases. When you and I have been infected by the same flu bug, do we suffer equal pain? No, evidently we don't. But beyond this, the crudest observation, we can't say much about our relative qualities and quantities of pain, any more than we can about other elements of our relative subjectivities, including our need for suicide. All one can say in this respect is that *at some point* suicide *may* become feasible in anyone's life. This is not saying much, and it doesn't satisfy our need for something conclusive in such a difficult moral predicament. We are left where we, as mundane and imperfect human beings, always are.

But in terms of what followed after the suicide, I don't see how anyone, even the doctors, can maintain it was a mistake, except in fare-thee-well doctrinairian terms, which I reject on every ground.

Another point: my suicide occurred at a moment in life when death would not have been ill-timed. I had done about as much as one is normally expected to do. This doesn't mean I had no obligations still outstanding; at any point in anyone's life responsibility is always present; but I had generally done what I could. In my writing I had concluded my best work some years earlier. Even in teaching, which for me was in any case a late development and not something that could be called professional, any time at which one chooses to depart is as appropriate as any other. Teaching is like working on the assembly line of an auto factory; the semesters go past, one applies an air-wrench here, a soldering gun there; but the task is repetitive and can be interrupted with equal felicity or infelicity at any point. Hence in every sector, disregarding the fortuity of what has happened afterward, my death at the moment of my suicide would have been as opportune as anyone's.[2]

If my suicide was a mistake, it was such a mistake as is a part of life. Suicide in this respect is like any death, a part of the experience of living, consequent upon one's original luck. It is something existing within the potentiality of life. Is this possibility of suicide therefore a reason for suicide? That's a conundrum. Given a sufficiently anxious sensibility, it might be. But our proclivity for mistakes is not a reason for not living. What I'm saying here is that suicide is a choice, a free act. Whether a mistake or not, whether it succeeds or not, it authenticates the freedom of the intelligent being who chooses it. It is a powerful indicator of our relevance to ourselves as human beings. We can and do choose whether to live or to die. Granted, the Mickey Mouse psychologists who are trying to legislate morality on this question and others—e.g., in the public schools— decline such a view of suicide and in general try to exclude as much dangerous human freedom as possible, but these people, these technologists of behavior, are anathema to me, just as my own freedom—to choose and to do other things— is crucially important to me. This does not mean I am in favor of what the papers call "teenage suicide," incidentally. Young people must be taught to think. Whenever they are inculcated with such Rotarianized precepts as "respect for life" and the "American way," from sea to shining sea, etc., their capacity for thought is diminished proportionately and in most cases irrevocably. This is not exactly relevant here, but it's important nevertheless.

---

2. All this, and indeed the whole essay, applies only to suicide in its relationship to the individual who resorts to it. Scores of good friends were grieved and angered by my action. And what shall I say about the pain inflicted on my two children, who, though grown up and out in the world, are still close to me? This is not only another consideration, it is a different topic.

Alfred Alvarez in his first-rate book about suicide[3] says at the end: "It [suicide] seems to me to be somehow as much beyond social or psychic prophylaxis as it is beyond morality, a terrible but utterly natural reaction to the strained, narrow, unnatural necessities we sometimes create for ourselves." Yes, it is natural. But I think Alvarez takes too much onto himself in this, too much guilt for the "necessities" that summoned his will to suicide. I assume this is an extension of his guilt in other things as well. My own experience is different. The pain suffered beforehand for sixty years was not created by me. It was forced, jammed, crammed, wreaked upon me by . . . by "Fate," and my decision to kill myself was a decision made in defeat. I no longer had enough strength to carry on, and I mean physical strength as well as emotional and spiritual strength. This happens. Though I had not brutalized myself, I was exhausted from years of brutalization, and exhaustion, as everyone knows, is what old age does: it steals one's endurance. So the suffering is what must be emphasized, without self-pity, the suffering of everyone. It can be documented. "Listen to the newborn infant's cry in the hour of birth—see the death struggles in the final hour—and then declare whether what begins and ends in this way can be intended to be enjoyment." So wrote Søren Kierkegaard, and it's the commonest human sentiment of all. Defeat. My students and people who read my poems will be discouraged or even angered by what I'm saying here. "Look at all those books he wrote. Can that be a defeat?" If it isn't a defeat, it's an irrelevance. One cannot live in the past. Nostalgia is an illness and a delusion. Nor can one live on one's former accomplishments, which belong fundamentally to other people. But beyond this, every artist of the second half of the twentieth century knows that his or her working life is in at least one sense a resounding defeat, for what understanding or explanation or solace can art bring to a people who are like animals being driven up the ramp to the abattoir and who know that their imminent, massive deaths are extraneous to any motion of human men-

3. A. Alvarez, *The Savage God: A Study of Suicide* (London: Weidenfeld and Nicolson, 1971; New York: Random House, 1972), p. 237.

tality whatever? Can poetry, painting, or music overcome the "greenhouse effect"? People say that a society which neglects its arts and artists will be impoverished, but this society is so impoverished already—and from hundreds of quite other causes—that the neglect of art can't make the situation any worse. Artists know this. They know that if they work simply for themselves, or even for some abstract ideal of Art, they and their work will become attenuated and parched. They yearn to be connected. But they can't be, and they are defeated, they are in a condition of unending degradation.

At least in small ways, however, connection is still possible. Since my recovery my good luck has continued. In fact some nearly unbelievably lucky things have happened. One result is that the house I had bought a few months before my suicide, an alien, cold, unfriendly place at the time, has now become a real home. Another is that I am planning to be married soon to a beautiful and loving woman. My life has changed completely, in other words, and in ways I literally could not have believed possible at the time of my sucide and that anyone would have thought extremely unlikely. Moreover I have been welcomed back to my university on a semiretired basis and apparently am teaching as well as ever. As we say, I'm *lucky to be alive.* But the most important result of my new luck is that I am enabled to perform acts of virtue once more. I have moved out of the isolation and alienation of my former life and back into the world, which is where acts of virtue occur. Because of this I am a better writer, whatever the artistic quality of my work from now on may be. Writing is first of all a way of being in the world, a functioning nub of relatedness. Hence my happiness, that frothy feeling, is now with me almost all the time.

Bad luck and unhappiness are what I remember from the time before, as they are what I see continually around me in the smaller and larger worlds. Like anyone else, I pay attention to the news. Nor am I foolish enough to think that bad luck and unhappiness may not return to me. I've reached the time of life when one's friends begin shuffling away, usually in pain and humiliation, and saying good-bye is a sorrow I find simply overwhelming; yet it is not incompatible with my happiness. I do what I can, everything I can, so that other people may have good luck and may know it when they do, and in this I'm an average decent sort of a guy. Not that it amounts to much; a few friends, a few students, a few strangers—one cannot hope to reach more. The many kinds of impotence, like the many mistakes, are a part of life. But I am happy even so, happy with my luck and my knowledge of it, with my virtue and the good I can do if I am strong enough.

This is what is important, surely. Happiness, this spiritual happiness, can and does come to people like me—the cynics, as I have called us—so that spirituality is as much a dimension of our pragmatic lives as it is of the exalted lives of the mystics. Maybe I haven't explained it, and maybe no one can. In investigating the expressiveness of a sonnet by Shakespeare one brings to bear every resource one possesses of language, psychology, and thought, thereby increasing one's understanding and pleasure, but in the end one's resources will be exhausted and one's understanding will run into the mystery of the poem. Not a mystery in the sense of an enigma, but in the sense of an unclassifiability. The poem is unique; it cannot be interpreted in any terms but its own, which means that no computer, let it be programmed ever so sophisticatedly, can discover or record all the combinations of nuance that make the poem. The same with personality. The same with my happiness and its spirituality. Yet these, like the poem, exist. I can identify them and believe in them, and believe in the connections they have made for me, as in the hospital when I began, after a lifetime of anxious withdrawal, to talk spontaneously with those around me, performing little acts of virtue. It is a connectedness that has continued. It becomes greater. And the feeling of happiness, which of course I do accept and for which I am truly grateful, is undeniable. It makes all the difference.

Fragments of
Autobiography

Fragments of Autobiography

Somewhere near Villeneuve de Berg in the Ardèche is a hill I visited a number of times when I lived briefly in that region ten years ago. Not a knoll or a cobble, but a good-sized hill, part of the system of foothills leading northwestward to the Massif Central. I don't remember its name.

At the base of the hill was a scattering of homes, the farthest fringe of the village, some of them old farmhouses, others more recently built. Gardens, cars, children's toys; the usual pleasant clutter. Farther up the slope were terraced orchards, mostly of polled mulberry trees, gnarled and ancient, with overgrown scrub oak, vines, and tall grasses; a grazing place for goats. A small broken-down *magnanerie* in a gully was evidence of the silk culture that had helped sustain the upland country of the Midi in the time before synthesized fabrics. The whole hill was strewn with jagged boulders of limestone, glacial detritus. Small hand-lettered wooden signs, the letters carved or charred, marked the boundaries of truffle-hunting grounds to which local people hold hereditary rights, not necessarily coinciding with other property lines.

At the top was a ruined village from the eighteenth century and earlier. Lines of sprawling, pale, angular stones marked the walls of buildings whose timbered parts had long since rotted away; longer lines marked a principal street and two or three secondary ones. There were larger rectangles too, which I took to be pens and corrals. It must have been a village inhabited by shepherds, perhaps only in summer.

Elsewhere indications of a still earlier culture remained. Toward its far end the village dispersed completely into rubble, reminding me of Old Oraibe and other ancient pueblos of the

American southwest. Beyond this, on the crown of the hill, I found fields of stone so dense that hardly any vegetation grew there, nothing but a few stunted junipers and oaks. At one place archaeologists had cleared the site of an Aurignacian dolmen, an impressive structure of huge flattish stones, three to form the walls and a fourth, still larger, laid over the top for a roof, what the French call *une table*. I believe the site of a menhir was also on that hill, though I may be confusing it with another I saw; menhirs, the upright columns we associate with Stonehenge, are less common than dolmens in southern France. When I walked farther, stepping from stone to stone—in this I had a certain skill from walking in my brook in Vermont—I found another dolmen, partly fallen, its site uncleared, and also the entrance to a cave, a black opening, two or three feet wide, down into the earth, so ringed by white, jagged stones that it could be called toothy. I nearly fell into it, but made no attempt to descend, being not partial to caves. Was it a big cave? Did it have paintings on its walls? Almost certainly not. The hole showed no sign of activity. My knowledge of archaeology and geology was—and is—slight. Did the Stone Age people live on top of that hill? At any rate they did *something* up there; no mistake about that. Then there were the moon-faces, as I called them, which I saw many times in that region, perfectly round, carved in half-relief on lintels, end-stones, herms, etc. I could learn nothing about them from the local people, but I presumed they were originally Celtic and late neolithic, a culture which in those hills might have lasted well into Roman times. Surrounded by all that history I felt my ignorance keenly. "Go read some books," I told myself.

But ruins were everywhere in that poor, devastated region. The village I lived in, Lagorce, was 80 per cent destroyed. All that remained of the old chateau were a few broken walls, a half-buried room, and signs of a moat. Many houses in the village were only broken walls. Most of the inhabitants were old people, or outsiders like myself.

Well, in a desultory way I did read a few books, mostly about the history and language of Occitania, but I am not a scholar. My curiosity is not the kind that can be satisfied by objective knowledge. Plato said that opinion is worthless and that only knowledge counts, which is a neat formulation, attractive to Mediterranean temperaments, including Yeats's (e.g., in "A Prayer for My Daughter"). But melancholy Danes from the northern mists understand that opinion is all there is. The great questions transcend fact, and discourse is a process of personality. Knowledge cannot respond to knowledge.

And wisdom? Is it not opinion refined, opinion killed and resuscitated upward? Maybe Plato would have agreed with this.

I liked to sit in a particular spot at the top of that hill near Villeneuve de Berg, on a wall of the ruined village, looking out toward the terraced slopes of other hills in the distance. Over my shoulder I could see the dolmen in its mute significance, could almost see the ancient folk struggling to raise and move those stones weighing many tons. All about me lay the silent remains of a village that had once, to judge by the number and complexity of its walls, been a bustling community. Both inside and outside the village were shallow diggings, evidence that hunters of wild truffles were still at work, though surely theirs is a dying trade. Down below was the silk culture, already quite dead. A few miles farther into the Massif I had seen beautiful chestnut orchards and the villages, now poor as dirt, of the people who in past centuries had invented scores of ways to use the hulls, shells, and meats of *le marron* and had lived on their inventions. A few miles away in Largentière I could still overhear women gossiping in *lo lenga doc* in the churchyard of what had been an Albigensian cathedral. Thousands upon thousands of ghosts whispered in the air around me; many layers and levels of culture. Even the living were assimilated, a sound of hammering and radio music from the foot of the hill, a jet overhead signing the blue sky with its contrail. The earth itself, the stony wreckage and rickety vegetation, was as clear in its significance as any slaughtering ground. Every natural thing is transitory and contained in its own nonexistence. Every species, the human as well as the rest, is extinct. Why? What for?

I was reminded of the time many years earlier when my family had spent part of each summer at the place of a close friend in the remote countryside of Dutchess County in New

York. This was in the twenties and early thirties. The town, named Dover Furnace after the old stone smelteries still to be seen there, which were said to have furnished iron for Revolutionary cannon, at that time had a railway station, store, and post office, now disappeared. Electric power was unavailable, so our friend had built a sizable dam, twenty-five feet high, across a stream on his property and had installed his own generator and transmission lines. I was a boy of eight or nine. The spot where I liked to sit then was on top of that dam between two spillways which controlled the flow of water and the level of the millpond; in other words I liked the roar of water in my ears, which effectively shut me off from the rest of the universe. It was a point of stillness, so to speak, in the immensity of action. The blade of grass being twitched by the current on the bank of the stream below me, the oriole flying across my field of vision to its nest in an elm a hundred feet beyond, were motions seeming vastly distant as I sat in the roar of eternity on either side. I was truly isolated. And what I thought about was: Why? What for?

The purposelessness of it all, of existence as such, had struck me at so early an age that I have no idea when it happened or how. Perhaps it came from a conjunction of my father's atheism and my mother's conventional Episcopalian faith. (I went to Sunday school because the other kids did. It seemed to me a strange place.) Or perhaps it came from some early, repressed encounter with personal death. More likely it was the result of many causes, too lost and intricate to be known. But I had always been aware that the universe is sad; everything in it, animate or inanimate, the wild creatures, the stones, the stars, was enveloped in the great sadness, pervaded by it. Existence had no use. It was without end or reason. The most beautiful things in it, a flower or a song, as well as the most compelling, a desire or a thought, were pointless. So great a sorrow. And I knew that the only rest from my anxiety—for I had been trembling even in infancy—lay in acknowledging and absorbing this sadness, as I did when I sat on top of the dam, a boy at the deafening instant between the future and the past.

Never then or now have I been able to look at a cloudless sky at night and see beauty there. A kind of grandeur, yes—but not beauty. The profusion and variety of celestial lights have always frightened me. Why are they there? Why these instead of others? Why these instead of nothing? And no received faith or reason has ever helped me one iota in answering.

What is the difference between a "natural object" and a "man-made object?" None. In ultimate terms—and I've never been able to think otherwise than ultimately; no wonder my scholarship is paltry—all things in reality are part of reality, and hence are equal; they all plunge equally into transitoriness and nonexistence. The only meaning, such as men and women pretend to find in mathematical or poetic statements, is the meaning of obliteration. The only absolute value is value itself inverted, turned inside out—the void. And long before I came intellectually to the realization that the notion of relative value implies inescapably a hierarchical structure, which thus tends toward illegitimate triadism, dualism, monism—and it wasn't easy to give up my pragmatic Yankee view, my agreeable fondness for Mr. Peirce and W. James—I knew that everything is equivalent, every pebble and masterpiece, every atom and thought of love: they are *precisely* the same in value. The idea of value is an invention. At its best a sick joke, and at its worst an inexpressible sorrow.

Many times in the past twenty-five years I have been called a "nature poet." I'm grateful to anyone who takes the trouble to read something I have written, of course, but I wish to say also, quietly but insistently, that if I am a nature poet, then the understanding of nature which I have suggested here is fundamental to my work; it is, literally, the foundation. I think it can be seen in most of my poems, except that readers are predisposed to overlook it. Naturally, like most people, I am prone to changes of mood; at any given time (but aren't they all "given"?) my cheerfulness in the face of existence may be more or, usually, less than at other times. But at all times my perception of what exists, the whole or a part, is of the absence of intelligence, except for the weak, insipid, tedious, petulant, and inadequate intelligence of human beings.

But to say this merely on my own behalf would not be enough to justify writing it here. I believe I speak for a good many others. Elsewhere I have explained my aversion to the lovelessness, arrogance, and egomania of Henry D. Thoreau in his book called *Walden*.[1] I won't recapitulate the argument here. But it is worth noting that many readers, though five women for every man, have told me that they understand my view and share it. They see the connection between Thoreau's so-called Transcendentalism, i.e., his flight from reality, and the violence and irresponsibility of the American frontier, which are now in a fair way to becoming the national way of life. My view is not extreme; on the contrary it is a middle ground between Thoreau's expropriative, solipsistic vision of nature and the systematic disdain we find, for instance, in the work of a European like Jean-Paul Sartre. Yet Americans have been so brainwashed by continual subjection to *Walden* that my moderative tendencies seem actually out of line. It isn't that when you pick up the book review section of the Sunday *New York Times* you will find that easily half the reviews emit a Waldenesque smell; it is rather that a great number of those who are reading the reviews will, once they put down the paper, go out on Sunday birdwalks with all of *Walden's* snobbery and righteousness and sentimentalism crammed in their heads. I believe no other book in English has been more widely read by the American middle class, by millions and millions of comparatively well-heeled and powerful people. It is a touchstone even for those who work with nature—scientists, forestry professors, veterinarians, state fish and game administrators, and so on. The one class of country people who have not read it is the farmers and farm workers, though they too have been affected by it from a distance and derivatively. *Everyone* had been affected—and infected. We need a national antitoxin.

That's what a small band of us is trying to provide. We are profoundly attached to nature, our lives are dominated by it and we write about it, we write about flowers, birds, the differing intensities of color in autumn, the venation of a locust's wing, about the greatest manifestations and the least (which

---

1. "The Man in the Box at Walden," *Effluences from the Sacred Caves* (Ann Arbor: University of Michigan Press, 1983), pp. 63–68.

are, in fact equivalencies), but we do so clear-sightedly. To the mass of the *literati* we say: Have the kindness to understand what we are trying to do, what we are actually writing, before you make pronouncements about it. (The "favorable" pronouncements are often as silly as their opposites.) Cling to your Thoreauvian TV if you must, to Walt Disney and John Wayne—those twins!—to the *National Geographic* and "Miami Vice." But please refrain from criticizing us in ignorance. Our number is small, but it is growing, and we have young, vigorous leaders, people like Audre Lorde, George Dennison, John Ashbury, Grace Paley, Cid Corman, June Jordan, Leo Connellan, Ray Carver, Edward Hoagland, and others, as well as some though not all of the essayists who write about specific matters of environmental understanding in the pop magazines, people as diverse in style and temperament as any you could choose, but they are clear-sighted. They know what the earth is and what it means. If we are to find a way to proceed beyond the violence that is crippling us now in every sphere, beyond the egomaniacal sentimentality that cripples us just as much, the main intention of these people and others like them must prevail.

∾ ∾ ∾

A number of women of my generation or earlier have told me that they were knowledgeable about the facts of sex and reproduction when they were children—five or six years old, say— but that they then repressed this knowledge so completely that later, when they were adolescent and necessity required them to rediscover these facts, they suffered an emotional trauma. This was an aspect of the general difficulty women have always had, but especially during the Victorian age, as it is called, and the time while the influence of that age continued in American civilization—as in some respects it continues even now—an aspect, but only one, of the difficulty women experienced in growing up in a sexist society. Probably in our so-called open society today most young girls are spared this kind of repression and trauma. Which is an important topic, but not what I want to write about here. Instead I want to say that I understand clearly how such strange repression and trauma can occur, though most young people today would find it unimaginable, because I experienced the same things with respect to my knowledge of personal death.

When does a child become aware of personal death? Some psychiatrists argue that for infants the experience of birth itself may be an experience of death, of the destruction of reality, which I have no trouble accepting. At the very least it must be an experience of radical vulnerability. But it occurs so early that we cannot consciously remember it happening; we think we were born with it. Thus I can't tell when my knowledge of personal death first came to me, but I do know from certain corroborative thoughts and images that if I did not have it "always," I had it well before the age of three, when my family moved from Waterbury to Woodbury in Connecticut. I know further that it was associated with the person of my father, the stranger who waited for me outside the womb. What I cannot know—one of the billions of things—is how long it took me to move from my virtually instantaneous knowledge of my own death to the inference that he, the stranger, would also die, and would die before me.

All our lives we are the accomplices of Time, our mortal enemy. It is the treason against ourselves that we cannot resist.

Though they are there in my mind, these memories are shadowy. The fact of repression is not. Of course I don't mean I completely repressed the facts of life and death, which would be impossible. But their urgency, their immediate and felt relationship to my personal existence, their enormous capacity to frighten me—these were "forgotten." And my parents did everything they could to abet this. One of the events of my childhood that now seems perhaps the most extraordinary of all was when I was told of my grandmother's—my father's mother's—death. This was when I was eight or nine years old. I had known her well. Although she and my grandfather lived more than fifty miles away—a real journey in the twenties; by car, when we were lucky enough to have the use of one, it took three or four hours, and by train more than that and a considerable wait to make a connection at Brewster—I saw them often on holidays and in the summer. I knew my grandmother as a kindly old lady with gray hair who wore shapeless dresses and black, lace-up shoes, a woman who was recessive in her household, did not talk much, spent her time baking pies and frying doughnuts, but who was friendly and welcoming and imaginative in her relationships with children. She paid attention to me. She told me stories and thought of things for me to do. When I was told of her death, I grieved. But not deeply nor long, because my grief was dispelled almost immediately by a sense of mystery operating on many levels.

I was told of her death not only after she died but after her funeral and burial. Yet she had died in our house. She had lived in our house for some time before her death, I don't remember how long, perhaps a couple of months, bedridden with cancer, cared for by my mother and father and hired nurses. Our house was not a mansion by any means; it was a poor man's house with seven small rooms. Yet I never saw my grandmother in her final illness, I was not permitted to go into her room. I was unaware of her death, I was unaware of the removal of her body, I had never even heard any suspicious noises, and the whole episode was kept from me until after her funeral by what must have been an almost inconceivably elaborate subterfuge, in which my grandmother herself, in her final suffering, must have concurred.

That was Victorianism. Death was taboo in our house. So was sex. These topics were never mentioned. I don't mean that they were casually omitted in a mutually acknowledged understanding, such as one can find in many homes today; probably in almost any home some topic—the father's birthmark, the mother's addiction to soap operas—will be unmentionable. But in our home death and sex were so systematically ignored that they could not exist. Our mutually acknowledged understanding was that if either of these topics were spoken of, some great catastrophe would ensue, reality would be shattered. When I was much older, in my mid-thirties, living for a few years with my parents because I was acutely ill and had nowhere else to go, the three of us were playing Scrabble one night—a game I soon despised—and I made the word *venery*. "What does that mean?" my mother asked. I had uttered only the first fragment of a speech-sound in response when my father, blushing beet red, broke in, "It means the art of hunting deer." Later I looked it up in the unabridged dictionary, and by God he was right—as he was so often when it came to questions of language: I had plenty of occasion to marvel at his vocabulary. The "art of hunting deer" is a secondary meaning. But here was my mother, a woman in her fifties who had been married for years and had borne three children, yet who, in America and in the fifties, could not be "subjected" to a largely archaic and in a sense technical, respectable term that in its primary meaning signifies fucking or sexual lust in general. (Etymologically they are two separate words, both spelled *venery*.) This is the degree of repression my father suffered from all his life, which he imposed on the rest of his family. What it meant was a peculiar shallowness in the quality of family experience, which I think was common in lower middle-class English homes during the Victorian and Edwardian periods, and in American homes that imitated them, resulting in all kinds of trivial and disguised and absurdly unnatural behavior.

Children were "Brownies," who lived forever. Sprites and fairies inhabited the woods. Santa Claus was the intimate friend not only of small children but of adults. The extent of such fancies is nearly unbelievable now. I had to pretend a belief in Santa Claus long beyond the time when I had been disillusioned, even until I was twelve or thirteen years old; in fact we *never* came to an open agreement that Father Christmas was a fantasy. The adult family was almost as deeply trapped in what my father might have called—if he had known the jargon of criticism—"necessary fictions" as the family of children had been.

All this was accomplished without resort to a religious base. My father had seen angels, but he was a proclaimed atheist. My mother's efforts to give me and my younger brothers at least some grounding in low-church Episcopalianism were smothered by my father's radical rationalism. Of course I did not discover until long afterward that this combination of rationalism and materialism with fantasized spirituality was deeply rooted in English Romanticism and post-Romanticism, from Shelley to Morris to Swinburne, and that my father, past the middle of the twentieth century, was still living in a watered-down pre-Raphaelite, Blakean (as in *Songs of Innocence*—his favorite poem was the first one in that book), *Yellow-Book*ish era. A spiritual element existed in our life, but it had no footing in the real cultural and historical place of the family, and hence was perceived by the children as tenuous and even anomalous.

Two books that were imposed on me when I was a child were *Alice in Wonderland* and Charles Kingsley's *Water Babies*. I loathed both of them. I knew this at the time and did everything I could *not* to be affected by them, even to the extent of hiding the books. (Destruction would have been unthinkable.) But only much later did I come to see that my loathing was a consequence of stifled fear, a profound mortal terror. To this day I cannot take pleasure in fantasy and have resisted such authors as Tolkien and C. S. Lewis.

As for the trauma, the necessary rediscovery, it came later in my adolescence than I would now have expected, and I don't know how to account for that. I was a freshman in college, seventeen years old. Perhaps this is substantiating evidence of the degree of repression I had undergone. I was a student at the University of North Carolina in Chapel Hill. I was living in a boarding house on the western edge of town, a large house with a pillared verandah next to a big magnolia tree, but it was a shabby house that badly needed painting and repair. This was in the depth of the Great Depression. The landlord was a peddler of cheap jewelry, a sharp dresser with a battered sample case who went from door to door in little towns, from farm to farm in the country. I remember once or twice when he sat with us, the students, in the evening, brushing his thinning hair with a silver-backed military hairbrush and telling us how this benefited the scalp and stimulated the growth of new hair. His wife was a drab woman. She was thin and had straight black hair that fell untidily around her face, which looked ravaged by work and anxiety; she wore old dresses and sweaters with holes in their elbows. They lived in the back of the house, I think in what had originally been the servants' quarters, and I slept in a small room, not much more than a closet, where I could hear them through the wall. One night she asked him if they could make love. I can't remember her words, and probably I didn't hear them clearly—in fact what I remember is her whispering, which nevertheless expressed urgency. Her gist was clear enough. "No," he said, "I don't want to, I'm too tired." From fucking all those farm women, I thought, after you've sold them pieces of trash for more money than they ought to spend. And then immediately I thought: *I am going to die.* Not casually, I'm gonna die someday like everyone else; but rather, I, this self, this focus of identity, all I have, all I am right now—*this* will be annihilated, *I* will become extinct. In my bed I bolted upright; my eyes smarted, my heart thundered, my breath was labored as if my own throat were strangling me. Plenty of times before I had been afraid, and as I know now all my life from an early age had been governed by hidden anxiety, but this was different. It was terror and panic. I made no sound, I did nothing but lie down again in the bed and pull the covers over me, but I was out of control. I did not sleep that night. And to tell the truth, during most of the thousands of nights since then I haven't slept much either.

Why this happened on that particular night is not hard to understand.

∾   ∾   ∾

Woodbury, the town in Connecticut where I lived from age three to thirteen, stretched for several miles along its Main Street, which was—and still is—the old U.S. Route 6 that joins Provincetown, Massachusetts, to the west coast. In the twenties it was a big highway; I thought living next to it was rather significant, though I couldn't have said of what. From our steps that led down the bank to the road, my friend Ralph and I watched the passing cars for hours, dozens and scores of different makes, which we could identify and upon whose qualities we held complex opinions: Dusenbergs, Stutzes, Pierce Arrows, Franklins (air-cooled cars with funny-looking hoods), Studebakers, Dodges, and so on, down to the lowly Model Ts that we called Tin Lizzies—when one went by we routinely hollered, "Get a horse!" Fairly often we saw cars with out-of-state markers, as we called the license plates; occasionally we saw a car from far away, from Florida, Colorado, or even California, and this was cause for rejoicing in our limited lives.

Like most towns in New England, Woodbury was extensive. Woodbury and North Woodbury, with perhaps three miles of Main Street between them, were the principal foci; they were fully independent and had their own post offices and town administrations. But the school district incorporated both of them. Other early settlements had been absorbed by the two towns but still were separate communities and had their own names, such as Pomperaug, Middle Quarter, Hotchkissville, the West Side, Sherman Hill, and so on, connected by many gravel roads and by the river and its system of tributary brooks. Other names were important too: the Green, the Dump, the Dam, the Blacksmith's, the Iron Bridge, the Indian Grave, the Quarry, the Cliff. This last was part of a granite ridge that lay parallel to Main Street and east of it. The Masonic Temple stood on top of the cliff, just at the point where the Indian maiden had jumped to her death in despair for her love of a white settler. Every town in New England, and for all I know in the rest of the country, has an Indian maiden in its mythology, and the meaning of these hapless women in American culture could not be charmingly extrapolated, I'm sure.

Farther back, on the highest point of the ridge, stood the Fire Tower. It was an open structure of steel girders and struts about eighty feet high with a railed wooden platform at the top, then a roof over the platform and a wooden pole rising from the center of the roof. I don't know what the pole was, perhaps a flagstaff or a support for a radio antenna, more likely just a decoration; the fact is that I never saw the fire tower manned. I suppose during times of drought the town or the state may have posted someone to keep watch, but I don't recall ever seeing anyone up there who looked like a fire-watcher, and the tower was clearly visible from Main Street. What I do recall is that every boy in Woodbury who was worth his salt had to have his initials carved in that pole, which was six-sided, not round. It meant climbing to the platform, standing on the rail, hoisting oneself out, up, and over the edge of the roof—eighty feet in the air—then hanging on with one hand and using one's jackknife with the other. And then, of course, getting back down. What folly for anyone. For a boy already afflicted with the acrophobia that would become pathologically extreme a few years later, it wasn't foolish, it was crazy. Nevertheless I did it.

No doubt by now if that tower still stands its pole is etched and over-etched with hundreds of initials. Which means that hundreds of boys have looked at that sloping roof in terror; they have looked death in the face and defied it. For what? Vanity. Yet perhaps it was not a bad thing for boys to do.

I was scared up there, and I remember my fear, but I remember also how beautiful the town looked from the tower, especially in the fall. Such an intensity of color—red, orange, yellow—rising from the woods and hills, from the great maples that lined the roads and shaded the houses. The October sky, brilliantly blue; the October air, its effervescent freshness. On a Saturday afternoon one could see from the tower scores of thin, blue columns of smoke rising from the town, spreading out at a certain elevation below the ridge-lines of the hills. The townspeople were burning their leaves. In those days we felt no remissness if we burned the leaves instead of composting them, and the smoke with its piquant smell was no pollution. On the contrary it was a sign of seasonal change, of ritual change, always welcome. The labor of summer was over, the harvest completed, the cows were in the barn (or soon would be). It was a time to put on our worn flannel shirts and old woollen sweaters raveling at the elbows, so comfortable, conformable. In our family we wore old clothes from necessity, but with a kind of gratification too, derived in part from ordinary Yankee feelings of thrift, but in part also from something more indistinct and perhaps especially important to the Carruths—a knowledge that we were common folk and that the common values, including those of common suffering, were worth noticing.

Even during the affluent twenties, Woodbury was a poor town. No one was starving, though a few families lived on the edge of it, especially in winter, those pitiful families whose genetic resources in the back country had dwindled over centuries. (Woodbury was first settled in 1636.) Many of the farms were too small, stony, overworked, and infertile to be productive. Some of these, especially north of town, had been taken up by Lithuanian refugees, who were struggling to make a foothold in America. Their children, with unpronounceable, unspellable names, came to school in tattered clothes, the boys in drab vests and the girls in more colorful ones, both sexes with strange crude haircuts and their stockings falling down. The rest of us shunned them. Children are not just cruel, they are barbarous. But in truth, if it makes any difference, the strangeness of the Lithuanians, not their poverty, was what made them alien to us. How remote and isolated Woodbury was—no Italians, no Jews, no Portuguese. The one French-Canadian family, the St. Pierres, had been there for several generations; and the one black family, the Fords, had descended from northern slaves freed before the Revolution. No, the Lithuanians, three or four families, were our foreigners, whose children were called *snot-nosed* as a matter of course.

But not in October. Who could be xenophobic in the midst of that glory? Autumn was a time of good health and clear thinking, so it seemed to me. People died in winter, spring, summer, but not in autumn. Autumn was beautiful, fleeting, touched with the premonitory sorrow that I somehow came at an early age to recognize as the fundamental quality of all existence. The trees, the stones, the stars: all were consummately beautiful, and all were condemned to mutability.

Perhaps the best of autumn was to sit on the cool grass at the end of afternoon while the piles of leaves still smoldered and eat concord grapes taken in ripe clusters from the vine that sprawled on the arbor of cedar poles my father had made for it.

∾   ∾   ∾

When I began to smoke in earnest I can't remember. It was well before I was thirteen, which is when my family moved from Woodbury to Pleasantville. I know I experimented with tobacco when I was five or six, stealing from packs of Lucky Strikes my Uncle Max left lying around the house. I can remember sitting in the sun on the hill that sloped down from our back fence, lighting cigarettes and blowing the smoke out in gusty huffs, studying the way a cigarette looked in my hand. I can remember trying to chew a pinch of my father's pipe tobacco. By the age of nine I was picking up butts from the street, saving them in the fold at the waist of my heavy sweater. My friend Ralph, who lived across the road and was a year younger than I, was a smoker too; we snagged butts and smoked them together in the loft of his family's barn, which was not used for storing hay, or in the woods. I can remember smoking in the icehouse that was near Sullivan's Pond. I can remember being taught to inhale smoke by an older boy in a gravel pit off toward the eastern edge of town; he took a drag on his cigarette, opened his mouth to show me the smoke, then breathed it down into his lungs. He handed me the cigarette and I tried it. Of course it made me dizzy, but I pretended I didn't feel a thing. Which, ever since, is what I have pretended generally.

I remember buying cigarettes at the drugstore by saying they were for my uncle. I remember when the druggist, having been alerted by some busybody, told me I couldn't have any more. I remember sitting on the girder of the steel-truss bridge over the Pomperaug River, thirty feet above the swimming hole, with Margaret Shean, a freckled, sexy-looking, intelligent girl from my eighth-grade class at school, beside me. We were in bathing suits, as we called them then; I was smoking and had a pack of Camels in my hand. Margaret was Irish and Catholic—she went to my school because Woodbury had no parochial school—and a little prim, and she was nagging me in a covertly flirtatious way, which was the only kind of flirtation twelve-year-olds could imagine in 1932. "Why don't you throw those cigarettes away?" she said. I turned my hand over and dropped the pack down into the river. It floated away. What an unusual and romantic thing to do!— that's what I told myself, and Margaret put her hand on my wrist. I can bring back to my mind without effort the sensations of her touch and the gratification and excitement and mystery I felt as a consequence of what I had done. But I'm sure I had got my hands on some more cigarettes, one way or another, before the sun went down.

Incidentally, the image of that pack of Camels falling toward the water, falling flat and without turning and hitting the water an instant later with a little splat, remains vivid in my mind for another reason. Why didn't I pitch myself after it and dash out my brains on the rocks below? At the time I don't believe I was tempted, but now, after fifty-five years of phobic, including acrophobic, conditioning, I am retrospectively—and powerfully—tempted. The vision, as vivid as anything in my memory, of that pack of cigarettes, which had been a part of myself, falling toward the water seems to draw me after it and makes me gasp every time I think of it. I suspect I have thought of it every day since it happened.

I loved to watch people smoking. The farm boys at the diner could drag in such riches of smoke from their unfiltered Chesterfields and Old Golds that it came out in ropes and loops from their mouths and nostrils. The local businessmen would light up their Luckies by striking kitchen matches, which they kept in the side pockets of their suit coats, with their thumbnails, then blow out the match with a long straight plume of smoke. Another of my uncles, who talked loudly, would smoke his Camels in a paper holder with a goose-quill tip, like FDR's, and he would talk and exhale smoke at the same time, so that the smoke came out every whichway, as if it were the ectoplasmic embodiment of his language. Mostly women didn't smoke in those days, but sometimes I saw a college girl from Vassar—in those years we often spent weekends at Dover Furnace, New York, not far from Poughkeepsie—who smoked or pretended to, dressed in a big sweater and short pleated skirt with her hair bobbed and a huge necklace swinging on her nearly breastless front. But such girls smoked effetely, holding the cigarette between thumb and index finger like a European, puffing the smoke out without inhaling it, batting their eyes. I scorned them. In the winter when my breath was visible I loved to blow out vapor as if it were smoke, using a twig or a pencil for a cigarette, and I studied the different shapes I could give my "smoke" by changing my mouth and the tilt of my head. In those years smoke meant more to me than marbles, hockey, my solitary reading and writing, or the glimpse of a girl's underwear when she was putting on her arctics, as we called overshoes. I was an addict before I had smoked five cartons of real cigarettes, five ounces of Prince Albert or Edgeworth. I was sold on smoke from the very beginning, the way some kids are sold on training for the Olympics or giving a recital in Town Hall at the age of thirteen.

Of course my family hated the idea of my smoking and rejected it absolutely. This was part of the whole mind-set of Carruthian secular and neurotic puritanism, as was the fear of talking about it, of talking about anything that might be charged with negative feeling. So the fiction was maintained for years, all during my adolescence, that I didn't smoke. I smoked out the window of my bedroom. I smoked when I went walking at night in the quiet streets of Pleasantville. I smoked behind the school with my friends or at the swimming pool in summer. By the time I was fifteen I had been thoroughly shanghaied by both cigarettes and pipes, a condition my family at last acknowledged when I went to college a couple of years later. By the time I was twenty-five I was knowledgeable about the grades of Havana filler, binder, and wrapper, East Indian and African blends, cigars from Connecticut like Muniemachers, Kafkas, and Judges Caves, pipe tobaccos such as white burley, bright leaf, Cavendish, perique from Louisiana, Latakia, and Turkish and Macedonian varieties whose names I no longer remember, etc. But mainly I smoked Camels, two or three packs a day. At age forty I gave up cigarettes and for about fifteen years smoked only pipes (twenty a day, mostly Granger Rough Cut) and cigars (two or three a day if I could afford them), and then gradually in my late fifties I succumbed to cigarettes again, though now the filtered, "low-tar" kinds. Today I smoke usually two packs of cigarettes a day, five pipes, and one or two cigars.

In other words I smoke all the time. Only rarely do I encounter a smoker like me. To smoke twenty pipes a day, as I did for years, one must live with a cindered mouth, a mouth no better than a charcoal brazier. To smoke as many cigarettes as I do one must cough continually, wheeze and pant, accept constant inflammation of lungs, throat, nose, etc. The pain is considerable. At night, when I go to bed after a day of smoking, I often have such pain in my chest, such difficulty with breathing, that

I become truly frightened and dream about suffocation, the death I fear most. And of course everyone knows now, though we did not when I was young, about the hidden damages, cancer, emphysema, heart weakness, clogged arteries—the deaths that smoking brings to us, 370,000 a year in America. I am writing this on the twenty-fifth anniversary of the first surgeon general's warning printed on cigarette packages; this news on the radio is what has impelled me to put such a wretched history into words. Now for twenty-five years I have been reading that forecast of my own death! And I believe my addiction is more profound today than it has ever been.

Every morning when I get up, no matter how rotten I've felt the night before, I reach for a cigarette automatically, and smoke five or six while I have my coffee. If I don't do this I begin immediately to feel a great psychic itch, untranslatable into any language, that prevents me from working or doing much of anything. I have no doubt whatever that this addiction is mostly "psychological"; it is in my head, so involved in my personality, like the innermost cog of a machine, that I am dysfunctional without it. The nicotine is unimportant. The symbolic and attitudinal significance of smoking is everything. My life depends on it.

A painter whom I particularly admire and whose work seems to me close to my own in poetry is Vlaminck, especially in his later paintings of French farms and villages. He was also a musician who played in clubs and dance halls and a competitive cyclist, a tough and independent guy. I have never seen a photo of him in which he wasn't smoking a cigarette, pipe, or cigar. He was a smoker like me. Maybe that's part of the reason for my attraction to his work, though certainly only a part. He was a damned good painter.

What is the reason for this addiction? Do I still get pleasure from smoking? Not much. Since the Cuban embargo, almost thirty years ago, I have never found a cigar I enjoyed as much as the double claro, candella Havanas that used to be common, and my favorite commercial pipe tobacco, State Express from England, was discontinued some time ago. Cigarettes give me almost no sensual enjoyment at all. No, the reason lies far back in childhood, I'm certain of that, though it's still impossible for me to distinguish all the causative elements clearly. In part I admired my father and his "literary" ways, and he was a pipe smoker; in part I hated him and resented the alienation he forced on me and all our family. Cigarette smoking was a way to cross the immense barrier between the Carruths and the rest of the world, which I wanted to do more than anything. I wanted to be "out there" with the others, away from solitude and fear. I never made it and never will. Precisely how this dynamic knot of attraction and repulsion evolved over the years and became an ineradicable component of my being, is unknown to me. I doubt anyone could figure it out except in gross, uninteresting terms. But I know it is there, close to the heart of my psychopathological life, creative and destructive, a strength, a weakness, a function of the basic energy that has always driven me.

∾ ∾ ∾

The Rome Theater in Pleasantville probably resembled most small-town movie houses in the 1930s all over the country. It had been built a decade or so earlier. By 1936 it was worn and shabby; it offered double features, bingo, giveaway chinaware, anything to attract audiences. Admission was fifteen cents for matinées and twenty-five in the evenings. I went as often as I could, perhaps once a week, and did not care greatly what movies were showing, with the consequence that now my memory is overladen with names, faces, and images of all kinds from the popular films of that era.

But sometimes I went furtively to a door in the back of the building. It opened off a slotlike alley. The other side of the alley was a concrete wall. Trash barrels. Broken furniture. Many shadows. When I was certain no one could see me, I slipped through the door, then up a steep, dingy stairway that brought me to another theater hidden on top of the one below. This secret theater was dark, small, filled with cigarette smoke. The seats pitched downward toward the screen at a sharp angle. The whirring of the projector could be heard distinctly, and the coruscant beam of light that shot down through the smoke to the screen was bright and straight.

Perhaps the audience numbered thirty or forty. No more than that. I remember little else about them. And what I remember of the films is only that they were different from those shown in the public theater down below: more serious. No sentimental comedies or tawdry musicals. I have the impression they were westerns, which my parents disapproved, but also that they were about real moral and metaphysical issues, probably with a political slant. They may have been a kind of super-newsreel, news raised to the status of myth, for newsreels were often what I liked best when I went to the movies. At any rate they were not, though one might have expected it, pornographic. As I sat in the dark and watched, my feelings were fear and excitement mingled together, a sense of growing confidence which I nevertheless knew might turn out to be false. I also felt pleasantly alone. I was aware that the others scattered among the seats were experiencing similar feelings.

Maybe after all it was a kind of pornography?

Now I have a clearer if still faint remembrance of those others. They were all men. They were older than I. The projector's light reflected dimly from white shirts and here and there from bald heads and eyeglasses. They sat mostly apart from one another or in groups of two and three, and in differing attitudes—some lounging, some bent forward toward the screen.

This dream began when I was about fifteen and continued until I was in my forties.

Auden wrote somewhere that the invention of photography was the worst of the disasters of technology. I don't recall exactly what he meant. Probably he felt that photography blurred the distinction between his primary and secondary worlds, as he called them, the worlds of reality and imagination, and since this distinction was important to him, photography—the preservation of reality outside of time, which had been a function of the imagination through all earlier epochs—was troublesome. I agree that keeping this distinction in mind is important, but not that the distinction itself means much. In fact the primary and secondary worlds are interfused, and we live in a fluidity of consciousness. What happens inside and outside a camera is merely a simplified analogue of what happens inside and outside a human head.

Nevertheless a filmed image, especially of a person, is a mystery. Not a puzzle; it can be rationalized easily. It is a variable awesomeness, sometimes poignant, sometimes frightening. Only rarely is it joyful. How can that person who is dead, or who is even twenty minutes older, be there? Jung emphasized the similarity, conventionality, and recognizability of archetypal images because it suited his purpose to do so, but individuality is what makes those images powerful. A burned-out ranch may be the sack of Troy, but it is still a burned-out ranch. That man in the newsreel running and dodging down the hillside, that Spanish Republican caught at the instant when the bullet smashes his heart, that death in its individual actuality forever: this is the mystery and awesomeness. And this, aside from the simple symbolic representation—the womb, the initiation, the secret identity—is what my dream was about.

When I was ten or eleven I had a BB-gun, a standard Daisy "air rifle," as they were called, although they were not air-powered but spring-powered, ordered from the Sears Roebuck catalogue and paid for with money I had earned. It was the only gun I've ever owned. (Gun, from the medieval Latin feminine name Gunilda, applied to a mangonel or stone-throwing machine, though I don't know what to make of that—or maybe I do.) I shot and killed two living creatures with it. One was a medium-sized green frog by the edge of a brook; it died immediately. A bubble formed on its back and grew larger and larger until it burst; then a second bubble, a third, etc. The other was a chickadee on a branch of the maple outside our attic window. I shot from well back of the window and in the expectation that I wouldn't hit the bird, and at first I thought I hadn't, for like the frog it didn't move. Then slowly—almost as if thoughtfully—it tilted forward from its perch and fell to the ground. I ran down the two flights of stairs, retrieved it, and buried it.

Both these episodes sickened me.

Once I also deliberately shot my younger brother Gorton point-blank. He was wearing a heavy, stiff, horsehide jacket that had once been mine. I was certain the impact of the BB wouldn't be felt through that thick leather—although if I was certain why did I try it? Gorton's face turned red and he began to cry—he was about six or seven at the time—and I could see he wasn't putting it on; he was stung. And no doubt shocked by my perfidy. So was I.

I was, or became, a first-class marksman. In the army I was given a Thompson submachine gun, which I'm glad I never had to shoot except on the firing range. I was also given a little medal for superior marksmanship with carbine and rifle. I had always been able to ring the swinging bell at the shooting gallery, ten times for the ten .22 short-shorts you could buy in those days for a quarter. Many years later when I was fifty and my son was about ten and had his own BB-gun, I picked it up one day and shot a small twig sticking up through the snow about twenty-five yards away. It quivered slightly when the BB struck it. The Bo was astonished, but I wasn't. I knew I could do it. Even so I was pleased.

Yet I hate the damned things. I always will, and I hope I'll never have to shoot another gun in my life, not even a BB-gun.

I remember in Woodbury an old, unused shed that stood on the ridge back of Pomperaug Road, beside the path to the river and under a hemlock tree. The wooden walls and door were weathered colorfully, all the shades of gray, silver, and brown that old soft-wood boards take on, with traces of ancient red paint still intermingling. One day I stood away from it and shot a pattern of copper-coated BBs into the door, and I can still see in my mind the points of new metal gleaming against the antique background, an effect that pleased me at the time. I think it still would. The particularity of it: vertical boards with knots and splits in them, square rusty nailheads, shadings of color, lichen, and then the design of the new copper BBs, a circle with a tricuspid in it.

Particular, related to *part, particle, partisan, partner,* and *parse*—all pretty good words.

☙   ☙   ☙

Stephen Spender visited Chicago while I was living there. I don't remember exactly when, but during the time I was active on the staff of *Poetry*, roughly between 1947 and 1950. His visit had something to do with *Poetry*, probably with raising funds, since that is what invited celebrities are invited for. What else? Most of the people connected with *Poetry* were partial to celebrities, but if they wanted one for private purposes, they were more likely to invite Governor Stevenson's ex-wife or Potter Palmer's granddaughter.

I had no part in entertaining Spender; that was the province of the poetocracy. A huge bash was organized, which I later travestied in my novel, *Appendix A,* but I remember almost nothing of it now. I was no doubt drunk. As for Spender, my impression is of a man taller by a good deal than myself, handsome, wavy hair, a good workmanlike British accent, an unpressed suit, a pleasing manner, etc. But the main point is that Spender was indeed a celebrity, one of the best-known and best-liked poets of that time in the English language. The names of Auden and Spender went together as inevitably as Laurel and Hardy. They were not only the young lions, who had baited Eliot successfully; they were the immediate and powerful influence on the foremost young American poets of the generation just before mine—Karl Shapiro, Randall Jarrell, Delmore Schwartz, and the other left-leaning poets who had begun to publish just before World War II. Auden's *Collected Poems* of 1945 and Spender's of 1942, which was titled *Ruins and Visions,* were on the shelf of every poet and every serious reader in the country, and they were well worn. I still recall the dust jackets on both books. Spender seemed to me then a literary giant, as he was, a man almost infinitely beyond my reach, and although I must have shaken his hand and may have tried for a moment or two to hold up one end of a conversation with him, I'm certain that my anxiety, which with a figure as exalted as Spender could not have been much allayed by gin, would have kept me as far away from him as I could politely get.

Many years later Spender gave a reading and talk at Syracuse University, and I introduced him. We chatted a little beforehand, but not much. Our main chance to talk was at breakfast the next morning, before I took him to his plane. We ate sticky pastry and drank coffee in the Something Room at the Hotel Syracuse downtown. In my introduction the night before I had said that in reviewing the letters of Wyndham Lewis I had learned that when Lewis went blind Spender was the first person who volunteered to read to him. "I have reason to believe," I had said, "that Mr. Spender cared no more for Lewis's rotten fascistic ideas than I do. But in those days a community of letters existed, to which one was admitted solely on grounds of talent and devotion, and within it a mutual respect or even loyalty that traversed ideological disagreements." Spender picked that up at breakfast. "You know," he said in that accent I like so well, though the majority of people who speak it are royal pains in the ass, "you hit it exactly—that business about the community of letters. If it hadn't been for that, how could we have stood Eliot?"

What surprised me most in 1982 was Spender's appearance. Here's a man in his eighties, I said to myself, remarkably fine-looking and vigorous, flying all around the country, giving readings and lectures almost every day. How does he do it? And I must have hinted something of the kind, because at one point he looked at me quizzically and a little sharply, his coffee cup in his hand, and said: "I'm only seventy-three, you know." Jesus! Only eleven years older than I. I was surprised; I was floored. In Chicago he had been as far beyond me as the stars. And here we were, two old men together, at bay, so to speak, before the immense pack of our pursuers.

Well, that's romanticizing, of course. What we were actually was something else: two elderly men eating a third-rate breakfast in a third-rate restaurant in a third-rate American city—what could be more commonplace? And we were enjoying it too, Spender as much as I. It was the kind of meeting that evokes a quick sense of kinship with someone you will almost certainly never see again and to whom you feel no obligation beyond the agreeable one of being ordinarily decent. It was a pleasure.

At his reading Spender had been at pains to separate himself from Auden. At one point he even said he had not met Auden until . . . well, I'm not sure when, maybe 1937. I had just read Chamberlain's biography of Auden, which contains a photograph of the two, a snap-shot, taken at a time well before the date Spender mentioned. Why? Why such misremembering? At breakfast I told him how grateful I was to him for publishing some of my poems in *Encounter* at a time when I needed encouragement. "I like those poems very much," he said immediately and rapidly. Clearly he didn't remember them at all, any more than I remember 99 per cent of the poems I have chosen as an editor over the years. No doubt the reasons for such misremembering are easy to understand in general and easy to forgive in particular; still I do my best, not always successfully, not to let them affect me.

In fact I think a good deal about these niceties of the relationship between ordinary egotism and the awareness of pure subjectivity that all artists need.

Spender's accomplishment on his own, as poet, critic, and editor, is creditable and good. The miserable outcome at *Encounter,* when it turned out that the magazine had been secretly financed through a front by the CIA, overtook him precisely because he is a good man. It was a classic case. He dealt with it honorably. I hope his poems and his reputation will endure for a long time, though that's in the lap of the gods. The best and nearly only thing one can do for the gifted poets one knows is to wish them good luck, as I do.

∾   ∾   ∾

Kenneth Burke was short in stature, maybe a couple of inches shorter than myself, but sturdy, straight-backed, a good face: handsome and rugged with graying hair and steel-rimmed glasses. He wore a rumpled gray suit, etc., and looked the typical intellectual of the 1940s, although in many respects he wasn't typical at all. To my mind his critical writing is the most independent, honest, and useful of that period; more reasonable than Winters's, more original than Ransom's or Blackmur's, and far more agreeable in manner of intellect than Edmund Wilson's. His writing was awkward, difficult to follow, but it was mind-work right there on the page, pushing itself always harder, ambitious for its ends but modest in itself; none of the mock humility of Eliot or Tate. Furthermore his ideas, deriving from the socially oriented criticism of Parrington but enriched by the writerly insights of the New Critics, prefigured many of the attitudes of the poststructuralists of the past two decades, and not only prefigured them but articulated them more fully and reasonably than the younger critics recognize. As far as I know, they don't acknowledge him, or when they do they dismiss him as a mere "humanist"—that dirty word, applied by every generation to the previous generation.

I met Burke only once, at a party on the south side of Chicago, I think at Harvey Webster's apartment in 1948 or 1949. I had fortified myself beforehand, as usual, but at the beginning of the party I was still very tense. I found myself on a sofa beside Burke. He chatted, I listened. I tried to act as if I were comfortable, as I supposed the editor of *Poetry* should, while the party began warming up and getting noisier. People standing in clusters, looming above us, talking loudly, etc. Burke leaned toward me and said: "I wrote a poem this afternoon. Would you like to hear it?" I said: "Of course." (What else?) He recited it in a low voice directly into my ear, and I didn't catch a word. Not one. But because the poem was brief, because the occasion was social and cheery, I assumed the poem was funny, some sort of epigram, and I laughed. Immediately Burke drew back. He looked at me with shock, indignation, and injury.

I had blundered. I saw in him instantly the soul of the devotee, as I had seen it so often in all kinds of people. Burke took his poems seriously, even if no one else did. And in truth they weren't great, I think, though I haven't looked at them for many years.

I accused myself bitterly. What stupidity! Here was a person I would have liked to know, to be friendly with—if circumstances permitted—someone I admired genuinely, i.e., for his work. It was more than that; it was the mind revealed in the work, the intellectual exuberance, which for me remains the most attractive quality of that era. How I miss it now, surrounded as I am—we are—by apathy and mediocrity. But my timorousness, unrelenting from infancy until this moment, had caused me to offend Burke, so that I had again lost the chance I wanted to know my own kind; and because I was so good an actor, like most anxious people, and could disguise my fear in suavity—though not real suavity, just the alcoholic kind—Burke did not conceive why I had done it. Laughter in the face of a beautiful poem. It was unaccountable.

I remember nothing more from that party. No doubt I either got drunk or left early and then got drunk. That was how it was.

∾   ∾   ∾

It seems to me I can remember the look of each bookcase in the Woodbury house, and in the Pleasantville house too, and the exact place of every title. I saw them often enough. But of course I can't remember them that well, and in my mind now, fifty years later, I see only fragments through a mist, the lower dark corner of the bookcase at the top of the stairs, the second shelf of the one with the glass front in the living room. They held dingy old books mostly, which my father had bought for nickels and dimes from the Salvation Army, part of his relentless self-education. *The Poetical Works of A. Pope, Mr. Britling Sees It Through, Adventures in the Andes, Memoirs of a Revolutionist, The Cricket on the Hearth, The Old Wives' Tale, History of the Conquest of Peru* (3 vols.), *History of the Netherlands* (6 vols.), etc.

I looked into these books often and read what I liked here and there. Sometimes a book like Bulfinch's *Mythology* would hold me spellbound and call me back again and again, in which case I was always a little surprised, because the general air of dilapidation about those books somewhat repelled and frightened me. A few books were so utterly fusty that I never touched them.

I remember one book on the bottom shelf of that bookcase at the top of the stairs. You couldn't miss it: there it was, dead ahead, as your eyes rose above floor level when you were climbing up. I saw it thousands of times. The title on the spine was:

NERVOUS

NESS

Another ghastly morality novel, I thought to myself every time, about some ghastly forlorn girl of the moors named Ness. And hadn't I already at age thirteen read all of Scott,

Cooper, Irving, Dickens, and even some of Hardy and Meredith, etc.?—and had enjoyed them too, though sometimes the enjoyment was an effort, a kind of dutiful effort. Enough, I said. I would read *Tarzan of the Apes* and the novels of Zane Grey in the public library on Wednesday and Friday afternoons, sitting under a big round table. I smell the dust and oil of the old wooden floor to this day. Never did I dare bring such books home; they weren't explicitly forbidden, but I knew they were "cheap" and "not the right reading matter for an intelligent child," as my father would have said. Once when I told him I had read a book of poems by Robert W. Service and had memorized a couple of them, he looked at me with patient condescension and said—but of course I don't remember the words. I remember the look.

Years later when I was in my thirties and was again living at home with my parents, I pulled that book from the shelf at the top of the stairs and sat on the step to look at it, still thinking, since I am literal-minded and not quick-witted, that it was a novel entitled *Nervous Ness*. I saw at once, of course, that it was a book of pre-Freudian practical psychology; the hyphen which had originally divided the title had been worn off. How many hands had held that book? I had no idea, but I was touched by the thought. I was myself ill at that time, unable to exist in the world, and I was thinking a good deal about my parents, especially my father, and my relationship with them. My father was ill too—I think I had known it intuitively since childhood—but he had hidden it all his life, and had found ways to live around his phobias, to exist on the edges of them. But he had not hidden his illness from himself. He had bought this old book and probably had read it. I thumbed the pages, trying passages at random, passages that seemed to me both ludicrous in their concepts and urgent in their sincerity. Had the book helped my father? I couldn't see how. But who knows what will help another person who is desperate enough?

I remember another time ten years earlier, when I had been in psychoanalysis in Chicago for a couple of years. I was on a holiday visit with my parents. At the dinner table I referred to myself, I don't recall in what connection, as "neurotic," as all young peole did in those days; the word was commonplace. At once and loudly and indignantly my father said: "You're not neurotic!" I shut up. I could see how deeply shocked he was. For him, like many of his generation, neurosis was equivalent to madness. His shock lasted a long time, and although later on, when I was hospitalized and then for a considerable period lived in total seclusion, he grew used to the idea of a neurotic son, I think he never overcame the feeling that I was therefore crazy and dangerous. One time when he visited me in the hospital, I became angry enough over my continued confinement to show it, which was rare for me. I punched a wardrobe and splintered the door-panel. My father ran from the room. He accosted the first attendant he found. "The boy's in bad shape," I heard him say, his voice shaking. Well, it's true, I was in bad shape, but not the way my father meant it. Punching that door—in effect punching my father, which I could never, never have done—was a very sane thing to do at that moment. None of the hospital staff complained about it at all.

I wonder if my father every punched a door.

Books. Lots of books. My childhood was surrounded with them. They reposed there on the shelves in their umbrageous hundreds. I believe I thought, when I was a young child, that they were alive, or had been alive, or were ghostly presences talking among themselves behind my back. At any rate I knew they were important, fusty or not, and in some way menacing. That knowledge has shaped my life.

∾   ∾   ∾

One time in the late sixties I had to obtain some arsenic. It had been prescribed by a doctor and it had to be in a suspension. I went out on a Saturday morning to the local druggist, but he couldn't do it. He would need to order the medicine, he said, and it would take some days to get it. I went to a pharmacy in a nearby larger town. The druggist there said the same thing. "A suspension is not an emulsion or a solution," he added, by way of condescending professional mystification. "I know," I said. "I worked in a drugstore when I was a kid. And in those days a pharmacist could compound a suspension right there in his shop." He was not fazed, nor was any other druggist in northern Vermont, from Burlington to St. Johnsbury, from Montpelier to Newport. For half a day or more I drove my pickup over the whole region. But I failed.

When I reached home, a strange car with Connecticut plates was in front of the house. I was not greatly in need of visitors at that point, but I went into the kitchen quickly, and there at the round oak table was Mark Van Doren. I recognized him at once from his photos on book jackets. The woman next to him, I knew, must be Dorothy, his wife. My wife Rose Marie, who was sitting with them and had served coffee and kuchen, began to introduce us, but already Mark and I had shaken hands warmly. And then, after I had poured myself some coffee at the stove and we all had sat down again, I learned how extraordinarily kind some older writers can be. Mark recited to me by heart a quite long passage from the second section of my poem called *Journey to a Known Place*.

At that time, as earlier and later, I scarcely thought of myself as a poet at all. I was living mostly in seclusion, though beginning to get around more than I had during the previous fifteen years. My work was largely, say 95 per cent, unconnected with my poetry, and much of it was outdoors in the company of people who considered me a laborer or mechanic, never a writer—at least it was never openly acknowledged among us. For long periods I forgot I was a poet. I needed visits (usually in summer) with my few friends who were writers, like Denise Levertov and Adrienne Rich, to remind me of my real function, to revalidate me. When *Journey* had first been published in 1961, I had been living in Norfolk, Connecticut, only a few miles from Mark's home in Falls Village. At the suggestion of James Laughlin, my publisher and friend, I had sent Mark a copy of the book, and had received a cordial and generous letter in response; I had said to myself that I should call on him, I had even driven a number of times past the house I thought was his—I never found out if it was—and tried to hype myself into stopping; but I was too shy, I couldn't do it. Then seven or eight years later he and Dorothy were there in my own kitchen, two hundred miles north of Connecticut, at my own table. I don't know if other people can understand the quality of that experience for me. It was astonishment, almost incredulity. It was the gift of unexpected faith, the opening of the heavens. I choose these words with care, for although I have no conventional religious belief, I think I know what those have felt who have witnessed miracles.

Mark liked my poetry. The visit, the reciting of my lines, could mean nothing else. And I liked his. The work of people like Van Doren has always moved me in a special way, people talented, intelligent, devoted, and humane—Archibald MacLeish was another—who have written superb, unimprovable poems, but whose work does not place them in the first rank and is perhaps in danger of being forgotten. Because the place of such poets in our consciousness is fragile, I hold them dearer than the titans, who can take care of themselves, and do. Mark was not a great poet, as the term is commonly understood, but he wrote a few great poems. And he was a great teacher, a great human being. Many others who knew him better than I, especially those who were his students at Columbia, as diverse as Thomas Merton, John Berryman, and Allen Ginsberg, have said the same thing.

After that visit Mark and I wrote brief letters back and forth, nothing high-powered or literary, just little notes of encouragement, bits about birds and trees—that sort of thing. Then Mark died. I exchanged a few notes with Dorothy, and then she died too. I felt the awful steadiness of the turning wheel—poets working, aging, dying, being replaced—the inexorability of it and the pathos. These were nothing new in my life, of course, but perhaps it was then, when I was in my late forties, that they began to enlarge themselves in my awareness exceedingly, as they have ever since.

As for the arsenic, our local druggist ordered it and eventually we got it. Not that it made much difference.

~ ~ ~

Once in a poem I called it the "blue house in the guttering chestnut forest." In fact it was painted gray with a bluish tint, and although some American chestnut trees still survived when I was a boy, we had no forest. The house was a farmhouse originally, plain and simple, built early in the eighteenth century, sided with clapboards. The roof was a modified saltbox. It had wide pine floorboards inside, an enclosed staircase, small-paned windows; some of the glass was original, and had wavy, rainbow-colored patterns in it, with the maker's initials scratched in a corner. The immediate surroundings—we owned four acres—still resembled a farmyard, the "north field," a grassy expanse with a knoll and a hollow, the "orchard" on the southeast, a plantation of eight or ten apple trees. The house was on a little hill, thirty feet above the road, and the front yard sloped downward to a steep bank. It had two immense sugar maples, whose roots ran along the surface and whose foliage shaded out the lawn, which was no more than wispy tufts of grass.

Beyond our property lay other fields, growing up to sumac, willow, birch, and locust. I don't know who owned them.

The original barn, across the road, was owned by a family named Fray, who had a somewhat more modern house, probably from about 1900, next to the barn. Ralph Fray, a year younger than I, was my closest friend. He was a strong, stocky boy, more than my match at wrestling, and a good-looking boy as well, with dark hair and brown eyes. The Frays believed they had Indian blood in them, as most rural New Englanders of that time did, and in spite of the fact that the idea of the "noble savage," having filtered down through who knows how many layers of romantic consciousness, was widely popular at that time, I see no reason to doubt that this was so.

My own people came, on my father's side, from Scotch-Irish stock, two brothers, John and William Carruth, who were refugees from King James's Ulster Plantation—to which they had been forcibly removed from Dumfries and where they had learned to starve as well in Ireland as they had in Scotland. They settled in Massachusetts in 1710. Other Carruths emigrated later to other parts of North America. The family here is larger than one might expect; many times I have found Carruths in local phone books all over the country. My own branch has no Indian blood, as far as I know, but over the generations it has absorbed plenty of English, Dutch, French, Scandinavian, etc. I don't know what real value resides in the notion of "nativeness," probably not much, but for what it's worth the Carruths, like the Frays and millions of others, are native Americans, if only because they can't be anything else.

Our house was supported by its chimney, the same principle of engineering used in many skyscrapers, the frame suspended from a central stem or core. My memory probably is distorted, but when I envision the cellar of that house, I see a chimney ten-feet square or more, occupying much of the space. It was made of rough stone and mortar, and the great hand-hewn beams, with the marks of the broadaxe on them, perhaps twelve-by-twelve-inches, passed through the chimney walls in both directions, north-south and east-west. I think those four great timbers carried the whole weight of the house. The outer walls of the cellar were made from field-stone without mortar and bulged inward. They were firm enough, they kept the earth from falling into the cellar, but clearly they did not support much weight. That chimney tapered as it ascended through the first and second stories, then in the attic became an ordinary brick chimney. For several years I slept next to it, sharing the attic with a colony of bats. At night the bats sailed back and forth over my head; by day they clung to the inside of the unplastered split-lath of the north gable. Red squirrels came in sometimes too, and in the big maple outside the window orioles nested in summer and tanagers flittered. I liked all these creatures. Indeed, I liked all wild animals, and some of my favorite books were by John Burroughs and Ernest Thompson Seton. But once when my father picked a green snake (*Liopeltis vernalis*) out of a lilac bush and was bitten on the thumb, I thought he got what he deserved.

When I was a soldier in Italy, the lizards there crept and ran all over our tents and mosquito bars. It was common to wake up in the morning and see, first thing, a lizard fifteen inches away, peering into one's eyes. Outdoors the lizards, which looked like miniature dinosaurs with ridged spines and bulky shoulders, played fighting games in the grass, often close to my feet when I sat under an olive tree, fierce games, though I never saw any injury beyond the loss of the detachable tails. If I lay down with my eyes at grass level and watched the lizards, I could see the rampaging dinosaurs and great ferns of the Mesozoic era. In the American west, the Rockies and Sierras, I have myself played games, mostly strife-of-the-eyes or who-can-be-dead-the-longest, with rattlesnakes. The snakes always won. Once near Buck-eye Flat in the Sequoia National Forest I came suddenly on a massasauga stretched out and sunning itself on a bank. I stood still. We looked at each other, green eye vs. black eye, for as long as I could stand it, maybe fifteen minutes, and during much of that time a newly hatched white lacewing walked waveringly up and down the length of the snake's back. The snake did not move a muscle; seeing it made my own back itch. Finally I turned my head for an instant, and the snake was gone.

When I was younger, I had a small bedroom on the second floor, with one window. The floor was humped and wrenched, almost convulsively. A couple of the wide boards were warped upward a good six inches above the general level. My father was a fine carpenter, and he had restored much of the first floor of the house, but did not get to the second before we had to abandon it. He had truly astonishing patience; I never saw him express the slightest irritation when things went wrong. My own experience, though I have worked a good deal with hand tools, is just the opposite. Nothing infuriates me more quickly than a rusted bolt that snaps its head off under the pressure of my wrench, or a board mismeasured, an eighth of an inch too short for the space it's intended to fill. I have the impression that my father never misjudged a bolt or mismeasured anything, and that all his boards were sawn exactly right.

In that small bedroom on the second floor I used to wake at five o'clock A.M. or earlier, often I think at three-thirty or four o'clock (insomnia has been with me lifelong), and I would lie in bed and read until the rest of the family got up. My father had taught me to read when I was four. He used an old primer, which he probably bought for a nickel at the Salvation Army in Waterbury, and the lessons were a half-hour every morning before breakfast. I learned quickly, and in my boyhood I read many, many books, for which I'm thankful now. But in those years it seemed to me that my father's instruction had merely placed me ahead of my class in school, and for a while—until I learned to play dumb—I was segregated from the others on that account.

∾   ∾   ∾

When my wife and I and our infant son moved to northern Vermont and settled in a location that seemed at that time remote, we did so because we had to. We'd have preferred to live farther south where our friends and relatives lived. But we had little money and little income, and our search for a place we could afford, which would also be immediately habitable, was unsuccessful in Connecticut, Massachusetts, and southern and central Vermont. We kept heading north, calling real estate agents who were listed in a guide published by the Vermont Development Council. After we crossed an imaginary line from Burlington to Montpelier to St. Johnsbury, real estate values declined remarkably. The north was at that time poor country, shabby, a region of marginal farms and small towns that looked worn out. Three miles into the hills from one such town, on a dirt road next to a brook, we found a five-room house and eleven acres of land, which we bought for $5,800.

We hoped we could afford it. We paid $3,000 down—all we had—and took a fifteen-year mortgage for the rest. Our monthly payment to the bank would be $27.54, and we thought we could manage that. We felt lucky and greatly relieved to have found a place where we hoped to live on our meager resources. For a while this had seemed impossible. Indeed it would have been impossible a few years later. When we settled in northern Vermont, land was selling for $25 an acre, but not long after we arrived an influx of well-to-do people began and land values were inflated by 1000 per cent in less than a decade. Extreme northern New England was the only part of the northeast that hadn't already been exploited. If I'd been smart—but I never am—I'd have borrowed money and bought a thousand acres, and today I'd be a yuppie.

Our new home was adequate, but no more. The house had no central heating, but a kerosene pot-burner in the living room and a wood-burning range in the kitchen; in winter we kept warm, though the two rooms upstairs couldn't be used for anything but sleeping. The water supply was a siphon-fed line from a spring located on a neighbor's place some distance down the road. The kitchen had one tap that gave a thin flow of water into a cast-iron sink. We did our laundry, including the child's diapers, in the brook, which was icy cold. About thirty yards from the house was a cowshed, in effect a one-cow barn, nine-by-nine feet, with a stall and stanchion and a hole in the wall, covered by a leather-hinged flap, through which to throw the manure. I put in a window, took out the stall and stanchion, laid a new floor, boarded up the interior walls, installed a small box-stove from the junk store, and the cowshed became my workplace for the next twenty years, giving us what amounted to an extra room. On wet days it always smelled of cow. At first I worked by lanternlight after dark, but then I ran a line from the house and gave myself electricity. It was a dusty, sooty, shabby, and extremely cramped place to work, but before long I became attached to it, and I still think of it fondly. Then before the first winter came I put a cattle trough in the cellar of the house to hold water, fixed up a pump and pressure tank, and bought a secondhand hot-water heater, so that we could have a washing machine and take baths without heating the water on the stove.

Over the years we made other improvements. I rebuilt the kitchen, and put in a new sink and new plumbing, though we always used the woodstove for cooking and heating. I hired a local person to install a new bathroom and a modern septic system. I built bookshelves. We repainted the woodwork and repapered the walls. All this took a long time, many years, because we were so busy with the daily routine that we could seldom take time for anything extra. And we continued to live poor, as country people say. We bought our appliances second-hand and our clothing from the church rummage sales. I learned to make all my own repairs; I became a country mechanic, plumber, electrician, and carpenter. After a while I even learned to sweat a copper fitting as neatly as a professional. I learned to repair my cars, even to the extent of complete engine overhauls. I cut, split, transported, and stacked ten cords of firewood each summer to run the stoves in the kitchen and cowshed during the winter; this took thirty days a year. I did evening barn chores with a neighboring farmer in return for milk. I built a woodshed, a chicken coop, a duck house. I made a big garden, 160-by-200 feet, in which we raised enough potatoes, corn, squash, green vegetables, root vegetables, etc., to feed us for a year; at first we canned them, but later we bought a secondhand freezer and froze them. We picked wild berries and ate fiddleheads and lamb's quarters. We kept a small flock of hens for eggs and meat, also ducks and geese, and we occasionally went in with friends to raise a pig or a cow, or we bought them cheaply from neighboring farmers. The one thing I did not do that poor country people usually rely on—and this may have been a mistake—was to hunt and fish. I had no liking for blood sports. But we grate-fully accepted venison, rabbit, trout, and perch from friends and neighbors.

All my life I have been a compulsive worker, but I've never worked as hard at any other time as I did during this period in Vermont. Usually I worked in the woods and fields or in the garden, or did errands and repairs and house chores, during the daytime, especially in summer when the big garden always needed attention, and then worked in the cowshed at night. I wrote book reviews for newspapers and literary magazines, I read and copyedited manuscripts and wrote ad copy for book publishers, I did rewriting and ghostwriting—at one time I had more books on the market with other people's names on the title pages than books of my own. I did anything I could and accepted every assign-ment that came to me, always afraid that if I turned one down the editors would cross me off their list. Once I was the sole staff of the monthly newsletter of an occult book club on Long Island. But I was no good at selling myself, and I could not go down to New York to seek jobs from the editors and publishers there; I had to do everything by mail. Nor could I turn out the kind of material that would be acceptable to high-paying magazines. I tried, I even had an agent who urged me to give him things to sell to *Holiday, Harper's Bazaar*, etc., and who suggested topics and approaches, but it just wasn't in me; after a while I quit trying. Consequently my income from my editorial hackwork was low. In the 1960s I averaged $3,000 or $4,000 a year before taxes, gradually rising to around $10,000 in the later 1970s when I was doing regular stints for the *Chicago Daily News, Bookletter,* and *Harper's*. In some of the bad years we had emergency grants of $500 from PEN or the Author's League, which helped immensely; I never knew who was responsible for them, but to this day I'm grateful. And other grants, fellowships, and prizes were helpful too. But by 1979 I was worn out, and my son was at the university. The System had snagged me after all; I needed more cash than I could earn, even though by that time I was spending eighty or ninety hours a week in the cowshed during the winters. Always before, when I'd been asked to teach at universities around the country, I had declined, because I knew I couldn't face a class of students, but in the fall of 1979, apprehensively, I went to work at Syracuse University. The semimonthly paycheck was a blessing. I knew nothing about teaching, of course, but my editorial and literary doctoring skills were useful in the creative writing program, and gradually I became comfortable in my new profession.

The truth, as readers of my work know, is that I've suffered all my life from chronic psychiatric disorders that were acute during my thirties and have been slowly and painfully overcome in the years since then. The decade before I moved to Vermont was spent in almost complete invalidism, including a long spell of hospitalization and a longer spell of reclusion. When I remarried at the age of forty, I was well enough to shift from reclusion to seclusion, but I still could not do what literary people normally do with their lives—work in offices or classrooms, live in a city, use public transportation, go to theaters, etc. So I couldn't earn much money and I needed a quiet and private place to live. That's why I found myself in the backcountry of northern Vermont with a young wife— who was a refugee from eastern Europe and had been cheated of her education by the war; during the following years she obtained a high school equivalency diploma and bachelor's and master's degrees—and an infant son. When our friends in the counterculture of the 1960s, many of whom had come from Bethesda or Greenwich and had nice little independent incomes, praised my wife and me for living in "voluntary poverty," we laughed.

When did I write my poetry? Usually at the tag end of the night, three or four o'clock. Occasionally I could steal a day for myself. But always I had to be sure that everything else was squared away—deadlines, chores, errands, fieldwork, maintenance, reviews, hack editing—before I could turn to my own writing; that was part of my compulsiveness. Or was it simple necessity? When the roof leaks you'd better fix it. When your wife needs something, you'd better get it for her. I learned to write fast and revise with lightning speed, like a newspaper deskman, which at one time and briefly I had been. I admire and envy my friends, people like John Haines and Galway Kinnell, who can spend months or years on a poem and can put their own work ahead of everything else. I can't do it, and perhaps this, as much as matters of principle, is what has influenced me to believe that artists should not be given any more consideration than other people: there's nothing sacred, or even all that special, about a poem. Though I owe much to Ezra Pound, I rebel against his idea of the poet as philosopher king, which seems to me both dangerous and a concomitant, if not a cause, of his foolish politics. Once in 1965 I was able to give myself a whole month. I don't remember how this came about, but I wrote "Contra Mortem," a poem in thirty parts, doing one part a day for thirty days. (Later I found the wonderful epigraph from Lao-tzu, which fits so well.) This poem remains my personal favorite among all the poems I've written, though not many share my feeling. Later in the seventies and eighties I was granted a number of residencies at Yaddo, the artists' retreat in Saratoga Springs, where I could put everything else out of my mind. Much of *The Sleeping Beauty* was written there, and many other poems and essays as well.

But voluntary or not, the life of poverty we lived in Vermont is what we would have chosen anyway six months after we settled there. This is what is important. It was a hard life and we could have benefited from more leisure and less financial anxiety—which were factors in the eventual separation of my wife and me—but it was in the fullest sense a rewarding life. And it was a possible life, nothing like poverty in the ghetto or in some ruined part of the world. Winters in northern Vermont are long, cold, and snowy, but we stayed warm in our banked and caulked little dwelling even when it was thirty or forty below, snug in our bed with all our clothes on and heated stones for our feet; I learned to love the winter, the cleanness and clarity of it, in spite of frostbite from the bitter wind and backache from shoveling snow. And this kind of adaptation occurred in every aspect of life there. What those years and that place afforded me was an opportunity to put everything together, the land and seasons, the people, my family, my work, my evolving sense of survival (for when I'd been in the hospital the doctors had told me I'd never again have anything like a normal life), in one tightly integrated imaginative structure. The results were my poems, for what they're worth, and in my life a very gradual but perceptible triumph over the internal snarls and screw-ups that had crippled me from childhood on. How gratifying it was! The process had begun before I went to Vermont, of course, with changes in my perception of myself and the world that turned me inside out and upside down, and it has continued since I was forced to leave (forced because no school in Vermont would hire me), but the time there was crucial. And I'm not sure I could have done the same thing to the same degree anywhere else.

In 1974, I think, I was awarded the Governor's Medal for Excellence in the Arts. Only one a year is given. No money is attached to it. But the ceremony in the governor's office in Montpelier was the first public occasion I had taken part in for twenty-five years, and that meant a great deal to me. Then having the recognition of my adopted state meant a great deal too. I still like that medal better than any other prize I've won.

In 1978 at the age of fifty-seven I gave my first poetry reading, helped and supported by friends, in a small art gallery above a bank in the town of Chelsea. It was a big occasion, all the more since what had precipitated me into psychotherapy the first time, when I was twenty-five, was a poetry reading in Chicago that I ran away from. Then in 1982 I gave a reading at the Library of Congress before a quite large audience. It was a fantastic private victory. I wanted to tell someone about it, but no one was left in my life who had known me well when I was twenty-five. In the motel I wrote a note to my first wife, who was probably astonished to get it.

A life of hardship that was nevertheless possible was the luckiest thing that could have happened to me in my middle age. If I didn't choose it, I quickly acquiesced in it. And in a way I did choose it because the instincts that were pushing me pushed me in that direction. My grandfather, whom I admired greatly and after whom I was named, had established himself in the Dakotah Territory in 1885, and had lived there, and written poems and stories there, in spite of similar hardship. I don't think I was consciously following his example, and in fact his life and mine have been distinctly different, but that strain of Carruthian stubbornness and adventursomeness was somewhere in me, buried and hard to find. In the end it saw me through—with lots of help from others along the way.

The young people I encounter today, mostly graduate students in the creative writing program at Syracuse, have nothing like this in their lives. In general they are too young to have it. But what worries me is that they don't recognize its value, they are aimed in the opposite direction, not toward the difficult but toward the easy. Everything in their upbringings and educations has trained them to seek the easy way, which is now the American way. Our lives are supposed to be "fun" and not much else. And for my young students the easy way is teaching; as quickly as they can they want to get their degrees and find niches in the academic world which will give them semimonthly paychecks in return for the least possible effort and discomfort. My friends, don't do it. Not when you're young, not even when you're middle-aged. It isn't because there's something intrinsically wrong with academic life, though I think now, as opposed to forty-five years ago when I was a grad student at the University of Chicago, this may be the case, but because it's too easy. You believe your writing can be a separate part of your life, but it can't. A writer's writing occurs in the midst of, and by means of, all the materials of life, not just a selected few. And if your life is easy, your writing will be slack and purposeless. I am generalizing, of course, but my main drift is sound and important. You need difficulty, you need necessity. And it isn't a paradox that you can choose necessity, can actually create necessity, if you seek the right objectives; not the great metaphysical necessity, but your own personal necessity; and it will be no less inexorable because you have chosen it. Once you are in it, your writing will be in it too.

Think of what Tom McGrath and Toni Morrison and Patrick Kavanagh and Cesare Pavese and Robert Frost have done with rural poverty. Compare their work to poems and stories about life in the academy. The latter are nearly all weak and foolish. Why? Because life in the academy is too easy. The authors of poems and stories about it do not react from it, they accept it, they go with it—they are conformable; whereas good writing is almost always against something. They take the values of the academy for granted.

Yet has not the corporate structure of education done us as much harm as the corporate structures of manufacturing, selling, and thought-control?

Myself, I think the aspect of necessity that helps the most is physical, and I don't mean jogging or tennis. Country people, primitive people everywhere, are healthy because their lives force them to be healthy. I don't mean they always eat the right foods or refrain from smoking, drinking, etc. I suppose most of them also take the easy way if they can. But artists who choose necessity do so in an act of intelligence, and intelligence will still be with them after their choice. Hard necessary physical work is the best aid to composition I know.

Maybe on the other hand the best part of necessity is loving. Young people who tell me they will never marry, never have children, worry me even more than those who say they want to teach. My son David, whom I call the Bo, was central to everything I did during those years in Vermont. He was growing as I was regrowing. Because his mother was often working or going to school, but also because I wanted it, we spent a lot of time together. My love for him and his for me infused all my work. I can't imagine that work without him— or his mother too. We were a loving family. I know many great artists have worked without this element in their lives, e.g.,

Van Gogh, Emily Dickinson; this was their hardship. But obviously they'd have been better off personally if they'd had it, and I'm not convinced that if they had had it, their work wouldn't be just as good as it is. For me, loving and being loved were necessities. My responsibilities to others did not make me feel less responsible to my work, as young people fear. On the contrary, the point of my life was to combine the responsibilities, to make them go together in one passage, one congeries of enactments, one passion, in spite of the stresses induced by lack of time and money. This was possible. It was done. Naturally it didn't last forever.

Well, there are many kinds of necessity. A discussion of the possibilities in particular lives would be useless. But I believe nothing worth much ever came out of easy necessity, and I believe this is true on all levels and in all spheres. It is something for young artists to bear in mind. Voluntary poverty is not such a bad idea.

More Essays

Paul Goodman and the
Grand Community

As an artistic personality Paul Goodman was so cohesive in his concerns and beliefs, so altogether yoked and bonded within himself, that one can make no analytical statement about him without falling into paradox, by which I mean opposites held in tension, and this is one reason why his writing has been little tested by the critics. For my part, I have always preferred to call myself a reviewer, not a critic, because reviewing is what I have had to do most of my life, and the distinction is important to me, not only as a matter of exigency, but as a disclaimer, for myself, of any systematic view of literature, especially as derived from sociology, linguistics, esthetics, or any standpoint outside literature as such. I do not mean to be falsely modest. It's no news that we live in a low and narrow literary age. My kind of spadework is what we need now, both to sort out our jumbled tastes and to make possible a future criticism that will be serious and responsive (as opposed to the Wimbletonian criticism we have now, the tennis match we can hear from somewhere on the other side of the hedge). More than eight years ago I began to attempt these sentences, and even now I do not know where they will lead. Nevertheless there is a point in my following my broadest impressions of Goodman's sensibility, since precisely these may lead into the self-enclosure of his remarkable fluency, which was not a matter merely of words, but of thought, feeling, perception, cultural reference; in short, the pattern-making awareness of experience that he himself called "the continuum of the libido." It was in fact his natural facility of imagination, driven always by his pervasive, many-tempered lust, and it never deserted him.

The first thing to be said about Goodman, therefore, is that his integrated sensibility was in some manner achieved; not imposed, not revealed, not fortuitously agglomerated.

And the second thing—still staying within one's broadest impression—is that Goodman's integrated sensibility nevertheless had two foci. Culturally speaking, Goodman lived in two places at once. More than any other important American writer of the twentieth century, he was European. Hemingway, Faulkner and the others of the "southern renaissance," Williams, Stevens (in spite of his mannered elegance), even Eliot and Pound (in spite of their European allegiances), as well as such members of Goodman's own generation as Schwartz, Jarrell, Shapiro, Lowell, Bishop, etc.—all were American, whether determinedly or unselfconsciously. It is not a question of style. (If it were, Stevens would be from Paris, circa 1880.) It is a question of vision, angle of approach, the way experience is seized and organized esthetically. Goodman was precisely *moderniste* in the European tradition, a companion of Kafka, Gide, Rilke, Brecht, Aragon, and Cocteau; especially Cocteau. He disdained the impersonal and conventional; he celebrated the personal and mythological. His procedure was that of dreaming awake, its wit as well as its profundity. He was absurd, practical, deeply moral, shocking, and polemical. He was a superb technician and had a philosopher's sensitivity to the humanity of language (somewhat akin to Heidegger, though I don't know if he had read him); at the same time he had little use for linguistics as such, for structuralism or concretism or any other conceptualist theory of art. He was devoted to *meaning*. In all these qualities he was a European man, and not simply European but Continental. He was a romanticist in the post-post-post-romanticism that this implies. I am reminded of the absolutely necessary apothegm written somewhere by Camus: "Classicism is nothing but romanticism with the excess removed."

Further, a point can be made about the deliberately "American" writers of the first half of the century, namely, that many of them, often including Williams (whose work I admire enormously), fell into a kind of rhetoric of America, exaggerated, in effect chauvinistic. The American Experience, etc. Goodman was far too sophisticated, too analytical, too well trained philosophically to fall into that. He knew how important the city of Paris was to the modernist movement. There really is a sense of place in the works of Cocteau, Gide, etc., to say nothing of Proust, whereas with American writers place tends to become exclusively subject, that is, to move from the background to the foreground. With Goodman, as with the Europeans, it is in both places. As for Whitman, I think at some deep level—below style, topic, and mode of thought—Goodman shared with him the bedrock humanism or artistic altruism, close to but never the same as messianism, that saved the older poet, if barely, from chauvinism. In some poems, though not many, I detect phrasings by Goodman that could have been taken word for word and rhythm for rhythm from Whitman.

Having said this about Goodman's Europeanism, however, I think at once of the ways in which he was so thoroughly American that my remarks seem crazy. No other American writer of his time dared to be patriotic in Goodman's fundamentalist sense. In the midst of his sophistication he was plain and straightforward, not to say homely; in the midst of castigating contemporary American civilization he would stop to proclaim, in tones of injury, his faith in the Jeffersonian archetype. It was almost a tic, but no less serious on that account. He truly believed that the Lockean presence in the American Constitution made it not only one of the world's most beautiful documents but still the best hope of mankind. He took off his hat when the flag went by. And his love of the American scene, urban or rural, was clear in everything he wrote. He called himself a "Jeffersonian anarchist." What's more, he made it stick, he turned the seeming contradiction into a unity. He was American even to the extent of accepting necessity in politics, moderating his revolutionary zeal and despair to a reformist optimism, at least from time to time—and what could be more American than that? Sometimes he seemed in danger of turning into an ordinary Anglo-American liberal, a fault his critics on the left were always glad to point out. At all events he made us see that *radical* and *conservative,* if they remain useful terms at all, are only so in combination. We cannot say one without meaning the other. He was practical and a pragmatist, like all Americans; but always haunted, like all Americans, by the ideal.

But I see that already I must correct myself, the difficulty of dealing with such a complex personality is so great. It was not that Goodman "moderated his revolutionary zeal"; he advocated short-term changes which in themselves were nothing basic but which he saw as necessary little elements of the social revolution (after Kropotkin) that would, if it were accomplished, make the later political revolution more secure. Something like that, at any rate. He felt that it would be a mistake to leap over these little changes because they were not revolutionary in themselves. He also felt—and this may be the heart of the matter—that it was important to avoid despair, depression, etc., since political activity, especially revolutionary, requires energy and hope.

Yet how many times, again in paradox, he castigated Hope as the enemy of reasonable endeavor!

Perhaps, refining the point further, it is possible to say that in effect Goodman believed in an underlying *nature,* in which human beings participate, though at the same time he recognized the danger of such a belief, its outworn transcendental simplicity. Cautiously but clearly, he believed that at all moments of political or social vitality (in history) one will see glimpses of this underlying nature, and one will be able to say why the particular political form sustains it, frees it, nurtures it, etc. This thought, and his preference for simplicity, entered actively into the aspects of his mind that can be called conservative. In an analogous recognition of its danger, he tempered his romanticism, his native libidinous exuberance, with a classical and historical mode of reasoning. And all this was deeply characteristic of Western intellectual life during the years of Goodman's active maturity, 1940 to 1970, though it obviously appeared in many shapes and colors.

In the back of my copy of *The Empire City* I jotted some of the names which occurred to me in my rereading: Rabelais,

Cocteau, Aristophanes, the Old Testament (but more *Genesis* than *Isaiah*), Swift and Hogarth, Proust, Joyce (but with a question mark), Twain, Voltaire, Handel, Poulenc, Thurber, "even in parts Francis Ponge," "the orchestrations of *The Critique of Pure Reason*" and Buster Keaton. A random list; obviously many others were tributary to Goodman's confluence: Aristotle, Villon, Wordsworth, Freud, Louis Sullivan—the names keep surfacing—perhaps Kafka most of all. Two temperaments so unlike, Kafka and Goodman, their positions worlds apart, their concerns scarcely touching; yet Goodman found in Kafka something necessary to himself. I think it was the figure of the alien first of all. If Kafka was an artist too, so much the better. But the isolated man, the cut-off imagination, these were the paradigms Goodman needed for himself. If he loved America, he did not love Americans, any more than he loved Libyans, Finns, or Trobrianders. Before each act of thought he had to touch, as if it were his talisman, his own freedom in all its chordal changes—independence, solitude, alienation, horrible messianic loneliness. Otherwise he could not think deeply at all.

(And was he, parenthetically, touched and reinforced by his own style of language and thought as it had surfaced in prior American civilization, in works by Thoreau, Alcott, the other tax-dodgers, or by Dickinson or Hawthorne? The styles were close to his in many ways, yet the distances were great. I feel that Goodman's cultural temperament made him think of his American forerunners as unwanted rivals, and of their Transcendentalism, especially in its withdrawal from social process, as too puny a human endeavor to warrant his attention. Yet Brook Farm was important to him.)

Now in the course of a couple of pages, following my sentences where they go, I have been led through a considerable number of opposing coordinates on the circle of Goodman. The European American, the socialized alien, the practical utopian, the radical conservative, the pragmatic idealist, the self-explaining mystery and self-disclosing secret; for like all writers, but more manifestly than most, he was an Indian giver. If he disclaimed, as he characteristically often did but sometimes did not, the conventional post-romantic role of prophet, *homme d'esprit,* and vatic spirit, nevertheless he promised what he could not deliver. This was not, as one might be tempted to say at first, the "unutterable" word; Goodman was too thoroughly Aristotelian and psychoanalytic in his bias to accept ultimately the idea of a secret, mystical, supraverbal *logos.* It was simpler than that. What he sought was the word, the combination of words, that could contain all his own contradictions. This was humanly impossible, itself a factor that would have to be incorporated in the "word," with emphasis on "humanly." So he wrote around it and around it, forty books on almost as many topics, explaining himself again and again, laying everything bare except the one real object of his and our desire, that which has no name though a thousand synonyms. Goodman is the perpetually fading echo that reverberates between the cliffs of consciousness. Call them being and nothingness. That inexactness will do as well as any other.

A system of opposites lined up like the intersectional point of diameters along the circumference of a circle. As with all metaphor, this from geometry is inaccurate in its application, yet it is useful, functional. In its typicality it represents one observable and so to speak certifiable aspect of the continual negotiation between reality and human mental capacity or incapacity; it is inevitable, it is there in our head, beyond the control of "reason" or "will," and its success in any particular operation will be relative. This Kantian view (though Kantian only to the extent that much else proposed by Kant himself is disregarded) would have been agreeable to Goodman. He was an anarchist, meaning by definition a mind limited and undoctrinal; a pragmatist, a relativist, a humanist, a moralist, a personalist. I don't know if he read Nikolai Berdyaev, but he would have gone part way with that philosopher's peculiar Catholic anarchism, as he would have gone part way or further with Tolstoy and Buber and many other religious radicals; and the points of separation from them would have come over disagreement about terms—the definition of the social context—more than from conflict of ideas. Part way was Goodman's perennial journey.

So he chose more and more to live in the countryside of northern New England where some half-articulate philosopher might be milking cows on the next farm down the road. He was a city Jew drawn like a moth to the light of backwoods Yankee nonconformity. His place (near Stratford, New Hampshire) was as far from Cambridge as he could get without leaving New England. He shunned as well the objectivism of William Carlos Williams, Louis Zukofsky, and George Oppen, with their insistence on the purity and autonomy of the thing-in-itself. Yes, he might have said to them, metaphor has its dangers, including the risk of phenomenological distortion; but lo! (for he was our only modern writer who knew how to get away with the marvelous archaisms) see that metaphor pure and shining in this poem by Wordsworth, and another here in Villon! They work, they function, they are useful. How can one deny so natural an expedience of human invention? He demanded to be taken as a "practical" man, the esthetician of the possible. And just as he shunned the objectivists, he shunned everyone else.

Goodman could make friends with no one who was not either a disciple or dead—and the longer dead the better.

One cannot avoid the inference that Goodman's oppositionism was as much a matter of temperament as of principle. Yes, he complained of loneliness and he welcomed new friends eagerly; but he could stick with no group for long. He preached communalism, yet was the last who could have accepted it. Notice how quickly, after he had attained success and had won a following among the young advocates of counterculture during the 1960s, he turned against them, or partly against them, and began writing books and essays to distinguish his positions from theirs. These distinctions were and are important, he was perfectly right to insist on them; but he could have written his books and essays as a leader, rather than as a critic. The chance of leadership was handed to him, the gift of history that most ambitious people pray for and that he himself had prayed for (e.g., in *Five Years*). But Goodman threw it away, abruptly, almost at times disdainfully. He knew what he was doing. Then was he unambitious? Not a bit; his need for recognition was enormous, a principal theme of his poems. But so was his need for independence. He was in conflict with himself—the point is worth repeating—and what is interesting, indeed crucial, is the way he kept his conflicts under control, brought them into the circle of tension that was his whole sensibility, and thus held himself and his work together.

But I have no wish to anticipate Goodman's biography. That job is being done superbly by Taylor Stoehr, whose work, when it is finished, will be an indispensable history of Goodman's era. (I knew Goodman only briefly in the time before his public success.) One point of biography is well known already, however, Goodman himself being always eager to publish it, and is important and worth emphasizing here. He belonged to the generation of New York intellectuals, mostly Jewish, who dominated much of American political and literary thought in the late thirties, forties, and into the fifties; such writers as Philip Rahv, Lionel Trilling, Hannah Arendt, Delmore Schwartz, Dwight McDonald, Mary McCarthy, and many others. A cardinal point with these brilliant men and women was precisely their alienation from the main currents of American life and thought; yet Goodman was alienated even among them.

It was an earlier instance of what happened in his relationship to the young people of the 1960s. But his estrangement from his own contemporaries was more fundamental, perhaps more painful, more damaging. He bitched about it endlessly. I think even he, however, knew how much he needed that damage, that extreme intellectual and even personal isolation. He continually took positions, consciously or unconsciously, that would reinforce it. No line could be laid down by the group, whether political, artistic, or philosophical, that Goodman would not bristlingly object to. He was an alien among aliens, ignored, scorned, refused access to the alien magazines and publishing houses. You might think he would have been published regularly in *Partisan Review,* the *New Leader,* the *Nation,* and the other radical noncommunist magazines of that time based in New York, but he wasn't. Irregularly, yes; but he never had ready access to any means of publication before 1960. He complained about this, bitterly and with justice, yet it was his own doing as much as anyone else's, more than anyone else's, and his complaints were triumphs of exuberance.

Goodman was the self-justifying, self-congratulating pariah; not quite a martyr, he knew he was too intelligent to play that rôle convincingly; but he was wily enough to know too that he could be comfortably downtrodden and make a public virtue of his perpetual, autonomic dissidence. Not that the "virtue" was "public" at the time. The factions within intellectual life in New York during the late thirties, forties, and early fifties were many and minute; but they themselves produced hardly any public impact. How could the one who dissented from the dissidents expect recognition for it, all the more since the dissidents, when he attacked them, failed to counterattack? They just ignored him. Yet Goodman knew himself well enough to recognize that he could function best as philosopher and artist in an attitude of persistent opposition, and he hoped—he always hoped!—that ultimately this private necessity would become a public virtue. This is exactly what happened in the sixties when all his works, earlier and later, came, however briefly, into public prominence.

Even anarchists, whose base in thought denies them the comfort of ideology, need something to rest on, i.e., that base itself, which thereby becomes a kind of ideal or absolute. It is, of course, the notion of freedom. Freedom complete and unconstrained by anything except considerations of "public safety." What ensues from this has been debated for a century and a half, with tactical and philosophical consequences to my mind both fascinating and illuminating; but I have no need here to try even the sketchiest recapitulation. Goodman's use of the idea is my concern. His freedom was less that of the utopian theorists of Europe than of the nostalgic theorists of America. He called himself a "Jeffersonian anarchist." But the term did not satisfy him, and elsewhere he equated "anarchism" with "libertarianism" and "rebel humanism" in the attempt to pin down in a word his own undogmatic and ideologically unideological desire for freedom, practicality, and love. His view of the early history of the United States was sentimental, perhaps wrong; but it was crucial. "During the first thirty years of the Republic only 5 to 10 per cent were enfranchised and as few as 2 per cent bothered to vote. But the conclusion to be drawn from this is not necessarily that the society was undemocratic. On the contrary, apart from the big merchants, planters, clerics, and lawyers, people were likely quite content, freed from the British, to carry on their social affairs in a quasi-anarchy, with unofficial, decentralized, and improvised political forms. It was in this atmosphere that important elements of our American character were developed." And those elements were kept alive today, Goodman insisted, primarily in his own writing.

Yet he never forgot "our moronic system of morals and property," nor that this system emerged constitutionally from the political forms of the Republic, nor that the only recourse of honest people in America has almost always been political illegitimacy.

Goodman was a radical who dreamed backward more than forward, and whose view of the present was more often vague than precise, more often anxious than expedient, in spite of his commitment to "practicality." "Perhaps it is because I am so crazy with hope that I live in constant terror," he wrote. But also: "I fail to experience myself in groups that I cannot immediately try to alter by personal decision and effort." Again: "To dance into the present with the force of the endurance of the world." And elsewhere still: "With much of the business of our society, my intuition is to forget it." Finally: "On the advice of Longinus, I write . . . for Homer, for Demosthenes, and other pleasant company who somehow are more alive to me than most of my contemporaries, though unfortunately not available for comment." But if Homer had been alive in New York in 1940, Goodman would have dismissed him as inhumane and doctrinaire.

Goodman was not divided, he was torn. All his writing, seen from this standpoint, was an effort to patch himself together. It worked, and that is what is so remarkable.

The temptation at this point becomes obvious, namely to reduce these various dualisms to the basic one that Goodman called his bisexuality. In one way or another sex is his tonic from first to last. Aside from the explicitly erotic poems and stories, sexual energy is present in all his writing; at least so I would argue. I don't know how to prove it. But when Goodman speaks of "the force of the endurance of the world," a statement that can be found in different formulations throughout his works, I believe he is thinking of a nature that by no means excludes Newtonian, Darwinian, Freudian, Einsteinian, or any other modes of "objective contemplation," but that nevertheless is basically and simply generative—he is thinking, however metaphorically or unconsciously, of sex. His dualisms are sexually informed. His manner of argument is the same. The sensuality of his style, by which I mean its "poetry" or "music," its syntactical sinuosity and almost tactility, is clear in even his most abstruse discussions. This uninhibited fluency, so remarkable in a writer given to making distinctions, is the one element that pervades all his writings: the fiction and poetry, but also the declamations, the private jottings, the philosophical and critical exegeses—everything. And he kept this sexual energy flowing all his life, through to the final poems of sexual melancholy written when he sensed death not far away.

Yet I find none of these considerations convincing when it comes to assigning reasons for the dichotomies of intellect and feeling in Goodman's work. First, although he usually called himself bisexual, in at least one prominent passage of his writing he called himself homosexual. Secondly, one cannot avoid seeing that among his poems, the expressly erotic ones are to, for, or about men, while those addressed to his wife (and to his children as engenderings of his marriage) are distinctly different in tone; the latter being warmly and deeply affectionate and companionable, so that often they move the reader more genuinely than do the former poems of lust. And thirdly, I dislike and distrust any of these quasi-clinical, reductionist analyses in literature, and I would not resort to them even if I were competent to do so. For Goodman himself, psychoanalysis was without question the single self-enclosed structure of concepts that most clearly determined his view of reality, yet he was prudent, as he would say, in his application of Freudian theory, even in the derived Gestalt-analysis he favored, to artists or their works.

To my mind Goodman's propensity for dualistic modes of experience was forced on him, as on most of us, by his own temperament or by human temperament in general, and perhaps also by his early philosophical training, his graduate studies at the University of Chicago when Richard McKeon and Neo-Aristotelianism were the vogue there. Aristotle's Pity and Woe, Pathos and Purgation, were important categories to the young intellectual of 1938 because, not only esthetically but socially and psychologically, they substantiated his awareness of art as a functioning thing, if not dialectical at least mediative. No doubt he found further support for his pragmatic view in the Kantian notion of a priori limits, popular with John Crowe Ransom and other New Critics. (Part of the avant-garde rejection of Hegel and Marx in general during the late thirties was expressed in a reversion to Kantian concepts, but bypassing the Romantic excess, along with new interest in such writers as Kierkegaard, Dostoyevsky, and Kafka, all of whom were important to Goodman.) But mainly Goodman had no interest in faddish philosophy. Conflict for him was a practical or procedural necessity, but he was always engaged in more or less holistic analysis, or at least the hope of it. He resorted, or was forced to resort, to dualistic modes in some books, e.g., *Compulsory Mis-Education* and *New Reformation,* but more often he regarded himself as a man in the main line of honest souls, from Aristotle, Longinus, Descartes, Spinoza (whom he reverenced), Kant, James, Nietzsche (though he discounted the superman as a form of neurotic yearning), Dewey, etc., down to his own knocked-together but generally unitary "system." He shows little liking for Cartesian or, in his own time, Sartrean modes of argument. And if it is true that the more he insisted on the ideal oneness of society and the individual person, the more he found himself pushed toward equations, dichotomies, and oppositions, nevertheless he held the ideal—a functional unity—before his mind as the only reliable goal for anarchistic and loving ways of thought. If this meant, psychiatrically speaking, some scarcely appraisable but pervasive form of sexuality, so much the better.

Goodman's sexuality, however, does remain a question needing further explanation. He did not explain it himself, which is significant. He explained everything else about his poetry, repreatedly and lengthily, but he ignored this. He is rightly credited for his courage as a forerunner in the movement toward gay liberation; that is, for his open, not to say belligerent, avowal of homosexuality in his poetry. But his silence elsewhere seems to indicate some deeper embarrassment. Goodman knew that his concept of love was unitary and that it was fundamental to his notion of the good community. Only love can hold people together (as Locke had said), and this love must be whole and wholly free. Yet community necessarily entails the ideas of fertility and generation, which were traditionally associated with the loving heterosexuality of the human animal. And Goodman himself was a traditionalist. He does not say, however, what his communalism means in this respect, beyond his insistence that love, like everything else, must be free.

It is as if the division of love into *eros* and *agape* dear to the Catholic theologians and invidious to at least some of the rest of us (so that we have denied it and said that the two are really one) does in fact exist in Goodman's life and work, and expresses itself in his attitudes toward his family on one hand and toward his sexual adventures with males on the other. Thus we come round to bisexualism again, but at a deeper level of meaning, and I think this is valid. Goodman tried to make a unity of *eros* and *agape,* and at times succeeded (or thought he did), but ultimately he really is stuck with some kind of separation. His inability to *rest* in any group and his obsessive need to keep talking, both of which he confessed readily, as well as his preference for being the critic in opposition, since he was always more adversary than advocate except in cases where he found himself in such primary opposition that he could "afford" to lean toward conciliation (e.g., his almost innate divergence from established religion and his final attempt to come to terms with it in *Little Prayers and Finite Experience*), all these elements of his own "nature" indicate a practical alienation from the social values of love. This would explain both his yearning for community and his inability to rest in a community. It was a deep duality, perhaps the deepest of all, far below his bisexuality. Nevertheless this is what I am talking about, this source, when I say that all his thought and writing are informed by his sexual energy.

Goodman was not famous, God knows, for laconism. By his own account he wrote "forty books," a nice round number such as authors frequently let fall. Yet in his case it seems that this may be an underestimation; his bibliography is huge, and since his death in 1972 newly uncovered works have continued to appear with regularity. He was a man of many words, for "to me it is panic to be speechless." At the same time he knew the values of brevity. (Sometimes it seems as if he knew *all* the values of *all* literary strategies.) As he grew older and consolidated and simplified his vision, he turned often to the Japanese hokku, for example, and wrote a few so poignantly right that they wring your heart.

> If they were to say
> that this hokku was the last
> poem that he wrote

Yes, he knew *all* the values: how the strict armature of traditional artifice glows and comes alive in the broken language of unutterable, or nearly unutterable, feeling; the sentence left unfinished eternally. Yet he had a sharp, epigrammatic wit at times.

> I must be thirsty,
> man, to make love to such a
> long drink of water.

In the prose too, which gives the impression of almost uncontrolled discursiveness, organization by caprice, one finds embedded apothegms, these less the consequence of conscious effort than of the unmitigated force of invention. Imagine him at work, hunched over the battered old Underwood, his pipe fuming and clenched between what remained of his teeth. The sentence, the *sentence*—it was for him an act of compression, though he knew how to hook them together and keep the cadence rolling. It was the ideal expression of a thought, a single movement of the mind, a single gesture of meaning. The sentence was for Goodman what the image had been for Ezra Pound. Here are a few that have struck me over the years.

The givenness of Creation is surprise.

•

This world is purgatory. I have plenty of proof that I am not damned—I understand that it is heretical to say so—but I am being tried, I have no notion why. Maybe that's what I'm supposed to learn.

•

Yet men have a right to be crazy, or stupid, or arrogant. It is our speciality. Our mistake is to arm anybody with collective power.

•

"Stand up for the stupid and crazy," Whitman said. Is there a connection? I can say only that either way I wouldn't be surprised.

•

When Isaac was saved on Mt. Moriah, Abraham must have gone into a towering anger. The Bible, written as God's history, tells us nothing about this. All that heartache for nothing.

•

There are too many missionaries among my friends.

•

Spite is the vitality of the powerless.

•

It is astounding how natural and few the fine arts are.

•

A style of speech is an hypothesis about how the world is.

•

Despite its bloodlessness, the tradition of literature is a grand community and, much as I envy the happy and the young, I doubt that they have as good a one.

•

The color of the Burning Bush is thought-passing-over-a-face color (but it must be a *thought,* not one of the vagaries of the likes of you).

•

Any workman putting away his tools is among the lovely dancers of this world.

•

For whatever is a human passion may be expresssed in music, and whatever is music is in the human throat to imitate it.

•

. . . the bondage of peace. . . .

•

The thing is to have a National Liberation front that does not end up in a Nation State, but abolishes the boundaries.

•

Literature is not a "linear" unrolling of printed sentences and it is not a crude code; it is artful speech. And speech is not merely a means of communication and expression, as the anthropologists say, but is a chief action in our human way of being in the world.

•

The case is that our society is in a chronic low-grade emergency.

•

In the breakdown of repression, the artists do their part by first dreaming the forbidden thoughts, assuming the forbidden stances, and struggling to make sense. They cannot do otherwise, for they bring the social conflicts in their souls to public expression.

•

Certainly we are in a political crisis, for, though the forms of democracy are intact, the content is vanishing.

•

Yet it is a melancholy but common thing in the world (and makes for a melancholy world) that while the one fighter is for some reason single-mindedly bent on destroying a man, that man does not want this fight; he does not believe in it, he does not think that it is worth the hurt and damage involved. He has been forced into it, and it happens that he cannot quit the field.

Goodman could never quit the field. He would stalk off, muttering his disgust, but the next day—the same afternoon—he would be back, his pipe fuming.

What made Goodman so blithe a philosopher was his understanding that philosophy is of the heart. He loved Kant almost because the Koenigsburgher was so often wrong; or rather not wrong but incomplete—stopped by the limits of mentality. And this is the pathos that makes the Beautiful, surpassing every secondary esthetic principle of inclusiveness, dynamism, control, or whatever. *The Critique of Pure Reason,* read in this way, is Western man's greatest oratorio of ideas, a triumph of art; so huge, so majestically orchestrated, touching so many of the unnotable, unsoundable limits.

In this Goodman was closer, on second thought, to his American forerunners than to his European. He was a little Emersonian, but of the jumbled Notebooks (though I don't know if he read them) more than of the finished Essays. An important distinction. In spite or because, whichever, of his haste and vitality, Goodman was always feeling his way, touching one after another of the objects, often books, presented to him by chaos, repulsing most, taking a few to himself. It was intuition at work, his rule of thumb, which left him sometimes in contradictions he cared nothing about. But we, his readers, may care. Inconsistency is no hobgoblin, but it makes strangers where there should be friends.

"My trouble is that I have to be that kind of poet who is in the clear because he has done his public duty. All writers have hang-ups, and mine is To Have Done My Duty. It is an arduous taskmaster, but at least it saves me from the nonsense of Sartre's poet *engagé,* politically committed. How the devil could a poet, who does the best he can just to get it down as it is whispered to him, decide whether or not to be morally or politically responsible? What if the Muse won't, perverse that she is? What if the Truth won't, unknown that it is?"

"The ability of literature to combine memory and learning with present observation and spontaneous impulse remarkably serves the nature of man as the animal who makes himself. . . ."

Strange. The terms are Sartre's yet the drift seems blindly anti-Sartrean. How is it that the "animal who makes himself" has a "nature"? Impossible, the Frenchman would say, unless mere self-consciousness is a "nature," which it is not. Can a person be both created and self-creating? Yes, Goodman would exclaim, why not! And then he would go on to say that the fact that a man "makes himself" does not contradict the idea of a prior givenness, or nature, but instead refers to the aspects of evolution that proceed from human culture. Science and technology, applied to agriculture, improve the diet, and after a few generations the average man is 5'10" instead of 5'8", and has bad teeth instead of good ones. But obviously this takes more intellectual, more spiritual, forms as well.

Sometimes it seems as if Goodman ought to have found in Sartre a companion-at-arms. Little necessary conflict existed between them. Was Goodman's rejection of Sartre merely vanity, parochialism, defensiveness, the feelings that made him flare up at anyone who seemed to be treading on his own ground? Yet if no necessary differences divided them, certainly practical differences did, stylistic differences. Sartre was an ideologue. In politics he supported the invasion of Hungary. To this Goodman could have uttered only a gigantic NO! Freedom and love come before ideas. And to Sartre's word-spinning, the house of cards built for Jean Genet, the tenuosity of "existential psychoanalysis," Goodman could have responded only with another negative.

For it is after all more than a question of vanity, parochialism, and defensiveness, and Goodman is closer to Emerson than to Sartre and the other European secular existentialists. The poet "who does the best he can just to get it down as it is whispered to him"—what is he but Kantian, Emersonian, Romantic?

I do not doubt for a moment Goodman's sincerity in avouching what was "whispered" to him. He is a poet of intuition. And yet—was he not as well a poet of "responsibility," of "authenticity"? Emerson had thought he was a Kantian, but was at best only loosely so. Goodman brought to American "Romanticism" the inner moral voice, the imperative, of Kant, the poet's due to the Greater Spirit, his *intuition*. Goodman repaired the ruin of Transcendentalism with an esthetic accountability that could have come, but didn't, straight out of Sartre's theory of literature. For of course and without the slightest question, large parts of Goodman's poetry and fiction are political. He was being only petulant, denying the obvious, to say otherwise. The notion that somehow his polemical writing, his participation in rallies and demonstrations, left him free to be a "pure" poet was at variance with many statements of his belief in the unity of literature and life. Even on the same page with the last quotation above he wrote: "The habits, genres, and tropes that have been developed in the long worldwide literary tradition constitute a method of coping with reality different from science, religion, political power, or common sense, but involved with them all. In my opinion, literature, although it is a method *sui generis,* is not a specialized department of learning but a good way of being in any department. It is a part of philosophy, which as a whole has no department."

Incidentally, watch out for Goodman when he says "in my opinion." It means a whopper—right or wrong—is on the way.

Yet, with nearly the whole span of twentieth-century American poetry before us—so many politically inspired poets who failed to transform their politics successfully into their poetry compared with the few who did—we can see how the trap that Goodman fell into was tempting enough. I used to think, indeed I said publicly, that Goodman's broadly political books which brought him to the attention of a wider audience than reads good poetry and fiction—and I had in mind such books as *Growing Up Absurd, Compulsory Mis-Education,* and *People or Personnel*—were in some sense a misfortune, though no one could honestly say they should not have been written; a misfortune because they distracted attention from his "creative" writing; and I expressed the hope that in the long run these polemical works would be forgotten and his poems and fictions would remain alive in American consciousness. I no longer make this distinction. His best poems and fictions *will* remain alive in the American consciousness (if that consciousness survives, which it well may not), but so will many of his other books. They go together. Goodman's topics were many, but his theme was always himself; and he could no more refrain from inserting into his polemical works remarks about his beliefs as an artist than he could refrain from breathing. He was an organic whole. No other writer in America of this century—not Pound, not Williams, not Olson, though these are more nearly identified with the concept—represents so well the organicity of thought and feeling, of sensibility, implied in the title he gave himself, a Man-of-Letters.

Which is not to say that everyone must read every book in Goodman's "forty." Some are more important than others. For my part, I feel that these are the minimum for every reader's bookshelf: *Art and Social Nature, The Copernican Revolution* (edition of 1947), *Kafka's Prayer* (extremely important), *Communitas* (written with his brother Percival), *The Structure of Literature, The Empire City, Growing Up Absurd, The Lordly Hudson, Utopian Essays and Practical Proposals, Compulsory Mis-Education, Five Years, Hawkweed, Like a Conquered Province, Adam and His Works* (collected stories), *North Percy, Homespun of Oatmeal Gray, New Reformation, Speaking and Language, Little Prayers & Finite Experience.*

All these were published during Goodman's lifetime. Since his death more systematic collections of his short works (stories and essays) have been edited by Taylor Stoehr and others, including a few pieces not previously contained in books, and also one whole novel found hidden away among other papers, *Don Juan,* written around 1940. Goodman always had a difficulty—a heartbreaking struggle; see his paean to despair and survival in *Five Years*—in seeking publishers for his work, and heaven knows (or maybe Mr. Stoehr) what further unknown works may still appear.

Finally, the *Collected Poems* of 1973. Goodman was working on this, assembling, cutting, revising, when he was struck down; the further work of completing the manuscript and seeing it through the press fell to Stoehr, who did his best to ascertain and follow Goodman's last wishes. He could do neither less nor more. But I have considerable doubt of the wisdom of Goodman's own revisions, as I shall explain hereafter. Probably the *Collected Poems* must be added to the list because it contains poems not included in any earlier books while some of the earlier books themselves are hard to find. But the original books of poems are to be preferred, at least for the present.

A month or six weeks ago I found myself needing a copy of *The Lordly Hudson,* published in 1962. Mine was in Vermont, but I was in Syracuse—Syracuse, New York, which is not exactly Alexandria but is still a big enough, rich enough American city, with some pretentions of civic intelligence. Well, the neglect of Goodman's work during much of his life and still continuing has been a source of pain to me, and of astonishment. I could not find the book in any library, public, academic, or private, in this city. And is it any different in Lexington, Kentucky; or Hot Springs, Arkansas; or Salem, Oregon? You other Americans (as Goodman would remark), you pious four-flushers and grandstanders, what the hell is one to say to you?

I don't know how to account for the neglect of Goodman's work. Time after time I've met people who should be attracted by his poems and fictions, young and old, rich and poor, male and female. They have heard of him, those who are old enough have read *Growing Up Absurd* or attended a symposium on alternative schools in which he took part, but beyond that he means no more than the statue of President Harrison in the park. They do not know, have not even heard of, his poems or *The Empire City* or his short stories.

One explanation has occurred to me, wild as it seems,

which is that Goodman's writing is too clear and that whatever exegesis it needs has been given by Goodman himself. The critics have nothing to do, and of course readers will not bother with anything that hasn't been hashed over a dozen times in the fashionable quarterly maggot-scenes. Another explanation, obviously, is that he makes too much good radical sense; people can't take it. Or maybe they can't take his homoeroticism, his political anger and patriotism—a Jewish anarchist saluting the flag?—and his other forthrightnesses. But all these are foolish reasons.

"As a man of letters, I am finally most like Coleridge," he wrote. Then in parentheses: "With a dash of Matthew Arnold when the vulgarity of liberalism gets me by the throat." It was true. There is, if I am not mistaken, a universal turning point between Enlightenment and Romanticism, in the histories of individual men and women as in the histories of civilizations. It is a dangerous point because, for the vulgar liberals, who are the majority of mankind, it devolves into sentimentalism. But for the few, including Coleridge when young, it is a point of extraordinary freedom, the well-trained mind releasing itself into spirit. That point was where Goodman lived.

"Poets contrive to make interjections an organic part of their language by inverting the word order, distorting the syntax, and adding rhythm and resonance. Ordinary folk in a passion give up on the language." To which one need add only Goodman's own innermost thought, that poets ultimately are ordinary folk anyway, and that poems ultimately must also give up, e.g., the hokku with no conclusion.

Kafka was Goodman's closest literary friend, the young Jew of Prague, the writer whose greatness was like a dreamt castle with its towers vanishing upward in the mist.

Why am I so polemical about recent language theory . . . ? Why don't I let those scholars do their thing, while I, as a man of letters, do mine? Frankly, I am made polemically uneasy by it, by the thrust of cultural anthropology, Basic languages, scientific linguistics, communications engineering, and the Theory of Communications. They usually treat human communication as far more mechanical than it is; they are technological in an antihumanistic sense. They suit State and corporate policy too well and have crashingly pre-empted too many research grants and university appointments. My own bias, to be equally frank, is to play up the animal, spontaneous, artistic, and populist forces in speech. These forces are both agitational and deeply conservative—as I think good politics is. And as a writer, I want to defend literature and poetry as the indispensable renovators of desiccated and corrupt language.

Agitational and deeply conservative: mind soaring into spirit. (Reason, order, objectivity submitting to love.)

A poem is one inseparable irregular conglomeration, chanted. The word order is likely to be twisted. The names are particularistic and anomalous. New metaphors are invented. There is use of echoic meaning and expressive natural signs. There is strong use of tone and rhythm, sometimes even meter. The syntax is manipulated more than is common, sometimes "incorrectly," to give it more meaning. The exposition of the sentence follows the speaker's exploration of the subject rather than a uniform rule. All of this is for the purpose of saying a feelingful concrete situation, rather than making discursive remarks about it.

·

A generalist is a man who knows something about many special sciences, in order to coordinate their conclusions in a system that has little relation to reality. A man of letters knows only a little about some major human concerns, but insists on relating what he does know to his concrete experience. So he explores reality. A generalist is inter-disciplinary. A man of letters finds that the nature of things is not easily divided into disciplines.

·

When I do what is called "thinking," muttering to myself, I never use words like God or Faith, and they are in no way premises for my behavior. When I talk to other people, I sometimes use them, but not authentically; I might use such language, as I have said, to facilitate earnest conversation with a believer, though I am not a believer; or I might use them to cut short a boring conversation with an unbeliever, when I am too tired to explain myself better. When I write, however, I readily use this vocabulary and apparently seriously. How is this?

•

In *Defense of Poetry,* I suggest a possible reason: "Maybe it is that when I think or talk to myself, I am embarrassed; but when I write, I am not embarrassed"—since writing is my free act. But there could be a simpler reason, more *prima facie,* more what it feels like; I use this language because it is a poetic convention, a traditional jargon, like wearing old clothes because they are comfortable. It means what is the genius of the language of billions of human speakers—not my business. As a writer my business is only to be as clear as possible and say a work that has a beginning, middle, and end.

So we see Goodman clinging to his web of contrarieties.

Poetry is an empty act that is unfinishable but that has a beginning, middle, and end. But it is an *act.* Thinking is not an act. When the catcher signals to the pitcher, this is a thought; when the pitcher nods his head and goes into his windup, this is an act. Mind and imagination are connected, but the connection is tenuous, sometimes unlucky. The pitcher may shake off the sign, in which case the thought is useless. Or he may throw a bad pitch, in which case the act is a failure. But in all cases the pitcher's act is free, empty, isolated, internal, and its consequences, whatever they are, do not change it; no, not even if he beans the batter, who then suffers irreparable brain damage. Failure is failure, Goodman would say; it is a condition of human (self-conscious) existence, and so are punishment and misery and guilt. We can and must act with good faith and clarity, though these will never save us.

Thought is an argument with an imaginary companion. Making poetry is an act whose thought and content come from elsewhere, performed deliberately and in a conventional manner; its concreteness comes from its singularity—no act completely duplicates another, and a machine does not act but only moves in a meaningless transference of energy—and from the style imparted to it by the particular combination of attributes in the poet. (A machine is closer to thought than to a poem. A machine cannot have style.)

One may think at times that Goodman has painted himself into the same corner as the linguists and poststructuralists, as when he insists on the conventionality of language and artistic form. Yet the whole force of his argument, to say nothing of his poems, is to distinguish himself from those who would dismiss meaning from poetry. He too insists that the poem is "concrete," but he goes further. One must always remember that the poet does not believe in meaning as thought. Meaning is morality; morality is right feeling; and right feeling in concrete language is beauty. Sometimes I think Goodman yearned for "purity" as much as Mallarmé before him. But I also think that such was not his case with poetry, no matter how he yearned. His poems are political. Impossible to think of them as anything but political, moral, practical acts, "empty" and "free" only in their disconnection from objective determinants. Poetry is given. But so is life.

Another distinction, which Goodman did not make (as far as I recall) but which I want to make for him is this: on the one hand, style with a small s, being the techniques of syntax, grammar, and prosody contained in the grand and good and almost immemorial poetic convention; on the other hand, Style with a capital S, being the self-consciously fabricated verbal idiosyncrasy of poetic caprice or, worse, poetic fraud. Goodman's style was the former, and in fact he does not think about style explicitly and rarely uses the word. Moreover, as he knew, as we all know, convention in Goodman's sense is not always reliable. John Berryman could compose his *Dream Songs* in a Style that gave them a consistent superficial tension and density, while Goodman's poems in a plain style, as fine as the best of them are, especially in comparison with Berryman's, are more uneven. The fact that Berryman has been the darling of the critics while Goodman has been neglected shows the insensitivity of critics, who are always suckers for artifice.

But if in his poems Goodman conventionally used the conventional signs of a conventional religious language, and if as an unbeliever he conventionally knew that they were conventionally worthless, this is by no means the whole story. He was a practical man, i.e., a poet, i.e., a man of faith. Often he adverts to the idea of the earth beneath him supporting his footsteps as he walks idly along, thinking of something else. *This* is his faith. He was able, I don't know how, to shrug off the immense apparatus of his learning, experience, and thought, and to put himself again into the attitude of a child; or, more rigorously, certain constellations of traits and actions in the mature man reveal a childlike quality, the panicky, needful child who is very much afraid, but at the same time reliant on an unselfconscious prudential wisdom and joy. A child does not touch a porcupine even though he has never seen one before. "Nothingness" is a useful concept, and it may well be that if one pursues it far enough it turns into the same thing as "somethingness." But Goodman was a practical man. He worked with his experience of "this only world," and for him "somethingness" was truly somethingness: the given reality upon which we unselfconsciously, faithfully rely. He worked with his experience, which was this simple faith, through years and decades, writing poems in which the conventional signs took on more and more a personal, independent significance. Astonishing how simply and clearly he could say his complicated relationship to reality.

> O God, there must be some way
> that he and I (and many another)
> can be a little happier.
> Whisper it to me in my ear.

He was like a child. A wise, suffering, hopelessly hopeful child. Neither a literal nor a mystical way exists to define what the word "God" says in this quatrain, except that it does not say what it says in the sermons of TV evangelists. Yet I know what it says, and I'm confident my readers know what it says too. I don't have to try to explain it.

Goodman was *like* a child. But this is not saying he was a child. On the contrary it is saying how he was in his yearning, which was how he was in the world. And the words of children were often—but others just as often—expressive of how he was. "Whisper it to me in my ear," he says.

And then many times this poignancy eluded him, and he spoke out like the tough existential man he was, the Jewish Yankee.

> For the beautiful arts
> are made of cheap stuff,
> of mud and speech
> and guts and gestures
>
> of animal gaits
> and humming and drumming
> daylight and rock
> available to anybody.

This also is saying how he was in the world. And the names in these eight lines are not as random as they may seem at first, but were chosen in wisdom and placed with care. How else could he ever say how it *really* was for him in this world.

As for how it would be out of this world, Goodman did not write of death as such as one might have expected, knowing his metaphysical consternations. When he did write about it, he took it for what his experience—e.g., as a motorist (he loved the road)—told him it would be, and put it down on the paper more and more simply (though simplicity was one of his virtues from the beginning), and so in some sense dismissed it.

> Chuangtze is dead as I shall die
> unnoticed by the wayside,
> his spirit does not haunt the world
> and his death-grip is relaxed.

So. Finished and decomposing, no haunting spirit. Chuangtzu, more than two thousand years ago, the great interpreter of Taoism to the world.

Returning again to the matter of style (with a small s), I wonder what poets were Goodman's models. He does not say much about this. Poets generally don't. Villon was obviously important to him, Wordsworth more than important—crucial. I know he read Milton's essays. I suspect he may have looked once at Donne's sermons and several times at Aubrey's *Brief Lives* and Pepys's *Diary*. And I am convinced, myself, that he must have read Bradford's *History of Plimmoth Plantation*, that great distressed American epic, though I have only intuition to support me. But one can multiply the inferred influences indefinitely: Anacreon, Swift, Woolman, Catullus, Burns, the "Shepherd's Calendar," Rimbaud, and so on. Is there no contemporary instance? I can scarcely think of one (still adverting to style alone), though a wild guess might be that his deep interest in Kafka came through the translations of the Muirs, and that this might have led him to seek out Edwin Muir's own poems earlier than other Americans did; more than a trace of dictional and prosodic similarity exists between the two. And then Robert Frost—what about him? In an astounding number of ways Frost and Goodman echo each other, in many more ways than the devotees of either poet are likely to let on. But see, for instance, Frost's "The White-Tailed Hornet," especially its conclusion, which is Goodmanian in substance, tone, texture, and style.

But the point needing emphasis more than any other is that Goodman's instinct for the tradition took him not to individual models as much as in the direction of a persistent subpart of the tradition, difficult to define but roughly identifiable in his own thought and feeling. It was the pathos and sweetness and power of plain song that held his loyalty. The mandarins, the official poets—from Virgil to Eliot—were not for him, though he could pick out a genuine strain from any poetry wherever he found it. Thus his poem in praise of his brother Percival is in the "manner of Pindar"; and some of his poems in couplets have traces of Pope's last epistles and satires, though not of the earlier poems or of anything by Dryden except his songs. But not to individuals did he attach himself; rather to the company of poetic craftsmen who fashioned the long sigh of humanity; before them he knelt in humility. In his polemical writing he could be as egomaniacal and offensive as anyone, and even worse in his private behavior if we are to believe those who knew and loved him best; but to the real achievements of human genius he paid nothing but respect. And shall we blame him if his respect was surer and more readily accorded the farther back he looked? Time in its passage clears away our doubts, and Galileo seems a firmer friend than, for instance, Darwin (as Darwin in turn seems a firmer friend than the authors of *The Double Helix*).

Yet the paradox persists. Goodman's esteem for the tradition is a conspicuous part of his poetic attitude, both in explicit statements and in the intimations of his style; at the same time he was distinctly an experimental writer, an individualist. He stood at the end of the long tradition but cut out his immediate predecessors; he insisted on standing alone. The generation of Pound and Eliot did not much appeal to him, the generation of Auden and Spender even less. Whereas with all his prominent contemporaries—Jarrell, Schwartz, Shapiro, Lowell, Bishop, Rukeyser, Roethke, and so on—I can perceive immediate derivations from their forerunners, with Goodman I cannot. In a few other cases I see experiment and individuality—William Everson, James Laughlin, Kenneth Patchen, Charles Olson—but even with these I can trace immediate influences more easily than I can with Goodman, and besides, they do not—for whatever reason, narrowness of view, smallness of output, confusion of cultural locus, quirkiness of temperament—stand in Goodman's rank.

The thing is that Goodman reached backward to go forward. He was a heretic, outcast in his era, like all his heroes of old. Better than anyone else he understood the poet's need to exist consciously in the continuum. Granted, Eliot and Pound in their own ways had said the same thing and to a certain extent had shared similar tastes; but their views of contemporary literary society were elitist and their politics disreputable. (Not that Goodman was free from elitism, the elitism of one, which he called—and so do I—independence.) Nor was Goodman a mannerist, not in the slightest degree, which is what one cannot say of Pound or Eliot or most of the other modernists. Goodman's archaism of diction and syntax came naturally, came from the sound of the great writing of the whole past, from folktales and legend, from hymns, from everywhere; and it was combined inextricably with the jargon and street talk of his own time. Goodman in fact levied upon every linguistic resource at his command, shamelessly raiding both the elegances of gentility and the argot of hipsters. He made it all his own.

> This lust that blooms like red the rose
> is none of mine but as a song
> is given to its author knows
> not the next verse yet sings along.

This is genius, not typographical confusion. Stein, Proust, Joyce, and Faulkner made languages out of cultivated complexity, hard to unravel. Goodman is as clear as glass. But you will not find any grammarian after 1700—and before that who cared for grammar?—to parse Goodman's sentence logically. To my mind, to my ear—I having read this stanza many, many times—these four lines are magical, balancing forward and backward on the fulcrum of "author," that many-meaning word. (And only two polysyllables, that and the final "along," in the whole quatrain.) This strange syntax is not, I insist, a mannerism. It is the spontaneous speech of a man as much immersed in *The Anatomy of Melancholy* as in *The Neurotic Personality of Our Time,* a man to whom Cardan, Emerson, and Whitehead were all contemporaries.

How much would I have to quote to convince the reluctant reader that this is *typical,* that Goodman does it again and again (though naturally he became more skillful as he went on)? Too much. But I will quote once more, this time an entire poem.

> I lustily bestrode my love
>   until I saw the dark and poured my seed
>   and then I lay in sweetness like one dead
> whom angels sing around him and above.
>
> I lay with all my strength embraced
>   then swiftly to a quiet grave withdrew
>   like a grotto with the sea in view
> surging and pounding, till the spell was past.
>
> Since then, my hours are empty of
>   everything; beauty touches me
>   but is like pain to hear or see;
> absent among the tribes of men I move.

I cannot imagine, after this, that I need say more about diction and syntax. The fourth line is a wonder. A few additional points may be helpful, however. First, I take this poem from the same place in the book where I found several other quotations used already, where the book fell open randomly on my table. Second, how rarely do poets have the courage to take up what seem utterly worn out metaphors—orgasm as death—and try to give them something new. Third, the stanza suggests, but only suggests, the English lyric of the seventeenth century, a poem by Herrick perhaps (for Goodman too is a son of Ben, among other things); yet notice how the meter meanders between tetrameter and pentameter and how the accents fall not quite in order. Many have tried it and some have succeeded—Louise Bogan, Theodore Roethke, J. V. Cunningham, Stanley Kunitz, Richard Wilbur, and others—but none quite as well as Goodman. He is, if only by a shade, the most himself within the tradition. Finally, notice the perfection of cohesiveness among the poetic elements, how archaism ("bestrode") and inversion ("swiftly to a quiet grave withdrew") and backward-harkening syntax ("whom angels sing around him and above") all combine without rhetoric, overwriting, or strain. It is the most natural poem in the world. And I think the reason for this is precisely Goodman's humility, which so many doubt; his capacity to write simply with little words, yet always in deference—to time, to poets, to the poem, and to the reader—never in condescension. At least never in his best work.

It is an astonishing poem. It has no "right" to succeed. Bestrode, my love, seed, angels, grotto, spell, beauty, tribes of men—this is a wierd, romantic/biblical vocabulary, of attitudes as well as words. The remarkable thing is that this vocabulary really is Goodman's, is not just literary. Yet one reads the poem, at first, with little tics of embarrassment along the way, embarrassment for the poet and his naive words, and then, such is the force of the poem that when one rereads it, as one inevitably does, the tics are gone. Something powerful is at work here, some strange alienation in the poem from the beginning, deeply underlying the words, so that the sexuality of it disperses quickly and one is drawn down into the deeper matrix—of what, one hardly knows. The whole poem is about utter aloneness, but aloneness drained of suffering. (Compare the *basic* mood with Frost's "Stopping by Woods.") Esthetically what happens in Goodman's poem is so complex that even in this apparently boundless essay I cannot try to analyze it. Why does the poem work? What is behind the poet's humility? Goodman not only respected experience, the what-happens of life, he was often enough overwhelmed by it, like a child exposed to too many things, too much to handle. He wanted to freeze it, hold it *out there,* control it; but he couldn't—he was too hungry for it. His earnest defenses continually broke down, and the world crashed through. Such pathos! On the other hand Goodman would have defined an academic as one whose defenses are, alas, entirely successful. The question for him was: how much experience can I stand?

But I pause, I haul myself down. As always when writing about poetry I become diffident and doubt myself. Do other people hear what I hear? And if not how can I explain? The first line of the third stanza in the above poem, for instance—does Goodman get away with that contrived enjambment for the sake of the rhyme? Can one read it with an accent on "of" and still read in justified, justifiable English? I know I could never do it aloud; my voice will not hesitate on that syllable with the precisely needed degree of indeterminacy, though people tell me I am a good reader. In my head I can do it. But I am not willing for this reason to admit that the weak final accent is a flaw. It is a contrivance, and not *all* contrivances are artificial. If Donne can get away with

> Love's not so pure, and abstract, as they use
> To say, which have no mistress but their muse. . . .

(and he does), then Goodman can bring off his irregular line as well. And if my ear is more attuned to convention, and my mind more ready to accept it, than is the case with many other readers nowadays, then I can only agree, though ruefully and wishing otherwise. Contrivance works when it is conventional; and convention works when it is (1) not presently so widespread that it is meaningless, (2) not followed slavishly but with daring and independence, and (3) not of voice alone but of mind and spirit. In short, the relationship between the artist and his convention must be inventive and must subsist in a nice proportion of humility and self-assurance. Contrary to popular belief, convention in itself is neither alive nor dead, these being objective and verifiable conditions. It is an attitude, a feeling, almost a fantasy. Only its effects are demonstrable, never the thing itself.

Goodman had, like most full-time, long-time poets, many voices and modes, and he was not shy in using them. I have already spoken of his hokku. Then there are his sonnets, the ballades and ballads, the blank verse, free-form poems, songs, especially the quatrains composed of two loosely rhymed couplets with the second indented below the first, to which he turned more and more for his prayers and elegies as he grew older. What were his attitudes toward these different forms? It is enough to say that he did feel differently about them and turned now to one and now another, half instinctively, as his moods changed and different topics occupied his mind. It is notable that in organizing his collected poems he lumped certain ones together by genre, the sonnets, ballades, etc., showing that he had a literary feeling for them, even though the stronger linkages throughout the whole collection fall clearly within thematic, not generic, configurations. The further question is, did he have a single voice observable throughout? And the answer is yes, definitely, although only the most painstaking statistical analysis could discover the particular verbal usages that embody it. They are there, I am certain of it. But beyond the few I recognize in casual reading and therefore do not want to put on display, I can only point again to his remarkable control of syntax as the one talent that permitted him to move readily among and within the various forms; for all but a few of his poems were occasional and extemporaneous. (Which does *not* mean that he did not work hard and with the utmost seriousness.) Syntax, meaning the art of putting together sentences, as opposed to grammar, the science of taking them apart: this is the quintessence. And perhaps his sonnets show it as well as anything.

For those who cannot perceive in the poems themselves Goodman's affection and respect for the sonnet as a special, long-standing convention that he could take to himself, among many other conventions, in his state of being as a poetic master—and I am not speaking invidiously, because I know many people today who through no fault of their own have tin ears when it comes to the great traditions—for such readers Goodman's analysis of Milton's sonnet on his blindness, done in the most caring manner of *explication du texte* and contained in *The Structure of Literature*, will be helpful, as, for that matter, will all the rest of that book.

Goodman did not have a tin ear—anything but. Of the sixty sonnets in the *Collected Poems*, only two or three seem unreadable. I have checked five as sufficient to stand in the first rank, meaning that for me they are alongside the sonnet by Milton or others by Shakespeare and Wordsworth. Another way to say it: Goodman and Cummings wrote the best American sonnets we have, though we have fine ones by Longfellow, Lizette Woodworth Reese, Edna Millay, and others. This is astonishing. Goodman wrote in a time when even the most determined traditionalists did not care much for fixed forms; the sonnet, in spite of its provenance at the center of Renaissance poetry, was still thirty-odd years ago too closely associated with *fin-de-siècle* hearts and flowers. Pound wrote many but published none. Even Yeats, who one might have thought would have taken to the sonnet eagerly, did not, but preferred instead the stanzaic forms of his own invention. And taking Goodman's poetic generation as a whole (1935–1970), its most popular model by far was precisely in Yeats's later work. To all this Goodman paid no mind, going his own way in his "only world."

The first sonnet by Goodman I ever read was "In Lydia," which was submitted to *Poetry* when I was a member of the staff, circa 1947–1950.

I am touring high on the Meander River
the scenery ever varying. The land
is Lydia, the wheat rich, the climate bland,
and very sweet the modus of the zither.
Our queen is Omphale, for never never
cut was the curving cord in which we end
—when shall we arrive? I round a bend,
the view is changed, and forward is another.

That's not a woman in the palace yard
spinning! unwillingly—breathing hard—

Hercules! here, for pity's sake
the thread is long enough, it leaves the wheel
and tangles, and the world is areel.
My hands have hold upon it; shall I break?

I don't know whether the wording here, taken from the *Collected Poems,* follows the original version, but I do know definitely (because it struck me forcibly when I first read it and influenced the invention of a form I myself have used often, which I call the paragraph) that I have printed the poem in its original shape, that is, with the couplet displaced from the end and set apart by space-breaks in the middle. I had never seen this before. It works beautifully. For reasons I can't fathom, Goodman chose to run the couplet into the last four lines for his collected edition, thus deemphasizing his re-arrangement of the usual form and giving his sonnet a conventional-looking sestet. Moreover I wish he had written "and the world's areel," thus making the thirteenth line a clear metrical equivalent to the short eleventh line, the whole final quatrain easier and stronger. But it's a fine sonnet in any case.

God damn and blast and to a fist of dust
reduce me the contemptible I am
if I again hinder for guilt or shame
the blooming of my tenderness to lust
like a red rose; I have my cock traduced
to which I should be loyal. None to blame
but me myself that I consort with them

who dread to rouse me onward and distrust
what has a future.
                    Let me bawl hot tears
for thee my lonely and dishonored sex
in this fool world where now for forty years
thou beg'st and beg'st and again thou beg'st
because this is the only world there is,
my rose in rags among these human wrecks.

Is it half jocular? Of course, all poems about sex are; this is the
human sensibility, "primitive" or "refined." But notice the
strong movement of the sentences through the octet, the
power yet naturalness of the rhymes, and then in the sestet
Goodman's giveaway, "the only world"; whenever he says that
he is serous. This is a sonnet so packed with tonal, metrical,
dictional, and thematic intricacies that I doubt a thorough expli-
cation could be made in less than many pages; I mean this—no
exaggeration. Yet any reasonably experienced reader will be
able to do it just in the reading. The poem is crystalline.

At the same time it's necessary to point out, not only in
prudence but in humility, that Goodman's sonnets do not ap-
peal to everyone, and that this sonnet in particular has been
attacked by an acute critic who was also one of Goodman's
most sympathetic, my friend George Dennison. The poem—I
paraphrase George—is dishonest and spiritually ugly. Only
an intellectual, full of ideas as well as hurt and having a long
history of attempts to heal the splits between mind and body,
passion and thought, etc., could be so arrogantly *loyal* to his
cock. "Rouse me onward," ha!—Goodman was compulsive
and fetishistic, self-aroused and continually so. How can dic-
tion, syntax, etc., be of any force when the poem itself (and
the evidence is in the poem) displays such a disgusting mess of
illness, attitudinizing, self-protective lying, etc. I can only an-
swer that to my mind the literary quality of the poem does in
fact overcome these ugly revelations, which are revealed in
plenty of other poems too. Goodman was a man of letters
indeed. He revered prosody. The arrogance and dishonesty
patent in the poem are retrieved by the prosodic power of the
whole poem and by the authentic universalization of feeling

in the sestet. A great many of us can "bawl hot tears" for our "lonely and dishonored sex." But see how crazy and silly the words sound when quoted outside the poem? They are. Yet the whole verbal, structural, and imagistic complex of the sonnet holds its substance together and elevates it, I feel, to the plane on which personal dishonesty and braggadocio become realized esthetic paradigms. It was a terribly risky sonnet to write. But Goodman took the risks. Isn't this what being a poet means?

> Grief how into useless age away
> ebbed youth and I was unhappy all those years
> I also do not feel, for now new fears
> possess me and I steel myself today
> today's pain to endure, so I can die
> without a reckoning and weep no tears
> for promises deceived. Maybe my peers
> or my disciples will this tribute pay.
>
> Oh, when He bound my arms behind my back
> and threw me in the sea, I heard Him call
> "Swim! swim!" and so I have swum to this hour
> breathless in the cold water rough and black
> where many have already drowned and all
> *shall* drown in the swells that sink and tower.

Is it necessary to point out the poetic self-faith expressed in the metrical irregularity of the two opening lines? Yes, they are crabbed, incredibly so, arrogantly and intentionally so. (It would have been child's play to put those two lines in "right" order.) To me the force of feeling in them is the force that justifies and demands them, and they are beautifully expressive.

> One thing, thank God, I learned, the grisly face
> of Hope to abhor, her eyes bloodshot with dreams,
> her hair unkempt with fury. Lying streams
> out of her mouth and men drink it. Alas,
> if you look ever in a looking-glass
> and see an ugly Hope in hungry flames
> devouring you, so the unreal seems

real and the impossible to come to pass
possible, see, when you look again
Disappointment! But *this* face of pain
is mine, which I and all my family have,
my mother wears it in her southern grave,
my sister grown old woman has it, and
my brother building buildings rich and grand.

The couplet at the end makes us think of the great tradition, and no one has better extended the sonnet's essentially Shakespearean movement in English, pushing the runovers and enjambments *just enough further.* Goodman's verbal instinct is here at its best. See "mother/southern" in line twelve: did it fall accidentally that way? or did Goodman think it up? In either case the force of years of poetic thought lies behind it. Note also the movement of imagery from horror and Dantean grotesquerie to the more human "face of pain" and ending in the last line—the reference is to his brother Percival, the architect, with whom he wrote *Communitas,* his most important early statement of social criticism and also, incidentally, a hopeful book—with "buildings rich and grand." Who could have expected such a swift, complex modulation of images and feelings?

Students have said to me that they dislike the inverted syntax and archaism because such writing seems to them awkward. They wonder why Goodman let himself be pushed around by form. But there is no question of being pushed around. Goodman was a *writer,* a *versewriter,* among other things, which entails a skill that young readers seem ill-equipped to recognize, even now when so many of them are turning back to conventional fixed forms. (I've read hundreds and hundreds of sonnets recently, from students, from people who submit to magazines, from entrants in contests, from quite well-known poets, but have not seen one with any hint of the tensile lyricism that the sonnet has required since the thirteenth century.) Goodman wrote his sonnet this way because he wanted to, because this was the effect consonant with his own temperament and the poem's feeling. He could just as easily have written:

Thank God I learned one thing, to abhor Hope's
grisly face, her eyes bloodshot with dreams,
her hair unkempt with fury. Lying streams
from her mouth and men drink it. If you perhaps
should look in a mirror and see Hope's hungry shapes
of flame reaching to devour you, your own schemes
raging there . . . , etc.

This would have accorded well enough with his usual rhyming
and metrical practice. Something like it may have been a first
draft of the poem. But Goodman *chose* the inversions, the ar-
chaic "Alas," the whole inner strategy, and his choice was inten-
tional, if not at the moment of writing, then certainly in the
long course of self-training that led up to it. In fact I am struck
now by the possibility that some of Goodman's contemporaries
may have had more influence on him than I suggested earlier;
but a negative influence, not a positive one. Delmore Schwartz
and John Berryman, for instance, were both writing sonnets at
about the time Goodman was beginning his. He may have seen
very early that he needed something different from their
styles, plainer than Schwartz's Marlovian grandness, simpler
and easier than Berrymans' contortedness. This would have
been in keeping with his desire to be separate.

This sonnet is called "The Americans Resume Bomb-
Testing, April 1962."

My countrymen have now become too base,
I give them up. I cannot speak with men
not my equals, I was an American.
Where now to drag my days out and erase
this awful memory of the United States?
how can I work? I hired out my pen
to make my country practical, but I can
no longer serve these people, they are worthless.

"Resign! resign!" the word rings in my soul
—is it for me? or shall I make a sign
and picket the White House blindly in the rain,
or hold it up on Madison Avenue
a silent vigil, or trudge to and fro
gloomily in front of the public school?

Clearly this is *ex tempore*. Goodman's spontaneous anger is too great, forcing him into egomania and dishonesty, permitting him to make the easy identification of "my countrymen" with the State, which elsewhere he would not have done. The rhymes are too easy; only a trifle, but noticeably. And why when force, measure, and colloquial value demand it did he not insert "out" after "gloomily" in the final line, to give it more weight in the pentameter? Nevertheless I include it among my five because it shows so trenchantly how the surplusage of feeling can drive through the poetic form in Goodman's flexible syntax and carry all before it. This it does *as* a sonnet: the movement from octet to sestet exactly what the original lyric impulse (back to Pier delle Vigne in the *trecento* as Arthur Symons said) prescribes; *pre-scribes,* the word is worth considering.

Finally—

> Foster excellence. If I do not
> who will do it? The vulgarity
> of this country makes my spirit faint, what we
> have misdone to our history and what
> to the landscape. The tasteless food we eat,
> the music, how we waste day after day
> child, woman, and man have stunned me to dismay
> like an ox bludgeoned, swaying on his feet.
>
> John, rescue me by becoming. I have well
> deserved of the Republic, though it has
> rewarded me with long oblivion.
> Make you me proud and famous as the one
> who thought that we could be what Florence was
> when angry men made rough rocks beautiful.

Notice how Goodman has no metrical force-of-habit, but starts off this sonnet in a totally different, short and punchy syntax. Also how the hackneyed images follow one another in perfect originality because the language will not let them slump back on their cushions of hebetude. Lastly how Goodman, like the rest of us, was grandiose and greedy in his demands on his personal friend, in this case John. Why should John do what the "Republic" will not? Because *some-*

body must! Who better than a lover to assuage the injury dealt by Time and the State. Catullus, Villon, Swift, Leadbelly, etc.

No consideration of Goodman's writing can be let go without at least a glance at the quatrains he came to rely on more and more. Here is a bit of a poem, a tag stuck on at the end of a sonnet about a glimpse of a handsome, inaccessible young man.

> Some happy folk their faith
> and some their calling doth
>   justify, but Lord,
>   I am justified
>
> by the beauty of
> the world and my love
>   of Your animals, though I
>   may not be happy thereby.

This is characteristic; the involved, pivoted sentences, the rhymes ranging from near to remote, the archaism both reinforced and contradicted by the irregularity of rhythm, and then the grand affirmation given and at once partly withdrawn; also the circular movement from "happy" to "happy," making a perimeter around which the contraries align themselves.

Here are two more, untitled:

> I ask the Lord, "Who are You?"
> though I know His name is "Spoken to."
>   Hoping but I am not sure
>   His name might be "I am who answer."
>
> With certain faith let me continue
> my dialogue with Spoken-To.
>   Hope has always been my curse,
>   it never yet came to pass.
>
> The crazy man that you meet
> talking to himself in the street
>   is I, please gently lead him home.
>   Creator Spirit come.

Again a small poem, probably impromptu or near it. Technically it is very fine, revealing Goodman's faculty for reducing brilliance to what seems offhand. Notice how in the second stanza "certain" and "curse" are linked internally, as are "spoken" and "hope," "always" and "pass," so that the stanza is aurally compressed and unified, and then how the rhyme in the first couplet, "continue" and "Spoken-To," an unaccented sound rhymed with an accented one that nevertheless is a very small word, assembles behind the meaning a huge power of prosodic reinforcement. "Spoken-To" is a term used by some orthodox Jews as a euphemism for the divine name, which is taboo, and so Goodman's poem is immediately rooted not only in his own people's religion, a backward reach emphasized by further biblical-sounding language ("come to pass," "lead him home," etc.), but also in the structure of spiritual taboo in all human consciousness, as amplified sophisticatedly in our awareness of cultural anthropology and Jungian psychiatry. It is a poem about fear and craziness and unnameability, the pathos of the human condition, profoundly Hebrew but also profoundly Greek; a poem which ends on our one solace as the poet utters his own euphemism, "Creator Spirit." This is no cheap-shot poetic aggrandizement; quite the contrary. The humility of utterance is plain. (Goodman did talk to himself on the street.) Yet the poem is no orthodoxy either, and it does almost heretically link mankind's esthetic mentality with the sense of religion. It makes no claim for the poet as prophet, but every claim for the poet inhabiting all human souls. It reaches back through the shadows of anonymity which gather around the early members of "the grand community" to the earliest, the greatest Anonymity. I cannot help thinking of the painting that shows God touching Adam's finger. In this poem Adam (one of Goodmans' favorite names) touches back. It is a poem as swift as a spark leaping across a gap, and is as succinct, lucid, and profound a statement of modern man's religious nature as Goodman or any other poet has written.

Now another in the same stanza, opening with the line that was the earlier poem's close, this one written a couple of months after the death of the poet's son, Mathew.

Creator Spirit come
by whom
   I'll say what is real
   and so away I'll steal.

When my only son
fell down and died on Percy mountain
   I began
   to practice magic like a pagan.

Around the open grave we ate
the blueberries that he brought
   from the cloud, and then we
   buried his bag with his body.

Around the open grave
I laid the hawkweed that I love
   which withered fast
   where the mowers passed.

I brought also a tiny yellow
flower whose name I do not know
   to share my ignorance
   with my son. (But since

then I find in the book
it is a kind of shamrock
   Oxalis corniculata,
   Matty, sorrel of the lady.)

Blue-eyed grass with its gold hexagon
   beautiful as the gold and blue
   double in Albireo
that we used to gaze on

when Matty was alive
I laid on Matty's grave
   where two robins were
   hopping here and there;

and gold and bluer than that blue
or the double in Albireo
   bittersweet nightshade
   the deadly alkaloid
      I brought for no other reason
      than because it was poison.

Mostly, though, I brought some weed
beautiful but disesteemed,
   plantain or milkweed,
   because we die by the wayside.

(And if spring comes again
I will bring a dandelion,
   because he was a common weed
   and also he was splendid.)

But when I laid my own forehead
on the withering sod
   to go the journey deep,
   I could not fall asleep.

I cannot dream, I cannot quit
the one scene in the twilight
   that is no longer new yet does
   not pass into what was.

Last night the Pastoral Symphony
of Handel in the key of C
   I played on our piano
   out of tune shrill and slow

because the shepherds were at night
in the field in the starlight
   when music loud and clear
   sang from nowhere.

Will magic and the weeks placate
the soul that in tumbling fright
   fled on August eighth?
   The first flock is flying south

and a black-eyed susan
is livid in the autumn rain
   dripping without haste or strain
   on the oblong larger than a man.

Creator spirit come
by whom
   I say that which is real
   and softly away I'll steal.

It was not so long after this that Goodman did steal away, joining Mathew, and he did it softly enough too, like the rest of us.

From this longer poem one learns not to care overmuch for the design one has chosen from artifice to suit one's poem; the seventh stanza is shaped differently to accommodate the change of rhyming, yet the next-to-last stanza, which has the same rhyme in *abba*, is shaped like the rest. In the ninth stanza he thought of an extra couplet—before or afterward? I don't know. He could just as well have used the third couplet as the first of a new stanza. He didn't. He wrote in spontaneity and left the poem as it came.

Another point. Goodman was his own closest reader. He remembered when he had found a scrap of language that suited him and compressed his meaning. He repeated it, using it as often as he liked, deepening its meaning in the variety of contexts. In this poem "we die by the wayside," just as in the poem about Chuang-tzu.

And for a while I thought I could leave this poem about the death of Mathew Goodman with no more than my few technical observations. I felt so fine a poem, so clearly embodying the elements of Goodman's practice, needed no further commentary. I was attempting—but not consciously—to disguise or dispel my own and the reader's sense of self-revealment after reading this almost unbearably moving work. Why are we overcome with shyness just as we find what we go to art to seek, this ultimate human actuality? I don't know, but I believe this underlies the predicament of the arts today, our willful concentration on mediocrity.

The poem is as fine an elegy as I know. Do I mean it is as good as the dirge in *Cymbeline* that I have had tacked to my cowshed wall for twenty years? Yes. How do I know it is as good? Knowledge has nothing to do with it; both poems are pinchbeck to the *cognoscenti*. I feel the goodness, and I speak to those who feel it with me, or who may come to feel it. Will one define the human heart in an essay?

At the beginning and again at the ending, the poem advocates magic, invoking our primal intellection. It is another reaching back; it is paleolithic. The opening and closing stanzas are the same, which gives the poem Goodman's characteristic circularity, but in this case gives it even more: the strict repetition is like the magician's clap at the beginning and end of his trick, for the poem occurs outside of time, outside of experience, as if in the science-fiction writer's favorite time warp. It is an act of ecstacy (ex stasis). So simple the device, known well to children; so complex the psychic action. Then while we are "away" we live only ritualistically, the bringing of flowers again and again, their parts and properties named in the magic of evoking a reality we can say but never understand, the music, the seasons. The references all appear to us like waves from the same source, the mowers, the lady, the star, the poison, the music "from nowhere": all the same, waves falling on our shore of consciousness from "nowhere," from far out, from grief as the *mythologos*, the word that cannot be said. It is a poem of transcendent negation.

Milton praised Lycidas, Shelley Adonais, Goodman says of his "only son," Mathew, no more than that he was a "weed" and "splendid" and that he "fell down and died," having brought blueberries "from the cloud": no more. Yet to my mind Goodman's elegiac intensity is greater, and on my ear his words fall, without loudness, without formal declamation, still with more sweetness and resonance. I call it "transcendent negation" because I cannot define it except by saying what it is not, and even then only imperfectly. An elegy without praise? It seems odd, yet now that I stop to think I see that this is the poem of our time, written again and again, by Ransom, Roethke, by many others, because our "hero" is always this young person who is "real." And "the oblong larger than a man" is real. But the reality is more than we can take, except in the time-out-of-time, the poem, the myth. This movement, as of mercury in a balancing tube repelled by negative magnets at either end, myth and reality falling toward and away from each other, is the magic of minds reverting through mankind's ten thousand years or a man's ten thousand days of reason, to unending agony and fatigue again.

Goodman wrote:

> I cannot dream, I cannot quit
> the one scene in the twilight
>   that is no longer new yet does
>   not pass into what was.

I feel in this the ache of implacability as in few other pieces of literature. I know its simplicity, its negative refusal to say more, is what makes it, technically speaking, so effective. But I cannot hope to understand the means of it much further. So much does not pass into what was. Stonehenge. Ozymandias.

"The soul that in tumbling fright / fled on August eighth"— was it Matty's? Yes. Was it Paul's too? Yes. Was it the Creator Spirit, was it Death? Yes. Will it be placated? No. Do affirmation and negation mean the same thing? No. Yes.

This essay has said almost nothing about Goodman's prose fiction. Goodman had great hopes for his novel, *The Empire City.* The first section, entitled "The Grand Piano," enjoyed a fair success when it was published separately in 1942. But Goodman's reputation fell off sharply after that. The second section, "State of Nature," was ignored. When the third section was completed, Goodman could find no publisher for it, though he tried and tried. At last he published "Dead of Spring" himself and sold copies to friends through the mail, as I recall, for $2 each. Strange books they were, printed on cheap stiff paper held in spiral bindings, apparently produced in some job-shop that normally did calendars and appointment books. Now they are collectors' items. It seemed at the time a pitiable effort. How many copies could he have sold? A couple of hundred if he was lucky. But now we see the courage of his persistence, a courage he needed all his life, for although the novel was eventually published in one volume— including the previously unpublished fourth section, "The Holy Terror"—by a commercial publisher and then later in a paperback edition, and although I salute Bobbs-Merrill and Random House for their editorial intelligence, *The Empire City* still did not receive the attention it deserves from reviewers or readers, and has not till this day.

Is it a novel? In historical terms it can with justice be called an allegory, a picaresque tale, a philosophical novel, a comedy of humors, a panoramic adventure, and possibly a tractatus. For myself, I am content to say that *The Empire City* is a phantasmagoria of ideas whose hero is Horatio Alger, whose secondary personages are a decidedly mixed group of imagined and real people, whose structure is random, and whose purpose is to investigate through episodes of comic pathos the truth of human life at the middle of the twentieth century in the greatest city on earth. Its antecedents are legion, but mostly from para-literature: *commedia dell'arte*, Rabelais, *The Canterbury Tales*, Hogarth, Artemus Ward and Mark Twain, Krazy Kat, Chaplin and Cocteau—the list could go on and on, and why do I call it "para-literature?" That is an academic way of putting it. What I mean is that almost anything you can take from outside the "main current of literary evolution," anything from Petronius to Damon Runyon, will find its echo in *The Empire City*.

As for the short stories, they are various yet mostly also of adventuresome intents and methods. They are not well wrought in the Mansfieldean manner, nor in the Hemingwayan either, but rather they effloresce from Goodman's exuberance with only his own cogent imagination to supply their limits. I cannot attempt to say in a paragraph how they were made. I think all of them are a delight to the mind, some a delight to the heart, and a few are, after the poems, extremely important. Some of the stories are lyrical, and some philosophical. Some almost turn into essays before one's eyes. But Goodman was no perfectionist, and he wrote at a dizzy pace, his sentences of prose (more than his sentences of poetry) scarcely able to keep up with his thoughts, so that sometimes he wrote stories which had no real purpose. Yet even those are interesting and the language is always a pleasure to read. His least successful work was the posthumously published novel *Don Juan*, which bears some connection to the early parts of *The Empire City* but becomes tedious after the first fifty or sixty pages.

A number of times in recent years I have complained about the mess of Goodman's *Collected Poems* and asked for a selected edition that would contain the best versions of the poems, not simply the last versions. I made an extended case for this in the present essay as it was originally published in 1983. Now, I'm glad to say, we have good news. Geoffrey Gardner, a writer, critic, editor, and friend of Goodman and his family, completely qualified to do the job, has put together such a selected edition, an ample selection which includes not only all Goodman's well-known poems in their best versions, but also previously unpublished poems found among the poet's papers after his death, notes, variant readings, etc. It is a fine piece of work and desperately needed. It will be published, if all goes well, in 1992.

But the case of Goodman's best-known poem, "The Lordly Hudson," is still worth discussing because it is so instructive. Here it is as it was printed in 1962.

> "Driver, what stream is it?" I asked, well knowing
> it was our lordly Hudson hardly flowing,
> "It is our lordly Hudson hardly flowing,"
> he said, "under the green-grown cliffs."
>
> Be still, heart! no one needs your passionate
> suffrage to select this glory,
> this is the lordly Hudson hardly flowing
> under the green-grown cliffs.
>
> "Driver! has this a peer in Europe or the East?"
> "No, no!" he said. Home! home!
> be quiet, heart! this is our lordly Hudson
> and has no peer in Europe or the East,
>
> this is our lordly Hudson hardly flowing
> under the green-grown cliffs
> and has no peer in Europe or the East.
> Be quiet, heart! home! home!

We all know ardent wordings for a river, mountain, highway, glen: our only world, the earth *in loco parentis*. After the wrack of sex, this is the singer's most passionate testimony. But I know no other that surpasses this in simple expressiveness. Such poems bear the authenticity of universal knowledge and feeling, beyond the bounds of judgment, in the realm of equivalence and essential anonymity.

This is the text as it appeared in the *Collected Poems*, revised by Goodman a few weeks before his death:

> "Driver, what stream is it?" I asked, well knowing
> it was our lordly Hudson hardly flowing,
> "It is our lordly Hudson hardly flowing,"
> he said, "under the green-grown cliffs."
>
> Be still, man! no one needs your passionate
> suffrage to select this glory,
> this is our lordly Hudson hardly flowing
> under the green-grown cliffs.
>
> "Driver! has this a peer in Europe or the East?"
> "No no!" he said. Home! home!
> be quiet, heart! this is our lordly Hudson
> and has no peer in Europe or the East,
>
> this is our lordly Hudson hardly flowing
> under the green-grown cliffs
> and has no peer in Europe or the East.
> Be patient, Paul! home! home!

By such small stitches may passion be clothed in art or left shivering and naked. Three alterations: the change from "heart" to "man" in the first line of the second stanza; the deletion of the comma between "no" and "no" in the second line of the third stanza; the substitution of "Be patient, Paul" for "Be quiet, heart" in the final stanza.

One can reconstruct Goodman's probable motives in making these changes. "Heart" is a genteel and banal word; how much better to generalize and universalize by saying "man." Or, more likely, "man" was addressed to himself in the street idiom of the sixties and seventies. But in his haste Goodman did not see that "man" points directly and reductively back to "Driver" in the stanza before, and is thus both a spoiling of the poem's universality and a misplaced colloquialism in a poem whose simplicity is still very formal. Moreover the effect of the original poem was exactly *in* its repetitions: "heart," "heart," "lordly," "lordly," etc.

The excision of the comma between the "no's" was in keeping with Goodman's later typographical style, and is not of much moment—one doesn't wish to be finicky. Yet for me the comma was part of the poem's celebratory, odelike, formal expressiveness, and I miss it.

The greatest damage is the final change. Yes, Paul wanted to get home; he was on a plane while he read and corrected the manuscript for his *Collected Poems*. He had been teaching in Hawaii. He had had a heart attack not long before. The exotic environment of the islands suited him far less than the plain hayfields and hawkweed of New Hampshire. But "patient" is not the same as "quiet," again the wonderful repetition is lost, and "Paul" is a long, long way from "heart."

"The Lordly Hudson" is an early poem, probably from before 1940. I am told its occasion was Goodman's homecoming to New York after an unhappy stay in Chicago. He was strong, his poetic instinct was working beautifully, and he was in no haste. More than thirty years later when he revised the poem, he was coming home again. He was weak and in pain; he knew his death was not far off. He made the three little changes and a great poem was reduced to an ordinary one. It was a misfortune. But now we can go back to the original version in the new *Selected Poems*, and the two versions do give us a fine example of the place and mystery of craft in poetry, an example every student should examine carefully.

To the two sequences of poems he wrote for Mathew, not including the elegy quoted above, Goodman gave the title "Sentences."

> "Great Tao is a ship adrift"—awakes
> at sunrise asking, where am I?
> and deviates forward slowly to nowhere.
> What does he know? to front afraid the gale
> and painfully climb the next oncoming wave.
> It is by an inevitable mistake
> that the ten thousand cheer and shake their flags
> lining the shore in the indifferent port.

Nevertheless, and Goodman would have said so too, to be one of the ten thousand is something.

A sentence is an always potential construction of language. Goodman gave it his devotion for a lifetime. It is also "the opinion pronounced by a person on some particular question" (*OED*). Finally it is what the judge hands down. Those who fail to recognize behind Goodman's "Sentences" the weight of all these meanings and the weight of some of his favorite word-works from the past, *The Testament* of François Villon or *The Trial* by Franz Kafka, will perhaps miss nothing essential. But those who do recognize these things will be enriched by them, and will become themselves in some part members of Goodman's Grand Community. For the tradition is what we as mankind travel on, the Tao, wherever we are going.

Lear

One line from *King Lear* that all poets remember comes at the end of the play when Lear, carrying his dead daughter Cordelia in his arms and struggling to take in the fact that he will never know her alive again, says: "Never, never, never, never, never." Is that a good line prosodically, or isn't it? In an early poem of mine, consciously imitating, I wrote, "O river, river, river, river, river." The effect pleased me then and it still does. But a friend of mine, a poet and playwright, told me recently that Shakespeare's line is bad, both poetically and dramatically. And I know that most younger poets today, my students and others, would consider such passionate and lyrical writing inadmissible.

When I was young we not only studied Shakespeare, we read him for pleasure—as we read all the good poets of his time. He seemed in a sense one of us, a poet in our immediate succession, someone from whom we could learn. To young poets today he is utterly remote, I think, as far removed as Virgil or the author of *Beowulf*—of no use at all to their own work. I have noticed that on their applications for admission to the graduate creative writing program at Syracuse, in answer to the question about which older poets have influenced them, students rarely name any poets born before 1940. They never mention Shakespeare. Perhaps they are, collectively speaking, the first poets in English since the seventeenth century who have not taken Shakespeare for one of their models.

Probably this isn't their fault. On any semester's list of graduate offerings, at least at SU, these days you may not find a single course on Shakespeare.

But going back to the line near the end of *King Lear*, contextuality, as the theorists say, is all. This play is an impassioned poem. Extreme diction, reiterative diction, is common throughout. At the beginning of Act I, Scene ii, Edmund says:

> Why brand they us
> With base? with baseness? bastardy? base, base?

Later in Act I Lear says, striking his own head:

> O Lear, Lear, Lear!
> Beat at this gate that let thy folly in. . . .

And again:

> O let me not be mad, not mad, sweet heaven!

At the beginning of Act IV Gloucester says:

> But who comes here?
> My father, poorly led? World, world, O world!

which may be the dead-center of the whole play. In Act IV, Scene vi, Lear says: "Now, now, now, now!" and a few lines later he says: "Then kill, kill, kill, kill, kill, kill!"—actually one more reiteration than in the line which disturbs my friend. Indeed, near the very beginning of the play, when Lear asks Cordelia what she can say about her love for him that will justify a share in his bequests, the little dialogue occurs from which the whole action derives:

> Cor. Nothing, my lord.
> Lear. Nothing?
> Cor. Nothing.
> Lear. Nothing can come of nothing. Speak again.

Thus the play is framed between five *nothings* and five *nevers*. What could be more indicative of Shakespeare's purpose in this gaunt but complex poem? And what could be more revealing of the lyric impulse behind it? From first to last it is about people who are suffering extremely. The language does not seem to me excessive.

Nor is lyricism, of whatever kind, a departure from real speech. At moments of heightened feeling we all use broken syntax and repeat the same words over and over. And sometimes we sing. Most contemporary poetry, on the other hand, gives us language that is intentionally false, a language that could never be spoken by anyone, hence, however plain, a literary language, an artificial language. Lear in his madness speaks with a naturalness that young poets today can't hear, apparently because their own verbal sensibilities have been warped away from naturalness by the academic milieu in which they spend most of their lives.

For that matter Lear, though very hard-driven in most of the play, especially in the storm scenes, is not as crazy as many readers think. He is "out of his mind," but not far out. Like others nowadays I have served a hitch or two in psychiatric hospitals, where I have heard and seen people whose speech and behavior were far more violent and irrational than anything Shakespeare assigned to Lear. What we get from our newspapers every day is what is excessive. What we observe on the streets of our cities is excessive. But not the language of Lear. And in response to my friend's feeling that the line in question is poor drama, though in some sense I am disqualified from answering since during most of my life I have been prevented from even entering a theater, nevertheless in my mind's voice, with which I sound all poetry, I can arrange those five repeated *nevers* in half-a-dozen ways that are easily enunciated and appropriate. It goes without saying that they should not be shouted. When the line is spoken, Lear himself is dying, and his words should be uttered in moans and whispers.

Some critics and dramaturgists, like A. C. Bradley and Harley Granville-Barker, have contended, against the majority, that *Lear* is feasible in dramatic production. In spite of my ignorance I must disagree. The problem is not the violence of the play, not the probability in Act III that the storm will drown out the dialogue, not the constant reference to fiends and monsters, not even the destruction of Gloucester's eyes in full view of the audience—"Out, vile jelly! Where is thy lustre now?"—

but rather the fact that these elements of the play and everything else in it are real. Any attempt to push them in the direction of fantasy, stereotype, or the surreal, which would be the tendency of most producers and directors faced by such horrors today, would weaken the play. Influenced as we are in our century by our own kinds of represented horror, Kafka, Brecht, etc., we can hardly think of *Lear* without turning it into a morality, an allegory, a parable, a symbolization or typification of some kind; that is, without giving it what we call "esthetic distance." But the blinded Gloucester says: "World, world, O world!" He means this actual world, our own, from which we have no distance at all. We cannot schematize the events of *Lear* according to psychoanalytical, sociological, mythological, Marxist, or any other abstract conceptions without destroying their validity in the experience of real persons. Shakespeare himself emphasized this by departing so far from the conventions of even the bleakest Greek or Renaissance drama. *Lear* from inception to catastrophe to denouement, if these terms apply, is entirely downhill; it is a straight-line disaster with no structure beyond the scene-to-scene interweaving of the two stories of Lear and Gloucester. Cordelia could have been saved at the end without weakening the tragedy of the old king, as indeed she was saved in the bowdlerized version of the play that was put out for general consumption in both print and performance for a century or more, and this would have seemed perfectly correct to most playwrights and playgoers of Shakespeare's time. Or Gloucester, Lear's counterpart in the subsidiary plot, could have been saved, which would not have weakened the tragedy either. But in the world Cordelia and Gloucester are not saved. No one is saved. Immediately after Lear's death Kent says:

> Vex not his ghost. O, let him pass! He hates him
> That would upon the rack of this tough world
> Stretch him out longer . . . ,

and a few lines later implies his own death in the near future. Albany, the goody boy, and Edgar, the juvenile hero, are the only ones left at the end. It is a "tough world" indeed. It is a cruel and absurd world. If at the ends of his comedies Shakespeare, following the convention, made everything right with the world, and if in his other tragedies, again following convention, he made everything wrong with the world, at least in those plays the world itself is left, and the suggestion is made that the larger order will endure in its essential rightness. But in *Lear* the world is condemned, existence is rejected, reality itself is scorned, and nothing persists anywhere but disorder and mindlessness, the human condition. Thus the play is not only Shakespeare's most realistic but his most existential, in our own sense of the term.

If we except, as we must, the original predicament of the play, Lear's irrational favoritism among his daughters—which in fact is not as unusual as it may seem in the play's foreshortened opening; vanity and folly are not unknown in our time either—then the rest of the play is altogether realistic, and this is the way it must be played if justice is to be done to it. I cannot imagine it on the stage. I cannot imagine a realistic reproduction of Act III, the storm and the dialogue and action of Lear, the Fool, and Poor Tom, on any stage I've ever heard of. Yet only strict realism can sustain our interest in Acts IV and V after the violence and insanity, the tension, of Act III. In film it could be done, I think, if the direction were good enough.

But don't we always say that Shakespeare's stage was anything but realistic? Yes, and I think that's wrong. It was a bare stage. It was the minimum of artifice. It was scarcely a stage at all, meaning that the scenes and actions of the plays were contained, either explicitly or by suggestion, in the plays themselves, the texts. Shakespeare's "stage" could represent anything. Moreover realism is not simply a matter of props and sets. It is a way of playing, a way of reading. It is an attitude. Everything in *King Lear* points to Shakespeare's conception of the people in the play as real individual human beings, not primarily kings, earls, dukes, peasants, etc. On a bare stage or in a naturalistic film this is what they can be. Anything in between distorts them.

Perhaps this in part accounts for the relatively fewer productions of *Lear* than of *Hamlet, Macbeth,* and *Othello,* and for the fact that many people think of *Lear* as an anomaly among the tragedies. It is without doubt the bleakest of them, meaning the most realistic; the others, as I've said, have about them at least some saving reassurance. *Lear* came from the center of Shakespeare's black period, written probably in 1606, after *Hamlet* and *Othello* and before *Macbeth* and *Antony and Cleopatra*. Lear is not a misanthrope like Timon, not a power-seeker like Coriolanus, not a sexualist like Antony, not a paranoid schizophrenic like Hamlet or Othello; he is an old man crushed by reality, destroyed by things as they are. We identify ourselves with Lear in a way that we never do with Hamlet or Othello. Lear comes closer than anyone else in Shakespeare to the sufferer of gratuitous adversity whom we encounter in so much of our contemporary literature; he is the alienated victim par excellence. Yet we should not make the mistake of classifying *King Lear* along with the novels of Céline or the later poems of Robinson Jeffers. Pessimism is not necessarily mean. *Lear* has an amplitude and scope of sympathy, in spite of its bleakness, that makes it, at least in my view, much closer to Malraux's *Man's Fate* or Paul Bowles's *The Sheltering Sky* than it is to the merely sado-masochistic strain in Western literature from de Sade to, say, John Berryman and Vladimir Nabokov. *Lear* is a work that leaves us devastated but still aware of our own humanity. We are not revulsed by the play. We may prefer to see performances of *Hamlet* or *Othello*, which move us to the leniency of pity, but we return as readers to *Lear* rather regularly for its horror and wisdom.

To say nothing of its language. *King Lear* is a poem more than it is a play, as I've said already. It is a lyric poem of great spontaneity, as evidenced by the large number of irregular lines, hexameters and trimeters, scattered through the basic pentameter. It flows. The wise insanity of Lear and Poor Tom on the heath has been imitated thousands of times by other writers in all kinds of contexts, but has never been given to us with the acuteness of Shakespeare's dialogue. Lear's Fool is the best—wittiest and wisest—Fool in all Renaissance literature. And in spite of the violence of action throughout the play we find many beautiful lyric passages, especially toward the end. When Lear, recovered from his madness but still feeble and confused, is captured with Cordelia and sent away under guard, he says to her:

> Come, let's away to prison.
> We two alone will sing like birds i' th' cage.
> When thou dost ask me blessing, I'll kneel down
> And ask of thee forgiveness. So we'll live,
> And pray, and sing, and tell old tales, and laugh
> At gilded butterflies, and hear poor rogues
> Talk of court news; and we'll talk with them too—
> Who loses and who wins; who's in, who's out—
> And take upon 's the mystery of things,
> As if we were God's spies. . . .

What marvelous writing. And notice that Lear does not abjure the court and its worldliness, as other Renaissance heroes in similar circumstances certainly would have. His personality remains consistent; no matter how feeble or mad, he is a politician to the end. In these two qualities, a gift for writing and boldness in verisimilitude, Shakespeare's genius predominates over all his Elizabethan and Tudor contemporaries. In fact it is interesting to note that in these two respects he is closest in that time, not to Sidney, Spenser, or Jonson, but to Donne, as far apart as they are in most others. But the play is a poem in all its aspects, perhaps especially in its unity and integration. This is not simply a matter of Shakespeare's skill in adding the invented story of Gloucester to the medieval legend of King Lear (Leir) and interweaving them so well together. Rather it is the way the whole work moves with such fluidity from beginning to end, as if the constraints of stagecraft and dramatic structure did not exist. It is a work written in the fullness of poetic imagination. It is propelled by the same concentration of vision and intensity of feeling that characterize the best lyric poetry, in other words by the same force and singleness that impel the best of Shakespeare's sonnets. And perhaps this is part of the difficulty of producing it in the theater.

One goes to the breadth of Shakespeare's accomplishment

for many different gratifications. No writer is more various. I can't say I prefer *King Lear* to his other works, and I would be suspicious of anyone who did. But I can say that I value *King Lear* especially because, among all the plays, it has the least artifice, and because it tells the truth.

Letter to Wallace Stevens

*You know, we have reached a point
with sex where you can put it in
your pipe and smoke it.*

Dear Mr. Stevens:

Yes, that's what you wrote—in a letter. Hard to tell how serious you were, as we find often the case with you, yet beyond the *facetiae* in all your writing we do recognize, or think we recognize, a fundamental attention to principle and ultimacy that seems to mean seriousness, even a kind of solemnity. When you wrote your letter you had just read in *Harper's* an excerpt from *Jurgen,* which you called "piffle," and of course most of us now agree with you about that, although at the same time it's worth noting that we still get a little enjoyment from the novel's kidding style and irony, an enjoyment not so different from what we get from your own fantastic stylizations in your poems—granting we find many other enjoyments from you that aren't so available in *Jurgen.*

But, but, but—put it in our pipes and smoke it!?!? That's an old-fashioned manner of speaking, since the smoking of pipes has almost died out in our culture, except among certain very old farmers and poets. Hence for a moment we see the trope literally, sex in our pipes and we smoking it; we are absurdly and not unpleasantly taken aback. After all smoking is a form of consuming. But then we think of what the expression used to mean, that something—whatever one is referring to—is futile and unimportant and indisputable, that one can do nothing about it except smoke it—ingest it, burn it up, get rid of it—and we understand the toughness of your remark. Were you a little jealous of James Branch Cabell, of the success he seemed about to embrace with his pretentious romance of theorized sex?

Maybe. But the fact is that sex is absent from your work. I infer a degree of disapproval, even of moral indignation. Your background in Lutheran Pennsylvania is showing. Along with your feeling about D. H. Lawrence et al. Sex is absent from your work, and so is politics. The two appear only in distant and I believe inadvertent implication. How did you do that—write so much from such trivial motives? Why did you do it? Speaking for myself, I can't imagine it—finding the strength and inventiveness to write all that poetry without eros or a concern for the mass. Fear of the godless universe seems hardly a sufficient impetus; for a few poems, yes, and I've written some of them too, but not for a life's work.

We conclude that you wrote for beauty. All those marvelous lines and phrases: done in a need for the felicitous bizarre, for kicks. You were the last of the poets who wrote for beauty, I think. And after all you were worthy of your predecessors, Keats, let's say, and du Bellay and so many others. You and they are what we mean by the "old days"—the good old days. Long gone. Eros and politics, romance and justice, these are the coercions that grind us small in our lives and works today, making us ugly. Making us desperate and disconsolate. Our time in its lovelessness and brutality drives us to seek their opposites, and mostly they are not pretty. How could they be?

Yet here is a salute for you, poet of beauty! I think we rely on you more now than other poets did in your own time.

Essays for Wendell

I write to you, brother, to tell you
that the young sycamore,
princely as a yearling elk,
is dying. The bedrock of this place
is too near the surface, I think;
the tree hasn't enough root-space.
Which is an observation, at best a reason.
But this is June, my soul is sore
to study such gracefulness, so well started,
sturdy and well-limbed, thirty feet high,
which now in the spring season
shows bare twigs and withered leaves.
How can I not feel downhearted
to watch the young tree die?

∾   ∾   ∾

Brother, our family is pretty large,
you might say enormous,
and we don't speak to most of them,
and they don't speak to us.

∾   ∾   ∾

Two-thirds of my barn
fell down long ago,
long before it was mine,
collapsed, the rusty
roof-metal now flattened
on the ground. It is worn
out. The loose loft door
in the remaining third
sobs in the wind.

The barn looks perfectly
natural among the cedars
in the tall grass where
flowers grow—dame's rocket,
stitchwort, and buttercups.

           ☙   ☙   ☙

And yesterday my wife found
at the edge of our woods the flower
of the May apple, suddenly there
on the ground.

Two big leaves, intricately cut;
beneath them the six-petaled
delicate white blossom shut
from the sun.

We could not recall
having seen it before, either of us.
It seems the May apple
often does not achieve flower hereabouts.
Or had we been too dull?

In flowers and all its natural
parts the world has kept
delight. Last night when we went
to our rest, we clasped one another
against insomnia, and slept.

I woke once, near dawn,
and her arm still held me.

This morning I saw—and marked well
on the windowsill—
a jumping spider. Such
a pretty thing.
Its two front eyes touch
and are as blue
as my wife's lapis ring.

           ☙   ☙   ☙

> *One cannot act well or beneficently in a*
> *place until one has understood its nature,*
> *precedent to human intention. Thus, in a*

country originally forested, the farmer must
study the forest, because, to be healthy, the
field must be an analogue of the forest; in
analogy its nature is remembered.

On its steep hillside your farm once, eons ago,
in nature's fierce competition came to stasis.
Trees, immense trees for your region, held
the slope against the water's continual surge
carrying away the brown dirt to the sea.
The river down below ran clear. For even
early woodland hepaticas can hold
a grain or two of soil in the freshening season.
You've contemplated this a many a time
in your walking and working—I know because
elsewhere I have too—and have found in it
propriety and the importance of propriety
in farming and in poetry. Then of course
you found decadence when the woods were cut—
those bleeding trees—and corn and tobacco
were planted on the hill. Your mythic river
runs muddy still, muddy and bitter. No
propriety in that. Yet your fields now
after extraordinary labor—brother,
I do not know how you can have done so
much—and after extraordinary thought
and study are secure, right with the world,
proper, and full of meaning, which is love
in action, as your poems are. And what
a blessing this has become for us all.

ᘐ   ᘐ   ᘐ

My place is on a hillside too, and looks
over the Stockbridge Valley to the opposing
hill ten miles distant, a remarkably
green and fertile American intervale.
In winter when my trees are bare I see
twelve working farms, their multi-tinted
meadows and pastures, woodlots and gravel-pits,

through the picture window next to my
computer. Leave out the army, leave out
all such aberrations, this is by my count
my seventeenth place in my life; I live here
with my fourth wife, who yesterday gave me
a watch that tells the time in seconds, the day
of the week, the date and month, and I can time
a horse race with it too—yet I've been called
a "farmer poet." I'm not. Alienation
has been my life, even though I've spent
most of it living and working on the land.
Now I'm too old. I write blank verse (sometimes)
not from principle but because I like it—
the privilege of a crank. I trim my fruit trees
and vines, I tend my flowers, mow my lawn,
my hayfield is sown to Panama grass,
timothy, and alfalfa, my woods are
grown-over pasture with too many thorntrees
but some friendly ash and maple on the upper
side, basswood, hickory, cherry, hornbeam, locust.
Now the orioles in the dooryard have fledged
two offspring, and vetch and daisies and hawkweed
are in the meadow. Summer is here. I can't
do much to help it, but, brother, I talk with it,
and what we mostly talk about is you.

ᘐ   ᘐ   ᘐ

You wrote: "The god I have always expected
to appear at the woods' edge, beckoning,
I have always expected to be
a great relisher of this world, its good
grown immortal in his mind." That
was in *Farming: A Handbook,* 1970. And how
wonderfully that idea works, your expectation,
like your analogy, permitting many
possibilities. I have expected that god too,
and I'm still expecting him, the joy
of the world like Pan or Sasquatch
risen among the flowers or in the pristine

winter morning with new snow on the mountain.
To you, as I know from more recent poems,
he has appeared. What a striking, original
event in any world but especially ours.
I am astonied, as they used to say, I am glad.
For you, he is. And I think for you he is also
a source of authority, what you wanted
all along, to make the system go. For me
the system goes by itself—not very well.
Last year a big asteroid missed us by only
a few million miles. Yet in marriage
the orioles possess, at least for this season,
what I would call "perfect authority," such
as one can know it objectively, with their two
fledglings, carnelian in the appletree.
Now the melilot has bloomed near the barn,
a fountain of feathery yellow, and its authority
has brought it all the way here from Transylvania.
As Edmund Husserl said, values are
the "objectivities of practice," properly classed
under the formal heading of "something in general."
Something. An existent. An objectivity of practice.
And an authority too, even from broken marriages.
From the orioles and the melilot one moves
among formal headings, searching, searching.
I am expecting the god any minute, somewhere
near the barn. I like your faith, brother, and your
authority, so beautiful and important in this world.

∽ ∽ ∽

One comes to a new place
with marriage in mind,
a new light on the belovèd face,
which one had expected to find.

∽ ∽ ∽

"What is left is what is"—
a few more years maybe
(one wants to finish at least

some of what one began),
a few moments of the fizz
of dawn in the east
before I go to bed,
a few more nights to see
my way in the dark. A man
like me likes to describe
things, who knows why?—
how the sunset's soft red
lights the orange lilies by
the dooryard, their coarse brocade
as if under a pink film
of pure imagination laid
upon them—a consequence
none could have foreseen
though it can overwhelm
anyone. And once a tribe
of ancients did see it. How
they responded I don't
know, except in their sense
they knew it, as I do now.
Flowers in the light mean
beautiful changes. I want
nothing more than these
that are what is. How still
are the leaves in the trees.
How quiet are valley and hill.
It is getting dark. The ways
of the night are memory,
new and transitory.
We are very remote here.
But in your Kentucky days
and in spirit you are near.

∾　∾　∾

Maybe the sycamore
will make it after all.
Its crown is thickening;
I think more dark than light

might show in a photograph.
And if it dies, come fall
it will make a modest store
of heat for this heteroclite—
about one cord and a half.

Emily Dickinson's Unexpectedness

Among the hundreds of "critical interpretations" of Emily Dickinson's work that have come along in recent decades, most are devoted to finding the origins of her poems in her experience, that is to say, in every foible from masturbatory fantasy to mystical vision to out-and-out schizophrenia. Who was Emily Dickinson, the scholars and critics ask insistently, not who is she. To my mind this latter question is the only one we may ask with any hope of a reasonable answer or for that matter with any regard for ordinary decency. The Dickinson who is important to us, or should be, is the woman in the poems. The woman in history is for genealogists; the shadowy figure in the upper window of the house on Main Street in Amherst is for tourists.

I am interested, more and more as I grow older, in the application of intelligence to the topics which intelligence itself informs us are the most likely to yield useful knowledge; and gossip, no matter how scholarly, is not one of these. Biography is a tawdry art—if an art at all. We have seen many, many examples of this in the past couple of decades.

No doubt Dickinson could sound her own verses in ways that made good sense and good poetry, and no doubt she did. Any writer knows this. But for whatever reasons—one can think of several, or many, but again one is not compelled to mention them—she wrote in an eccentric manner with respect to both punctuation and grammar that does not help anyone else to sound them. People often complain that her use of the dash as her primary mark of punctuation was inconsistent. Yet in fact it was the opposite, quite consistent within the poetry, because she used it to signify anything and everything that any mark of punctuation can signify, with the result that it signifies next to nothing at all to readers who have not heard the poems in her voice, i.e., all of us. Similarly with her compacted, twisted, sometimes Latinate syntax, which may or may not have been influenced by the Protestant hymnal and the religious prose of the seventeenth and eighteenth centuries. (You can find the same grammatical constructions commonly in Bradford's *History of Plimmoth Plantation* and in the poetry of Paul Goodman, for whatever this is worth.) Because of these idiosyncratic usages— and because she apparently wrote without expectation that her work would be published—some critics have referred to her poetic language as a kind of shorthand, notes jotted hastily for herself in the language that came most easily to hand. But the woman who is evident in the poems is anything but a stenographer, and the critics of various occult persuasions who suggest that Dickinson was in fact setting down materials "given" to her by agents outside her consciousness are doing the woman in the poems a grave injustice. Whether and to what extent she revised individual poems, she did work at her writing, she worked hard, and the density of her language, in sound, syntax, and sense, will permit no other inference.

This is true of her rhyming as well. One cannot doubt her ability to make rhymes as exact as those of Christina Rossetti or Alfred Tennyson or any other poet of her time. She chose to let her aural imagination range freely, and one result is that her off-rhymes, which vary from close to distant, together with her reliance on well-known rhyming patterns (hymns, ballads, etc.), force the reader to hear rhymes where none exists. The first three stanzas of the poem numbered 410 (in Thomas H. Johnson's edition of the *Complete Poems*) are a good example, though you can find others even more extreme:

> The first Day's Night had come—
> And grateful that a thing
> So terrible—had been endured—
> I told my Soul to sing—
>
> She said her Strings were snapt—
> Her Bow—to Atoms blown—
> And so to mend her—gave me work
> Until another Morn—

> And then—a Day as huge
> As Yesterdays in pairs,
> Unrolled its horror in my face—
> Until it blocked my eyes—

The progression from "thing/sing" through "blown/Morn" to "pairs/eyes," from full rhyme to no rhyme, is remarkable in its manipulation of the auditor's rhyming sense, making one "hear" what isn't there, and except for one student in the graduate writing program at Syracuse University, who came by it independently, I know no one else before or after Dickinson who has attempted just this, and I do not forget Yeats, Ransom, Muir, and the thousands influenced by them.

In short, the reader confronting a poem by Emily Dickinson must make a few decisions on the spot, perhaps to a greater degree than with any other premodernist poet in English, though Donne, Herbert, Hopkins, Hardy, etc., come to mind as possible rivals. Obviously Professor Johnson was correct in reproducing the texts of the *Complete Poems* as they were found in Dickinson's holographic manuscripts, not as they were "corrected" by her friends after her death; but just as obviously— though it has rarely been suggested—the reader must change these texts in his or her mind to make sense of them. This is especially true of the poems written in the early 1860s, which often do seem to have come tumbling out of the poet's imagination in a kind of careless verbal exuberance, left unrevised. Yet I feel that these poems are anything but careless. They have great power, and part of their power is their strangeness. Here is number 422.

> More Life—went out—when He went
> Than Ordinary Breath—
> Lit with a finer Phosphor—
> Requiring in the Quench—
>
> A Power of Renowned Cold,
> The Climate of the Grave
> A Temperature just adequate
> So Anthracite, to live—

For some—an Ampler Zero—
A Frost more needle keen
Is necessary, to reduce
The Ethiop within.

Others—extinguish easier—
A Gnat's minutest Fan
Sufficient to obliterate
A Tract of Citizen—

Whose Peat lift—amply vivid—
Ignores the solemn News
That Popocatapel exists
Or Etna's Scarlets, Choose—

There it is, a genuinely great poem, but left hanging on a dash, like so many others. The dashes do not help at all. To my ear they impede and confuse a good reading. The capitalizations don't help either. Some adjectives are capitalized, like "Ordinary," "Renowned" (which surely she pronounced with three syllables), and "Ampler"; others, like "finer," "keen," and "vivid," are not. Some readers are certain that the capitalized pronoun in the first line refers to Christ; but if this is so, then the poem leads radically, not to say irreligiously, away from this first reference as it proceeds. In any event the capitalized "He" cannot necessarily indicate a divine person, as it would in most other Christian poetry. The rest of the punctuation, three commas and a period, is capricious. And how is one to read: "So Anthracite, to live—"? It is utterly extragrammatical, so that the dash for once really does indicate broken syntax. But how is one to distinguish this dash from the others? Well, the poem is full of surprises, but it is clear. What the reader must do, I believe, is reduce the poem to something like the following more conventional arrangement, which is perfectly legitimate provided that he or she then returns to reading the poem as Dickinson wrote it. A sufficiently adroit and experienced reader will perform these two operations so nearly at the same time that they are effectually simultaneous.

More life went out when he went
Than ordinary breath,
Lit with a finer phosphor,
Requiring in the quench

A power of renownëd cold,
The climate of the grave,
A temperature just adequate
So anthracite may live.

For some an ampler zero,
A frost more needle keen,
Is necessary to reduce
The Ethiop within.

Others extinguish easier,
A gnat's minutest fan
Sufficient to obliterate
A tract of citizen,

Whose lift[ed] peat, amply vivid,
Ignores the solemn news
That Popocatapel exists
Or Etna's scarlets. Choose!

I use an exclamation point after the last word because the
ending is such an astonishing, commanding leap out of the
syntax, point of view, and tone of the rest of the poem. At first
it seems to say that we must choose between Etna and Popoca-
tape(t)l, which is not much of a choice; we are thrown with
some violence back into the body of the poem, forced to re-
read and understand, e.g., that the "some" who require "an
Ampler Zero" are to be identified with the intentionally cam-
ouflaged "He" of the first line, as differentiated from the "Oth-
ers" who may be extinguished by the wind from a gnat's wing.
Is the poem saying that some people die out of this world
harder than others because they love—or esteem or compre-
hend—it better, and that we are with the poet in having the
capacity, at least theoretically, to choose which kind of person
we shall be? Yes, this is part of it. But whose is the power of
"Renowned Cold," whose is the "Gnat's minutest Fan" that
obliterates—stark verb!—the "Tract of Citizen?" (The poem
was written during the Civil War when "tracts" of military

graves became common.) Is it God's? Is the woman in the poem capable of throwing dust in our eyes with that capitalized "He" in the first line and then reversing our expectations, leading us to blasphemy, and hiding the whole maneuver beneath her "carelessness?" I believe this is the poet Dickinson's sensibility in a nutshell.

Why did she do it? What reader was she anticipating? Only herself? These are not biographical issues. If we could answer such questions we'd go a long way toward a better understanding not only of her poetry but of all poetry. But our answers can be only conjectural.

The reduction of the poem to conventional syntax and punctuation spoils it and leaves us with a relatively insipid piece of work. Part of Dickinson's power, though a secondary part, really is her quirkiness. And what a fine poem it is. No careless mind came up with "Ampler Zero," "A Tract of Citizen," or the rhymes in the first and fourth stanzas. This is what we mean when we talk about poetic genius, or at least what we ought to mean. Even more extraordinary is the way such simple words as "amply vivid" in the last stanza are lifted into brilliance—in this case brilliant horror—by the strangeness of "Peat lift" just before them, and the way this in turn sets up the extreme irony of another commonplace word, "solemn," in the next line. We know what "Peat lift" means; it cannot mean anything but burial (or, even more horrifying, exhumation); and yet it means much more. The commonness of peat suggests not only the commonness of huge graveyards but perhaps the ancient, anonymous graves of anthropological "digs" in the peat bogs of Europe. Moreover "Peat" picks up and contrasts to "Anthracite" in the second stanza, since both are fossil fuels, one distinctly inferior to the other. Notice the subtlety of "needle keen," which brings to mind not only the sewing needles of nineteenth-century housewives but the frozen needles, almost equally sharp, of spruce and fir in a New England winter. The force of concentration in this one poem is such that we would not believe it if we didn't see it before our eyes. Nor can we analyze it sufficiently. One could say that fire is what holds this poem together from "Phosphor" to "Etna's Scarlets," though the word itself is never used. Or one could say just as well that blackness holds it together (granting the misfortune of "Ethiop" in our regenerate consciences), though black is never mentioned. What is happening is simply too numerous to be seized in any single reading. And as far as I know this poem has never been much considered by scholars and critics.

Emily Dickinson, whoever she was, is the most significant woman in Western literature after Sappho. I don't mean she is "greater" than Jane Austen or Simone de Beauvoir. Who knows about greater? Nor do I mean to emphasize gender, which usually seems so obvious that it is not worth talking about in literary terms. (Politics is another matter.) But Dickinson is the only poet in our language, as Sappho and Lady Murasaki may be the only ones in other languages, or at least in what we call major languages, who forces us, actually coerces us—though this could not have been her objective—to think and imagine in feminine modes, which she accomplishes through the nearly absolute power of her artistic sensibility. She arouses in us an almost extravagantly heightened consciousness of metaphysical issues and existential emotions, such as we associate only with the supreme intelligences of our species. She convokes our being, so to speak, and she does it as a woman. I am not fool enough to try to define that womanness, but I am confident that all willing readers can recognize it.

Who the "He" in the first line of her poem may be is unimportant. She says everything about him that needs to be said for her purpose. In a similar sense the problems of Miss Dickinson of Main Street, whether she was afflicted with chronic agoraphobia, religious hysteria, sexual frustration, or none of these, are unimportant. That is, we are affected by Miss Dickinson in the same way and to the same degree that we are affected by Miss Farquahr, the great beauty of the other side of town, who died painfully at the age of nineteen from scrofula and shingles. The poet Sappho exists only in her poems. Likewise the poet Dickinson.

Here is poem number 443, which I've not seen much commented on either:

I tie my Hat—I crease my Shawl—
Life's little duties do—precisely—
As the very least
Were infinite—to me—

I put new Blossoms in the Glass—
And throw the old—away—
I push a petal from my Gown
That anchored there—I weigh
The time 'twill be till six o'clock
I have so much to do—
And yet—Existence—some way back—
Stopped—struck—my ticking—through—
We cannot put Ourself away
As a completed Man
Or Woman—When the Errand's done
We come to Flesh—upon—
There may be—Miles on Miles of Nought—
Of Action—sicker far—
To stimulate—is stinging work—
To cover what we are
From Science—and from Surgery—
Too Telescopic Eyes
To bear on us unshaded—
For their—sake—not for Ours—
'Twould start them—
We—could tremble—
But since we got a Bomb—
And held it in our Bosom—
Nay—Hold it—it is calm—

Therefore—we do life's labor—
Though life's Reward—be done—
With scrupulous exactness—
To hold our Senses—on—

Another quirky poem that leads us a long way from its open-
ing. The rhythm is more jog-trot than in the other poem I've
quoted, and the imagery is less exotic. In some ways it is a
rather ordinary poem about ordinary actions and feelings,
and I'm sure this was intentional. But it comes from the same
period of acute poetic endeavor. Like the other poems it

moves from the commonplace to the expressly personal and original, the "Telescopic Eyes" and the "Bomb": what could be more compelling? And notice the precision throughout, from the emphatic "do" in the second line to the "stinging work" in the middle and then to the tiny, momentous "on" at the very end. This poet is a woman immersed in womanly concerns, but at the same time left, by the power of life confronting spirituality and death, in a condition of undiluted exigency. This is rare enough in our frightened and evasive species; to find it combined with eloquence, with a verbal resourcefulness beyond our wildest dreams, is unexpected, unexpectable. Facing this, the critical mind is reduced to stammering, which is what I am doing here.

Isn't it a penetrating poem? One is tempted to call it free, because it moves so directly toward its object. But then one notices all the constraints, and one is tempted to call it artifice. The fact is that it shoots between these opposites like an arrow splitting a leaf, and between many other pairs of opposites too.

Finally, a poem written about a decade later, number 1259:

> A Wind that rose
> Though not a Leaf
> In any Forest stirred
> But with itself did cold engage
> Beyond the Realm of Bird—
> A Wind that woke a lone Delight
> Like Separation's Swell
> Restored in Arctic Confidence
> To the Invisible—

The cadence has become calmer, the language more spare but more fluent and spontaneous too, without any syntactical resolution. (Surely she is the first poet in English to use the uncompleted participial phrase as a comprehensive verbal gesture, and to do it repeatedly.) The movement of these lines embodies the movement of existence as simply and purely as words can. Was Camus the one who spoke of the "dark wind" always blowing toward us from out of the future? I believe so.

The coinciding of Moment and Eternity, Dickinson's invisible cold wind that does not stir the leaves. Have the spinster from Amherst and the workman from Algiers anything in common? Almost everything, I'd say. The loneliness of a village room and the loneliness of the desert are not much different. The artist knows that this isolation is madness (see poem 410), and that madness is the same as ultimate insight, which inevitably is of the limits of insight. Hence the Greeks' anthropomorphizing condescension to their gods. And Tertullian's to his? This is the absurdum. It is a glory in the mind, a gentle glory pervaded by sorrow, but beyond hope and despair, far beyond ego; it is the person become impersonality, the nobody to whom the finest genius assimilates itself. How different from the procedures of ordinary fine poets! What the mind makes, even in ecstasy, in fury, is always implicated in nonbeing, the void of God; and thus when Dickinson writes in dialect— poem 426, for instance, in which her writerly ear for speech-sounds is working beautifully—she does so partly to humanize her mythos, but more largely to humor, to placate, her ignorance, which is my ignorance too. And that is as far as I can go in responding to her poems.

It is far enough.

Donald Hall's House of Virtue Built in the Woods and Fields of Time

Throughout Donald Hall's writing the aspect of personal el-
egy has been predominant. His first popular book, *String Too
Short to Be Saved* (1961), which has been recently republished
and remains popular today, is an account in prose of his grand-
parents' farm in Wilmot, New Hampshire, as he knew it when
he was a boy, a discourse on the values represented by his
grandparents' generation of rural Americans, also on the val-
ues of his parents' generation—they lived in southern Connec-
ticut and were urban professionals—and on the impact of
these conflicting understandings upon the mind of a boy
growing up in the thirties and forties.

And these have been his persisting, almost obsessive con-
cerns in all his writing for more than thirty years, poetry, fic-
tion, literary essays, and even in his newspaper and magazine
articles about sports, travel, and anything else he has been able
to think of that might sell—Hall has supported himself and his
family as a free-lance writer and editor for a long time. Autobi-
ography, in the broadest sense of the term, has been his bread
and butter. Maybe he was influenced by Lowell, Berryman,
Jarrell, Shapiro, and others of that group—Hall's first book of
poems, *Exiles and Marriages* (the title is exact), was published in
1955, only a couple of years after Lowell's *Life Studies*, and Hall
is a Harvard graduate, a New Englander oriented toward Cam-
bridge and Boston—but I don't see a necessary connection,
and in any case many of Hall's contemporaries—Plath, Mer-
win, Rich, Kinnell, Creeley, Berry, and scores of others—were
doing the same thing. After the programmatic impersonalism

of much of the modernist movement between the two big wars, autobiography was, so to speak, in the air. Relationships within families, between families and locations, among conflicting ages and cultures and sexes: these became the staples of American poetry after midcentury, as we all know.

And we know the dangers of elegiac autobiography: nostalgia, sentimentality, and ultra-subjectivism or solipsism. These are said to be diseases; they infect and weaken the human spirit. Myself, I'm not sure of this, as I've argued elsewhere. But whatever the merits of that argument, if nostalgia, sentimentality, and subjectivism are diseases, then so is being a writer, especially a poet, in our time. Nostalgia, sentiment, and the self are what we all write about almost all the time. Perhaps we can say that the dominant traits of any era are the diseases of the spirit which must be accepted and transcended by the writers of that era if they are to succeed, e.g., Whitman's progressivism and optimism (with which he wrote the greatest elegy in American literature), Pope's rationalism and pan-deism (with which he wrote the greatest mock-epic in English literature), and Dante's Thomistic, not to say Gothic, determinism (with which he wrote the greatest humane lyric of all time).

Those who survive a disease are those who have felt it most—Marcel Proust wrote: "Illness is the most heeded of doctors: to kindness and wisdom we make promises only; pain we obey"—and those who have transcended it—George Dennison wrote: "Perhaps all sufferers are victims, but victimization cannot create a figure of suffering, there must be some principle of transcendence—courage, persistence, endurance—for otherwise the sufferer has collapsed and does not represent suffering, but defeat." Most of the poetry of our time registers nothing but defeat. But more than courage, persistence, and endurance, I think, though these are necessary, must go into real transcending. Dennison has also written of "the imperishability of the boundary at which consciousness becomes aware of itself gazing at the inexplicable." *This* is transcendence, just as it is the limit of transcendence. To survive is not only to reach that boundary but to live there. I don't think it can be reached through nostalgia, sentimentality, and subjectivism, which, collectively misnamed faith, are all that religion and patriotism, our famous American instant cures for everything, can offer; and courage and persistence are only elements of subjectivism. To live at the boundary, to create a figure of suffering, a figure of passion, is to live in history, including the future, and in the mind of the species, not simply in one's own mind.

I'd say 99 per cent of the current poetry I've read is written in the present tense and the first person, both the tense and the pronoun signifying one consciousness, compacted and odd. No wonder young poets speak of one poem being "more unique" than another.

A couple of weeks ago I drove from Utica to the interior of Maine, where I am now, and I stopped in Wilmot to spend a night with Donald Hall and Jane Kenyon; we have been friends for some time, and both of them are writers whose work is important in my life. (They have each published two fine books in the past year, Kenyon's translations from Ahkmatova, the best in English, also her new book of poems, *The Boat of Quiet Hours,* and then Hall's books of stories and poems, *The Ideal Bakery* and *The Happy Man.*) The drive from Utica to Wilmot is depressing and much of it is infuriating: the poverty and squalor of the Mohawk Valley, the tawdriness of Albany and Troy, the prettified gentility of towns like Manchester and Arlington in Vermont, the expensive ugliness of ski resorts, and so on, which doesn't mean that sections of admirable farmland and functional year-round villages can't still be found. Wilmot, where the main line of the Hall family has lived in the same farmhouse for five generations, with cognate branches in nearby houses and towns, is such a place, though the developers are already at work there, inevitably, as the mess in eastern Massachusetts spreads outward in all directions.

I had read Jane's and Don's new books. This is not the place to review them. They are splendid books and contain authentic and important work. At least three of the stories in *The Ideal Bakery* are as good as any short fiction I know, and the poems in *The Happy Man* are clear, strong, original, beautifully voiced and cadenced, and they give me much pleasure. But what struck me most in these books, as it has in nearly everything I've read in recent years, work by my students, my colleagues, my friends, myself, is the elegiac mode of thought and feeling, the governing elegiac *gestalten* in all our imaginative attitudes. Tragic or comic, journalistic or surrealistic, witty or earnest, we can write only about the things vanishing from our lives. This is the predicament of the young as well as the old, of westerners as well as easterners, of everyone. Science fiction and spy fiction are full of elegy; poetry the same; it's a constant in television and the movies. We are the saddest people on earth. I suspect we are the saddest people who have ever been on earth. This is what I said to Jane and Don when I was in Wilmot, and they agreed. Everyone agrees.

Since then I have driven on into the north country where I've found the coves of rural poverty which are, for me, more beautiful than any of the "beautiful places," untidy (though by no means messy) farms, shacks and trailers, gravel pits and cut-over woods. Yes, plenty of spoliation, yet nature appears to be holding her own. (One needs to look closely to see the effects of the major pollutants, like acid rain.) I am living by a pond which I share with loons, cormorants, great herons, black-crowned night herons, kingfishers, ravens, warblers, turtles, porcupines, moose, bears, and many other creatures, including six or eight human ones. The only jealousy here is sexual and confined to youth. I haven't heard anyone insult anyone else. Trading is a sport, not a *casus belli*, meetings are held to reconfirm humane values, not to publicize the contentions of avarice, and in one week I have been the grateful recipient of more generosity than I've found in the whole past year as a member of the institutional academic community, which is not a community at all. Ollie North, goddamn his eyes, is the kind of posing, whining egomaniac who gets thrown out of the real communities of backcountry Maine.

And this is backcountry, literally. It is not Boothbay or Deer Isle. Not many places like this are left. The rest of the country, the rest of the civilization, has been turned into a nightmare of greed and suffering. And what resources have we who are reflective personalities to fall back on except sentimentality, nostalgia, and our subjective identities? These have become not only our virtues but the substance of all our conversation, most of which is comic in intent. When twilight gathers in the foliage of the white ash trees, the swamp maples, the butternuts, the cedars, people come together and drink and tell stories, and their conversation falls and crests with laughter, magnanimity, and affection, like the tree swallows playing with a feather. This is what we do to preserve ourselves in our daily lives. But art is something else.

Art is what transcends virtue. This is a radical idea, but inescapable. Nostalgia, sentimentality, and subjectivity, though they are the flesh and bare bones of 99 per cent of what is called poetry today, are only the beginnings of realized art, which is unanalyzable and generally indescribable. Dante's love for Beatrice was nostalgic, sentimental, and subjective in the extreme, but it was his virtue that made possible the failure of mind and language—virtue's own failure—in the self-transcension of the extraordinary final canto. The love, the virtue, was only the beginning. In a very different but recognizable way, turning emotion into rightness, Donald Hall's best short stories do this, like "The Figure of the Woods" and "The Ideal Bakery." But to my mind his three-part poem called *Build a House* is Hall's very best work, in which virtue fails beneath transcendence.

The first part, "Shrubs Burned Away" (the title later changed to "Shrubs Burnt Off"), is contained in *The Happy Man*. The second part, "Four Classic Texts," I read in manuscript about a year ago. I was given the manuscript of the whole poem, revised and including the third part, "The One Day," when I visited Wilmot. It is as completely right and natural and *there* as the laughter of the loons. At the same time it is as comprehensive, as transcending as any recent writing I know.[1]

Commonly people say a work of art is timeless. This is what workshop students believe, what they aim at with their reliance on the present tense and ridiculous participial phrasings. But a work of art eats time, consumes time, obliterating everything else. True, it can exist forever on a shelf or in a museum, but its meaning and essence become apparent only when it is functional in consciousness, in time, and then it is totally func-

---

1. The entire work has been retitled *The One Day* and published in one volume by Ticknor & Fields, 1988.

tional. *Build a House* contains many, probably most, of the materials in Hall's earlier work, his grandparents and parents, the farm, the people in his life today, his own thoughts and feelings about "marriage and exile" over the years, his education in classical literature, all his sentimentality and nostalgia and subjectivity, but it is not a summary of these things; far from it. It is a poem of the evolved human species from its beginning to its present to its end. And its language is not written but given. I don't mean this in a mystical sense, though Hall might. I mean that the language of this poem is given in the same way that the top of a mountain is given once you have climbed it. One knew it was there but not what it looked like.

Donald Hall is a public man. He was a teacher for a long time before he became a free-lance, he frequently does readings and lectures, his critical and editorial work have made him a well-known person whose efforts on behalf of serious writing are widely appreciated. But he wrote *Build a House* in another compartment of his mind entirely, in solitude, where the public man with his gestures and responses—which are the inverse of those of a private man, both having been created as diffractions of the ego from reality—is supplanted by simple undifferentiated heterogeneity, the consciousness of the womb or outer space, call it what one will, and where the world turns into the act of knowing. History is part of it, but so are all significant things—voices, dreams, places, especially a particular place, the house. Hall loves to show his visitors around his house in Wilmot, where every room and nearly every object have a tale attached, which he expounds with a kind of modest enthusiasm. His big poem is such a tour, but conducted as if by the voice of the house itself and all its objects, that is to say, by the world and all its history, apart from such human predicaments as pleasure and pain, intelligence and stupidity. Yet the poem is expressive of a personality. And in the end we are reminded that personality is a structure of transcended values.

So the poem, like all considerable works of art, moves circularly or, to say it more accurately, in a helix, a constantly rebounding ascent or transcent within the cylinder of consciousness hemmed in by the inexplicable. The human mind rising out of itself, content with ignorance, content with a faith that can in the full realization of our existential condition be nothing but perfunctory, but content as well with experience, our own mysterious but undeniable being. *Build a House* is a complex, solid, and very habitable piece of work.

A Salute in Time

Old people wish they could recreate the quality of their early experience because they feel this is a value in the world. A value slipping away, yet needed. But such recreation is not possible. The quality of yesterday is already gone, and that of forty years ago—it might as well be four hundred. This is part of the sadness that pervades all our lives.

Teachers will know how I feel when I say I'm appalled by my own repeated failure to give my students an emotional awareness of the near past that they cannot possibly apprehend.

When I first read Karl Shapiro's *Person, Place, and Thing* (1942), which was his first full-fledged book of poems, I was excited by it in a way I never had been before. It may have been the first book by a contemporary poet I had encountered; I don't remember clearly. But I do remember how fresh, new, vigorous, and pointed the poems were, how they awakened me to perspectives of poetic possibility I had never suspected before. Here were poems taken from the American actuality I knew, from the technological world, cars, radios, industrial blight, the terrifying impersonality of death—and life. Other American writers had been Realists and Naturalists, of course; but writers like Sandburg, Anderson, even Hemingway, even such "proletarian poets" as Kenneth Fearing and Langston Hughes (if I had read them, which is unlikely, and it wasn't until after the war that I first encountered Williams, Pound, and others of that generation), seemed to me spoiled by sentimentality. Nothing like that could be found in Shapiro's poems about totaled cars and smashed people. No weakness at all.

All the poems were beautiful. I had always felt an impulse

toward the work of Alexander Pope, an impulse I had felt I had to suppress in the face of the romanticist bias of my teachers and fellow students. But here was a poet, a contemporary, writing beautiful poems in a manner that I instantly recognized, the beauty of good, hard, varied meter and tough, functional rhyme. Appropriateness: that's what hit me. I was excited. And I wasn't the only one. When Shapiro's second major collection was published, *V-Letter and Other Poems* (1944), it was awarded the Pulitzer Prize. I had written a good many v-letters myself during the war, and I knew the fear, bewilderment, loneliness, and boredom that were so well brought out in Shapiro's poems. Later I encountered Jarrell's war poems and Tom McGrath's and others'; but with me and with many young people Shapiro's were first.

Shortly afterward *Essay on Rime* came out, Shapiro's book-length poem about poetry. Again the crispness and appropriateness of the writing took hold of me powerfully, and the acuteness of the theoretical concepts. Between Pope's *Essay on Criticism* and the present, only Shapiro has produced an essay in verse worth reading, and I wish more people would pay attention to it.

Of course we knew—or came to know—that Shapiro had been influenced by Auden and other English poets of the Oxford group. But it was an influence we could celebrate. Shapiro was derivative but never imitative. He was American. None of that twiddly stuff we detected in even the most stringent of Auden's or Spender's verses. It made all the difference. And when Shapiro went on to rebel against not only prevailing attitudes but his own prior tastes and styles, as he did several times, we applauded. In *Poems of a Jew* (1958) we welcomed the new lyrical quality, somewhat Yeatsian but again definitely of the New World, and the prosaic poetry of *The Bourgeois Poet* (1964) seemed to us quite wonderful in the way it hit a rebellious tone that was not like Whitman or Williams or the Beats, but something new and different.

In 1946 when I was a graduate student at the University of Chicago, I had a few poems accepted by *Poetry*. I was as green as a new poet could be. One day I was walking down a corridor at the university and looked up to see Shapiro approaching me, accompanied by Judith Bond, who was the university's librarian in charge of contemporary poetry. I knew she would introduce me. I was pathologically shy, however, and my instinct was to turn aside, to escape. I couldn't; there was no place to escape to. When Mrs. Bond stopped me and introduced me, Shapiro told me he was visiting Chicago and had just had lunch with the staff at *Poetry*. He had been shown my poems in manuscript, he said, and he liked them a good deal. He spoke warmly, spontaneously. This was my first meeting with a well-known writer, someone I could recognize from his photos on the dust covers of his books. I can't say this was what confirmed me in my desire to become a poet—who can be sure of such things forty years later?—but I can say it easily might be the truth, it certainly is part of the truth.

Shapiro's more recent work, the lovely "Aubade" and the other erotic poems of the past fifteen years, seem to me altogether fine and fitting, though again they are a departure from the poetry he had written earlier. Shapiro's poetic courage, his willingness to change, his insistence on it, has been a great example. Similarly his criticism, especially in *In Defense of Ignorance* (1960), which contains some outrageous judgments, has been determinative for me. In fact the two critics who have influenced me most during my lifetime have both been men whose particular judgments often offended me, Yvor Winters and Karl Shapiro. With criticism the intention is what counts, and both men in their intellectual and moral anger wrote with a selfless, enthusiastic devotion to poetry that carries more weight than mere judiciousness. But most of all I learned from Shapiro that you can look out your window and make a poem from what you see. You not only can, you must. This is the responsible poet's obligation. All else is bluffing. And no one has demonstrated this more convincingly than Karl Shapiro in all his work.

Carolyn Kizer

I can't and won't pretend I'm able to write about Carolyn Kizer or her work "objectively." She has been a friend of mine for more than thirty years. She has been of such significant help to me—in many ways, which I won't elucidate—that I cannot imagine my life as anything but worse without her. I mean this literally, although in the whole thirty years we haven't spent that number of days in each other's actual company.

But indeed the entire poetic community is in her debt almost as much as I. When she was editor of *Poetry Northwest,* the magazine she founded in Seattle in the 1950s, she published the first work of many young poets and she opened her pages to older poets who were experimenting with new modes. When the NEA was established in 1966, she served as the first director of the literature program and had much to do with getting it off to a good start, meaning a fair and sensible distribution of grants—something the program has not always sustained in the years since then. She was also active in the general discussions preceeding the establishment of the NEA itself, which was the first federal venture into the arts after the controversial awarding of the Bollingen Prize by the Library of Congress to Ezra Pound in 1948. Now that we're used to the presence of the NEA in Washington it's easy to forget how vexed was the question of governmental participation in the arts at that time. Many people believed, with good reason after the Pound/Bollingen fiasco, that the government in a democratic country simply could not play a role in the arts. In addition Carolyn, as a reviewer and editor, also as cultural attaché to the American embassy in Karachi and USIA lecturer, has done much to bring attention to American poetry both at home and overseas. She and Donald Hall have done more in this respect, though in different ways, than any other poets alive. As a visiting teacher at many universities she has brought her enthusiasm for poetry to thousands of young people.

From the start Carolyn's poetry has been various and brilliant. Like some other romanticists she is a confirmed neo-classicist, and her characteristic mode is a witty, intelligent eroticism that puts her in a direct line with Catullus. But she has mixed in a considerable dash of the classical Chinese masters too, their slyness and spiritual sentimentality. And as a person of our own century she is sufficiently neurotic and metaphysical. Her writing has a flexibility that permits her to turn from public invective—how few have even tried this in recent times!—to personal meditation or lyric celebration with scarcely a shift of voice. Her work delights me. Obviously it delights many others as well because it has won a large audience and for Carolyn many honors and distinctions.

She wears her laurels well. Carolyn Kizer is a great lady. She combines the role of great ladies of the past with that of a responsibly liberated woman of the present, and does it magnificently. In her home in California she is arbiter, impresario, author, friend, succorer, facilitator. This could be a great burden to her, and no doubt it sometimes is, but she is so absolutely honest and just in all her dealings with the literary world that she is relieved of the mess in which lesser players of the literary game find themselves. Unlike them, she can repose in the acuteness of her sensibility and the goodness of her work, her own personal genius. This is what will sustain her prominence in the literature of America for a long, long time to come.

Elegies

Difficult and Ticklish

Life in the Stories of Raymond Carver

Raymond Carver died last summer. His friends were truly grieved and will remain so for as long as they last themselves because he was an exceptionally attractive person. He loved to tell stories, usually on himself, and he was good at it. He loved gossip, though not vicious gossip—he would back away from that. He was not a joker, but he loved humor and laughter and happy occasions. At the same time he was serious about things that matter, the basic human values, and could talk about them, as he often did, seriously and unabashedly. He was frank, open, honest, and receptive. Above all he was kind. His affection for and generosity toward his friends were unceasing. He was everything that anyone, man or woman, would wish a male friend to be, I think, though men and women responded to him differently. Women told me they thought him sexy, but I myself, and I expect most men, did not consider him handsome, not at all the roguish type. He was anything but suave. In fact he was ungainly and boyish, sometimes almost to the point of physical helplessness. But perhaps this is what appeals to some women.

One could recount many, many anecdotes that would epitomize Ray Carver, the stories that his friends tell one another when they are remembering him and placating their own feelings of loss. But I don't want to do that here. My memories are so clear and forceful that they could only lose in the retelling, and I have lost enough already. Yet thinking about this is what has moved me to write an essay about his work. For if the friends of Ray Carver are more grieved by his genuinely untimely death—he was only fifty—than most people are grieved by the deaths of most of their friends, which I believe is true, then at the same time they, the friends of Ray, have more reason to rejoice than most, because they need not rely simply on the anecdotes they circulate among themselves in self-diminishing repetition to sustain their memories of the man; instead they may turn to the undiminishable evidence of Carver's individuality in his writing, especially in his short stories.

Of course this is not to say that a one-to-one equivalence between the man and his work exists any more in the case of Carver than in the case of any other author. Carver's life was a good deal broader in scope, and in substance a good deal more complex, not to say contradictory, than any story or bundle of stories could possibly be. Nevertheless his short stories do represent the breadth and complexity of his imagination, and to my mind the breadth and complexity of Carver's imagination, not to mention the finesse, musicality, humor, emotional and moral consonance, or a score of other qualities, are, in an easily perceptible degree, greater than one may find in all but a very few other writers of his time and place, meaning the past two decades, or possibly three, in America. This is what makes Carver important, viz., his place in literature, not his friendship with me or anyone else. This is why my mind has turned from the man to his work in spite of my personal feelings about losing him. This is what makes writing an essay excusable.

Much nonsense has been written and talked about Carver. He has been called a minimalist, for instance. I don't know and can't imagine why, unless merely because the term, which came from painting and music, is in the air, one of those fashionabilities that beset literary consciousness. It's true Carver's stories are short, but not unusually so; some are not really short at all; they average about the same as Chekhov's. Was Chekhov a minimalist? If the term means anything in literature, which I doubt, it must have to do with narrative manner or some other component of style, not with structure. Is a haiku minimalist? Most people would say not. Carver's narratives are quite conventionally presented, usually in a consecutive sequence of scenes or actions with a clear chronological connection. Note how many of the stories, especially the earlier ones, begin with a statement about time: "It had been two days since Evan Hamilton . . . ," "Jack got off work at three . . . ," "Early that day the weather turned . . . ," etc. Carver oriented himself in his narratives the same way all of us do. Almost all stories, including reports in newspapers, begin with when. Nothing minimalist about that.

Is it that Carver's stories end without concluding? This is a common feeling about them, I've heard it often, but it just isn't true. Maybe Carver's stories don't have climaxes and dénouements in the classical sense, but neither do most short stories written in the twentieth century; this idea of the Maupassant-like "fixed form" of a story was abandoned years and years ago by Hemingway, by Mansfield, by Chekhov himself. Carver's stories end with a completed action; the fact that many people in his stories are essentially paralyzed and unable to act does not change this, because the action of a story is in the story, not in the people, it is a movement of spirit, of recognized and acknowledged feeling, which lingers over or in front of the story and is the combined response of every human sensibility engaged in the story, including the sensibilities of all its readers. A work of art that appears "minimal" in its concrete structure may in fact be open-ended in the more real structure or metastructure of its symbolic, parallel, inferential, affective components. This is elementary.

Another thing I've heard is that Carver's original manuscripts had more ample endings, which were cut down by editors when the stories were published in books. This is the kind of gossip that is both attractive and believable; nobody likes editors, and everyone knows that editors do take delight in red-penciling their authors' manuscripts. But I have looked at the endings of all the stories in *Where I'm Calling From* (1988) that were taken from earlier books—*Will You Please Be Quiet, Please* (1976), *What We Talk about When We Talk about Love* (1981), and *Cathedral* (1983)—and have compared the endings, and I have found only two stories that show appreciable changes: "So Much Water So Close to Home" has an expanded ending, and "A Small Good Thing," originally called "The Bath," is amplified in a number of ways. These stories were from the two earlier books, and it does seem likely that both books were edited more stringently than Carver liked. But two stories are not enough, when compared to the number left unchanged in the final book, to sustain a generalized conclusion about Carver vis-à-vis the editors. More important, none of the stories supports the notion that Carver's endings are inadequate. *Where I'm Calling From* is in effect Carver's collected stories. He told me, and I'm sure others, that it contained all the stories, thirty-six in number, which he wanted to save and that they were in the form he wished them to have. If his endings had been clipped by editors in the earlier books, he could easily have restored them in his last, which was published when he had quite enough clout as a writer to insist on his own preferences. He did change the two stories mentioned above, he retitled a number of others, and he rearranged all the stories in a new sequence. He corrected typos and made editorial revisions and amplifications in the interiors of some stories. He omitted a fair number of stories altogether, including four from *Cathedral,* which is unusual—writers tend to favor their recent work when they put together collected editions—as well as several of my own favorites from the earlier books, especially the title story from *Will You Please Be Quiet, Please.* (In spite of what Carver told me, this may possibly have been the result of an agreement with the original publisher, McGraw-Hill, not to strip so much from the earlier volume that it would become commercially redundant, in which case we must hope that the agreement will be called off soon, so that somebody can assemble a true collected edition.) But Carver altered the ending of only one story and made large-scale revisions in only one other. In these cases, it's true, the alterations do seem to be reversions to an earlier, ampler, remembered state, but they do not suggest that Carver had any real problem with the endings of his stories in general. He didn't.

What we have in Carver's work is the contrary of minimalism. We have the fullness and richness of an imagination not stinted at all. A few stories are distinctly hideous, in the strain of American gothic, stories such as the one about the deaf-mute who kills his wife and commits suicide because—though of course the reason is much more than this—a flood washes out his stockpond of mail-order bass; it's called "The Third Thing That Killed My Father Off." Some stories are almost pure farce, like "Feathers," the story of the ugly baby and the peacock, or "Elephant," the account of a man driven to despair by the demands of his relatives. These are so funny in parts that they seem like episodes from *Huckleberry Finn;* like Twain's masterpiece Carver's stories occur in a larger, darker context, making everything in them, even the funniest bits, reverberations of the greater understanding in which all our lives participate. I think, for instance, of the conversation between Huck and Jim about the French language, a moment of sheerest comedy which is, even so, rooted in the tragedy of the white boy and the black man, the tragedy of America and the world. In stories like "Nobody Said Anything," about the little boy who takes home with pride one half of a huge old fish he and another boy have caught together only to be yelled at by his father for bringing such a thing into the house, Carver writes both adroitly and touchingly of the humiliation consequent upon being human. "Where I'm Calling From," which he chose to be the title story of his final collection, is about what alcoholism means. "J.P. and I are on the front porch at Frank Martin's drying-out facility," it begins. "Like the rest of us at Frank Martin's, J.P. is first and foremost a drunk." We know that Carver himself was a reformed alcoholic, and this story, however its events and characters were derived, is indeed where he is calling from. It's a desperate story, a dark and disconsolate story; it's the truth. Yet it begins with a quip. Carver's mastery of colloquial idiom—and *mastery* is the exact word; that "first and foremost" is indelible in its rightness, and anyone who thinks coming up with such a phrase in such a narrative location is less than genius doesn't know much about writing—gave him the means by which he could say the truth, articulate the truth, which itself has no language. There are other ways to do it, especially if one is writing in Japanese. Carver's way is American and is aimed, though I think half-unconsciously, at the understanding of Americans, at least those living west of Worcester.

But most of Carver's stories are about the sorrow and pain

of failed romance. Again and again his couples separate, almost as if they were blind organisms in a test tube genetically programmed to divide. Some of these stories too are hideous ("A Serious Talk"), some are pathetic ("Are These Actual Miles?"), some hilarious ("Intimacy"). Many of them are simply relentless; they are unsparing accounts of the drivenness of sexual and antisexual behavior. "Menudo," for instance, gives us such a succession of romantic brutalities—nothing violent, nothing that doesn't happen in the house next door or in one's own—that we are ready more than once to cry "uncle" and ask for mercy; but the story goes on. It is a marvel of compression, like many of Carver's stories, relating an extraordinary length of time and many events in a few pages. And we read it to the end, not because we relish brutality, though perhaps we do, but because again and again Carver gives us, in a touch of idiomatic speech or gesture, those intimations of understanding that come out of the dark context to retrieve humanity and articulate the truth. Am I saying anything more than that he generalizes from the particular and particularizes from the general, as all artists do—or so we were taught in high school? Perhaps not. But the *way* he does it is important.

He did it by being funny. Carver himself complained about the academicization of literature in America and the solemnity, not to say pedantry, it has induced among writers and readers. What we have come to call workshopping was for him, though he himself enjoyed teaching, a sort of up-to-date dilettantism, which he deplored. In his last letter to me, written about two months before his death, he wrote: ". . . the things you said in the second half of the letter, about the humor and so on, well, according to my lights you are right in remarking on this . . . ; it gets talked about . . . rarely, if ever, by critics and reviewers." I have heard Carver read from his work to academic audiences a number of times, where getting a laugh was like pulling hen's teeth. Yet I myself can scarcely read his work aloud to my wife because I have to stop so often to wipe tears of laughter from my eyes. I keep breaking up. This is true of even his grimmest stories. They have funny moments. "Cathedral," about the husband who is jealous of his wife's old friend, Robert, who is blind—certainly one of Carver's most moving, most eloquent pieces—has such a moment, i.e., when the wife comes downstairs and smells pot-smoke in the room where the husband and the blind man are sitting.

"What do I smell?" she said.
"We thought we'd have us some cannabis," I said.
My wife gave me a savage look. Then she looked at the blind man and said, "Robert, I didn't know you smoked."
He said, "I do now, my dear. There's a first time for everything. But I don't feel anything yet."
"This stuff is pretty mellow," I said. "This stuff is mild. It's dope you can reason with," I said. "It doesn't mess you up."
"Not much it doesn't, bub," he said, and laughed.

It is a moment only, not a hilarious moment, what I suppose would be called a light moment, and these occur repeatedly in Carver's writing, moments of common insight created so to speak by the characters themselves for their own easement in the discomfort of their lives. These people are generally not as smart as we are, often they speak a language we would not use even in our most casual modes, yet we do not look down on them, we feel on a level with them, because they have in them the sharpness of common American humor, which is frontier humor. We participate in these people's discomfort and easement in a corresponsive way, and Carver presides over all of us as a tutelary presence by means that we may discuss and discuss, as we do, but will never altogether figure out. "Cathedral" must be the first piece of American writing in fifty years or more in which one person addresses another as "bub." But the blind man knows this, as well as we know it, he knows it exactly as well as we know it. This is evident in his whole verbal and rhetorical posture. He knows it and we know it, and each knows the other knows, each knows the exact nuance and savor of the other's knowledge; and Carver has made this happen. It is rare in literature, this degree of identification, and the fact that it does occur makes a decided difference in the quality of our lives.

Later in "Cathedral" the wife has fallen asleep on the sofa while her husband and Robert are talking late and smoking dope. "Her head lay across the back of the sofa, her mouth [was] open," the narrator says. "She'd turned so that her robe had slipped away from her legs, exposing a juicy thigh. I reached to draw her robe back over her, and it was then that I glanced at the blind man. What the hell! I flipped the robe open again." A Chaplinesque touch in this, many complexities compressed in one simple gesture. Yet "Cathedral" is in its whole effect a story of great pathos and seriousness.

Am I right in saying this is American? It would be hard to prove. Everyone knows about Carver's debt to Chekhov, and Chekhov has light moments too. No doubt Carver learned from them, and perhaps from the light moments in Kafka, Ionesco, Beckett, and many others as well. I have no fear that his European antecedents will go unexplored. For that matter, Chaplin, who has influenced so many American writers, came from England. But I believe Carver had equally strong roots in American humor of the nineteenth and early twentieth centuries, in Artemus Ward, Mark Twain, James Thurber, and William Faulkner, for instance, perhaps especially William Faulkner; the Snopes family, though more vicious and less attractive than most of the people in Carver's stories, was capable of light moments. This has not been mentioned. It's as if a break, a hiatus, occurred between Faulkner and Carver, fifty years when American humor, derived from the earliest native product of the white settlers, fell under the domination of foreign influences, the period of the joke, the one-liner, the *New Yorker* cartoon, the TV monologuist, and now for some time this hiatus has ended. In television the sitcom has replaced the monologuist, for instance, which is an unimportant exchange of equal dullnesses, but in literature Carver has replaced . . . well, let's say S. J. Perelman and Philip Roth, and this actually is important. He gives us a humor based, not on reversal of expectation, but on exaggeration, understatement, character, and incident, and above all on an American wiliness of attitude which we know well from Twain—and from still extant frontier storytellers from northern Maine to the uplands of Oregon—and which is funny precisely in its never-stated recognition of what is not funny.

In the same letter from which I've already quoted, Carver wrote: "What a life! But it's the only one we have, which makes it that much more difficult and ticklish." Difficult and ticklish, a perfect description of life in Carver's stories, especially in the context I have pointed out above, the greater context and the lesser, the general and the personal, in which we know that "difficult" means "impossible" and "ticklish" means "unto death."

The abundance of life in Carver's stories, in spite of his comparatively small output, is of a kind with Twain's and Faulkner's. Critics and creative writing students would love to be able to say that Carver's stories are formulaic, one of their favorite words. But the opposite is the case. *Where I'm Calling From* contains thirty-six stories, and similarity exists among them, but never anything like identity of structure, concept, attitude or anything else. Sometimes, it's true, one feels that a formula must be at work, for the stories have a seamlessness that can hardly come from life; but I challenge anyone to produce it. The stories really are, after all of Carver's technical accomplishment has been taken into account, spontaneous. I don't believe it would be possible to reduce the terms of any one story to the terms of another, as we can, for instance, with T. S. Eliot's *The Waste Land* and "The Hollow Men." These thirty-six stories are thirty-six distinct instances. I've heard people say that Carver's stories are not as rich as those of his mentor, Chekhov, because the life of our time is poorer than the life of Chekhov's or because Chekhov, as a doctor, had access to more strata of the human community than Carver had. But to me the point seems unimportant. Granted, Carver cannot introduce European aristocrats into his work, and the conflicts in his stories are not between disparate classes (as in Chekhov's story called "Heartache," for instance); but if one takes pains to detect all the levels, intellectual, social, economic, linguistic, etc., that Carver's characters inhabit and to discriminate all their degrees of urbanity and rusticity, the wide range of Carver's work will be apparent.

Which is simply to say that American life in the latter part of the twentieth century is indeed as "rich"—various, complex, particular, inconsistent—as Russian life a century earlier or probably any life anywhere. Richness, like beauty, is in the eye of the beholder.

Two or three decades ago Wallace Stegner wrote a number of essays about the literature of the American West, in which he deprecated the tendency of western writers to rely on stereotypes of frontier mentality without bringing present society and culture into their fictions. He did not mean the present of Las Vegas or Dallas; he meant the present of Grand Junction and Winnemucca. As a western writer himself, "I hope," he wrote, "we will find ways of recognizing at least parts of ourselves in the literature and history the past has left us, and I hope we will find ways of bringing some of the historic self-reliance and some of the heroic virtues back into our world, which in its way is more dangerous than Comanche country ever was." Stegner's hope has been met. Not only by Carver, of course; one thinks of Jim Harrison's *Dalva*, the work of Evan Connell, poets like Tom McGrath and Gary Snyder. But Carver is the master. The best. His stories are the most perspicacious, the best-written, the fullest of any we have from his time, and I know no serious writer, even those who are theoretically at odds with him, who would dispute this. *Where I'm Calling From* is the only certifiable American masterpiece—produced, paradoxically, in a time that thought it had disclaimed the masterpiece—of the last thirty years.

A masterpiece is not simply a work of intrinsic excellence; it must appear at the right time, it must answer an artistic need. Already we see Carver's imitators. In a short while, less than a decade, they have multiplied astonishingly, and the example of Carver has become a principal factor in the evolution of American literature. This has happened during a time when efforts to revive the avant-garde, through deconstructionism, language poetry, etc., have become rather stridently desperate on one side, while the further stultification of academic writing has continued on the other. Carver's stories do not fall in either camp. They are politically, linguistically, and esthetically "pure," meaning independent, and they have the sanction of popularity in every sector of the literate community. They are a liberating influence, in other words, and this is something for which we can and should rejoice.

George Dennison

One winter night, about 1972, George Dennison and I walked up the old logging road that led from his house to the cabin where he worked, about a quarter-mile through the woods. This was in Temple, Maine, a small village, no more than a hamlet, where George's place is situated east of Temple Stream, remote in the hills that rise from the intervale, which is pronounced in Maine as if it were spelled *interval*. George lived there with his wife Mabel and their three children. The night was moonless, but deep snow in the woods reflected starlight. We could see our way clearly enough. The road sloped upward. At the top was an open field, not large, where a few contorted appletrees, remnants of an orchard, stood irregularly, leading toward George's cabin at the far end. At that time, though it has since been enlarged, the cabin was only one room, and I don't recall what it had originally been built for. Perhaps it had been a shed for a cider press. George's place is a farmstead that was first established by Finnish immigrants a century or more ago. George had converted the shed into a workplace for himself. It contained a woodstove, a large work-table, other tables, several chairs, a number of kerosene lamps, and shelves of books and papers. In fact, books and papers lay untidily on every surface, including the floor.

George opened the stove and inserted—which for north-people is the word exactly—a couple of sticks of firewood, lighted some lamps, and sat down at his table. He wore a heavy sweater, which had a dark zigzag pattern against a lighter background in the Scandinavian style, and a dark blue watch cap. He lighted a Gaulois; he poured a half-ounce of Metaxas into a shot glass and sipped it. Then he bent forward, frowning, actually scowling, over the manuscript I had brought him to read, a sequence of poems called "Paragraphs."

A fierce guy. Everyone spoke of it. I had seen him in action with other writers a couple of times, and he frightened me. His language could be vicious; his ideas and perceptions were acute. But I felt strongly that I wished to present my work to him. Something in him—not simply intelligence, but some quality of person—compelled me to seek his assessment of my poems and, beyond that, his understanding, his validation of my sensibility in the larger world of ideas he inhabited. In my uneasy way I was looking for comradeship.

George's good looks are the kind that other men admire, and women too, it seems—he has attracted many—this being not a necessary combination. Black hair, very dark eyes, strong but somewhat irregular features, his nose slightly aquiline, his mouth and jaw firmly set. He has a powerful body. He played football seriously when he was younger, and was a boxer in the navy, and his interest in prizefighting continues even now. He speaks of Archie Moore, Mohammed Ali, and Sugar Ray Robinson with the same intensity of feeling that he has for great writers, and he smiles as he searches for the right words to describe them, a smile that lights up his face, makes it glow, changes his expression entirely, though I wasn't to see this until later.

That night in his cabin George tore my manuscript apart, left it almost literally in shreds. My poem had comprised sixty or seventy sections, typed with care, when I showed it to him; when he had finished, only a few sections remained intact. On page after page he struck down my lines with his black ballpoint pen, leaving great scrawls and wiggles of contempt, which stood accurately for what he was saying to me at the same time. I don't remember his words, but something like, "No, no, goddamn it, you can't do that, it's mush, it's utterly commonplace!," etc., again and again. He smoked more Gauloises and sipped more Metaxas. The stove emitted little burps of grayish fume, because he hadn't cleaned his stovepipe recently. Soot sifted finely onto the pages of my manuscript. We left the cabin in the early light of false dawn. A few chickadees were beginning to chatter in the woods. The stars were fading, and so was I.

Somewhat later I patched together twenty-odd sections of "Paragraphs" and published them in a book called *Brothers, I Loved You All.* The other sections were, for better or worse, discarded. Recently, when he and I were remembering this episode, George accused himself of a critical blunder and said he had been looking in my manuscript for the poem he would write, not the one I had already written, and this is true. But at the time I believed—and still do—George's criticism had been partly motivated by unconscious but real malice, some massive neurotic compulsion. George is a superb writer, and I think always has been, at least since his student days; in the 1960s he had published one extremely successful book, *The Lives of Children,* which had brought him a good deal of attention; but at the time I am speaking of he was blocked, writing only fragments and notes, unable to bring anything to completion, and he was frustrated and angry.

Yet in the years since that time he has become one of my closest friends and without doubt my most acute, most helpful critic. His letters have given back to me the essential purport of my own writing in all its modes and nuances, but from a point of view that neither I nor, I think, anyone else could imagine. These letters are beautifully written. Without wishing in the least to distract him from writing fiction, which is his main work, I have urged him to write criticism, to make his letters into essays—not much change would be required—but he hasn't done it. He says he is unable to find the right voice for it, though I believe the right, exactly right, voice is what he naturally possesses; searching would be unnecessary. But who can blame an artist for his successes? George is a hesitant and slow writer; I am so grateful for his fiction, which in fact is always critical in intention, that I can't complain if he hasn't written something else.

Once when I was passing through Saratoga Springs on my way from Syracuse to Vermont, I stopped to visit George at Yaddo, the artists' retreat where he was a guest. This was in winter too. The ponds were frozen, the woods filled with dirty snow. George had asked for the "Composer's Tower," a studio at the top of a round stone building by the edge of one of the ponds, separated by a short walk through the woods from the other buildings, and although this studio is not normally used in winter and is assigned only to composers in summer (because it is isolated and the piano-banging won't bother other guests), it was given to him. It was a big room with windows all around, looking out on the gray gloom. A woodstove had been installed in the fireplace, and George had it fired up. Everything was coated with ash and soot. Papers and books were scattered recklessly. I always wondered—and still do—how George can write a paragraph, say, on a page of the yellow paper he likes, how he can make that effort of mind and imagination, then let it lie on the floor where it is soon covered by other papers and lost to mind. I have seen hundreds and hundreds of such papers in a jumble. He prefers to write on closely ruled yellow graph paper, sheets lightly printed with little blue squares, although his handwriting—small, strong, fluent—runs without regard to the lines, and the left margin slants toward the center as it proceeds down the page. He and I were close friends by the time of this visit at Yaddo, and we talked animatedly on who knows what topics. Our talk has always been wide-ranging. At one point George jumped up and rushed to the piano against the far wall, and stood there, his feet braced widely, while he rattled out five choruses of Meade Lux Lewis. George couldn't read a note and had never learned to "play the piano"; those five choruses were all he could do, except for a few similar passages of Pete Johnson, Albert Ammons, and Champion Jack Dupree. But these choruses were perfect, not just in technique but in spontaneity and vigor—as far as they went, they were splendid jazz. George threw back his head and hollered. He loves that culture, or any expression of uninhibited but formed humaneness. More recently he was describing to me a time when he went with his friend Ivan Tolstoy to a Christmas Eve service at an émigré Russian church in London, where he saw a burly, roughly dressed workman come into the church and immediately throw himself on his knees and spread out his arms to the cross above the alter, his face radiant with ardor and sweetness. George began to cry while he was telling me this. "Anything that made me cry in the past," he said, "makes me cry even more now."

By "now" he meant the short time since he learned he has cancer. A serious metastasized cancer. What a misery! More than anyone else I know, George has changed himself, in both his work and his person, in the latter part of his life. I have heard him in recent years, though never before, contest the stupidity of an academic fool with great reasonableness and originality and keenness, and without the least anger. The same qualities are in all the writing he has done during the past ten years, much more writing than he had finished in the first fifty years of his life, and they are in his personal relationships as well. When I first heard of George's illness, I called him. He was in hospital, heavily sedated; he had just received his first dose—if that's the word—of chemotherapy. He felt awful, physically and emotionally. He could not control his voice, which was soft at one moment, too loud the next, rising and falling in pitch. He told me the nurses had spoken to him of his "good attitude." "What attitude?" he said. "When I feel like crying, I cry—until I can't cry any more. Then I laugh." This is the elemental Dennison, beneath the anger and anxiety, an embodiment of humane intelligence. It is the person I detected when I first met him. His favorite authors, whom he talks about often, Melville, Tolstoy, Proust, Paul Goodman—what are they but great independent minds at the mercy of love and concern for all people?

One summer night in Temple—I don't remember how it came about—George was projecting slides of paintings on his living-room wall, speaking to us of the qualities he found in them. One was a painting of a young woman by Vermeer. George pointed out how the perspective shifted a little, so that the figure is shown more roundly than it could have been when seen from a single viewpoint, as if the painter had moved his easel sideways a foot or two while he worked. I had never seen this before. Now it seemed to me more important by far than the properties of light, color, and line I had associated with painting of the northern Renaissance in the past. This is the real sign, I thought, of independence in an artist; not romantic ego, not solipsism, not the power of "voice" or "style," as so many people persist in thinking, but this subordination to the object that comes only in the ability to look from two angles of vision. Love and concern. And then intelligence, the connecting factor.

After I wrote the above, which I think—I don't date my manuscripts—was done after I came home from a quick visit to him in April, 1987, i.e., in the first shock of learning about his illness and seeing him so weak and changed from the chemotherapy, I visited George several more times. In May I was in Temple for a few days. In August I went and stayed a month, living in a camp on Varnum Pond. We had hoped to see each other often during that month, but before I reached Temple George had left for a special hospital in Illinois to undergo a treatment which entailed raising his body temperature to something like 107°. His heart and brain were somehow blocked off and the rest of him was wrapped in high-powered electric blankets. It was a desperate measure and it didn't work. I suppose the theory was that the high body temperature would kill the cancer cells but leave enough undamaged tissue to reconstitute his physical being; but when he came home, he was greatly weakened, thin and gaunt, looking at least twenty years older than he was. He was sixty-two. He went almost immediately into a hospital in Lewiston, Maine. During the remaining days of August I visited him each afternoon for three or four hours. I left Maine myself on August 31. In September George went home from the hospital and I talked with him two or three times on the phone. The last time we spoke he was too feeble to say more than a sentence or two. His last words to me were, "I'm going down, Hayden." He died on October 8.

George wrote three "short stories"—I use quote marks because these are anything but conventional stories in structure and intent—that I believe are among the best ever written, "A Tale of Pierrot," "Oilers and Sweepers," and "Interview with the Author of Caryatids." I know this will seem improbable to many people, that three works by a writer not very well known should be ranked so highly. But I am serious—why shouldn't I be? His other stories are good but not that good. His long essay about his dog, his hometown, and his place in the world, titled "Shawno," is a superb example of its genre. His novel, *Luisa Domic,* is finely written and one of the best political novels I know, political in the broadest sense, tying together the particulars of fascistic Latin American politics with the general political, social, and cultural degradation of our time. His first book, *The Lives of Children,* a work of social criticism and theory, is a modern American classic.

When an artist dies before his time, people always say what a pity it is that he didn't finish his work. It gets rather tiresome. I won't make a big point of it. But what George and I mainly talked about during those last days in the hospital in Lewiston was the novel he had been planning for years. It was to be a novel about the people of central Maine, especially the older people (he had interviewed many of them), and about their interrelationships with the young people of the counter-culture who came to the region during the sixties and seventies. He had written dozens of episodes, both in handwritten notes and fragments and in his head. He quoted them to me verbatim. Some were hilarious. The work was to have been a comic epic almost in the classical sense. George could scarcely raise his head from his pillow during those last days, but he was enthusiastic, he talked animatedly, he laughed and wept. He still believed, part of the time, that he could beat the cancer and write his book. And without doubt it would have been a marvelous book.

The friendship between George and me took a long time to mature. We each were suspicious of the other, often reinforced by third parties, which had to be overcome. But during the last ten years of his life George was my best friend and by far my most helpful reader, in both letters and conversations. I came to depend on him as I have never depended on anyone else; he was the only person with whom I felt truly free to discuss my ideas and aspirations. His death, now more than a year and a half after the event, still seems to me insurmountable.

I hope his work will be remembered. I hope especially that those three stories will be recognized and accepted as part of American literary achievement during the twentieth century. They deserve it, and so do we.

Joel Oppenheimer

During the years when I made part of my living from editing and reviewing poetry, I thought I was obliged to keep up with everything of importance that was happening in American poetry. It meant reading every new book, not just those by poets with established reputations but those by young poets who for one reason or another seemed promising. Of course I couldn't do it, and as the years went by and the current of new work became a flood, I did it less and less. Even so I read an astonishing number of books, many thousands. And naturally I was bored by most of them, and I began to look out for books that were in some way—in topic, attitude, intention, or whatever—different from the rest. I began to look out especially for books by Joel Oppenheimer.

Oppenheimer's poems were always direct and clear, often amusing, often in a mode of political radicalism that was attractive to me, and moreover written with a kind of generalized erotic affection for everything and almost everyone that diverged from the tedious irony of most American poetry in this century. Not that they were simple poems; many were poems of ideas, of argument; some were even poems of learning. But they presented themselves simply and confidently and were a pleasure to read. They were, literally, a refreshment. They combined the most ordinary idiomatic speech with both poetic and intellectual language to make poems that were natural and tricky at the same time, as all really fine poems are.

> believe it, believe it.
> the song sings for

spring as in other
seasons, only more so.

Of all the poets directly influenced by William Carlos Williams—and I think immediately of a very diverse group, including Denise Levertov, Robert Creeley, Wendell Berry (his earlier poems), David Ignatow, James Laughlin, and others—the one who comes closest to Williams in line-structure and syntax is Oppenheimer. I don't know how to account for this. It doesn't appear to be a question of imitating; Oppenheimer's poems are not at all studied or labored. And the sensibility of the Jewish boy from Yonkers who grew up to be a peacenik and flower child in the sixties and seventies is certainly different from that of the pediatrician from Rutherford who was born nearly twenty years before the end of Queen Victoria's reign. But maybe the two poets had the same ear, or as close to it as poets can get. That's how it seems. Their poems move in the same way. Oppenheimer's poems on the whole are simpler, their humor is more abundant and distinctly Jewish, their sexuality is far more evident; but the rhythms and phrasings are noticeably similar.

Because Oppenheimer's poems are simple and direct in language, it's easy to make the mistake of reading them too fast, as if they were prose. Here are a couple of his short poems.

For David

eyes wide, we
have dumped it
in your lap. you
do not know that
yet. hands opened
and closed, the
panorama stretches
before you. you
do not know that
yet. lips ready,
you will take all
we have to give you.
and will survive.

and will pay us
back in our own
coin. even love,
if we come to deserve it.

Happy New Year

i thought it would
be a different place, this
year at this time,

still the poem promised is
the poem to be delivered.

sing a different song then
from the one intended.

ah well if it hadn't been
the goyim, it would've
been somebody else, right?

next year, the promised land.

And here is a poem by Williams:

Approach to a City

Getting through with the world—
I never tire of the mystery
of these streets: the three baskets
of dried flowers in the high

bar-room window, the gulls wheeling
above the factory, the dirty
snow—the humility of the snow that
silvers everything and is

trampled and lined with use—yet
falls again, the silent birds
on the still wires of the sky, the blur
of wings as they take off

together. The flags in the heavy
air move against a leaden
ground—the snow
pencilled with the stubble of old

> weeds: I never tire of these sights
> but refresh myself there
> always for there is small holiness
> to be found in braver things.

The superficial differences are obvious, punctuation, diction, etc., but I hope the more fundamental similarity is obvious as well. The phrasings that make us continually come down with a thump on the last and first syllables of the lines. The occasional epigrammatic tightness of line-structure. The simplicity of description against the complexity of abstraction. But one doesn't want to push the comparison too far. Oppenheimer had nothing like the ambition of the older poet, produced nothing on the scale of "Kora in Hell," "The Clouds," "The Pink Church," not to mention *Paterson*. Oppenheimer never, as far as I know, experimented with long lines or more complex strophes. He was content with the short-line lyric. And of course he never attempted the stories, novels, plays, or extended essays that are such a considerable part of Williams's accomplishment.

Yet Oppenheimer wrote many fine things and they have not been sufficiently recognized. He was a founding editor of the *Village Voice* and wrote for it steadily over many years before it sold out to kitsch and pot-boiling; a book of selections from his newspaper pieces is to be published before long. He wrote a charming book about Marilyn Monroe. He wrote about sports and pop culture in many contexts. But the main thing is the poetry. His poems have for me the same freshness that they had years ago, the same immediacy. They are varied and fall into the classical modes: elegy and satire, love poems and diatribes, anniversaries and celebrations. He was an occasional poet with a classical mind who wrote in the language of intelligent discourse, including street language. I don't know how many books and booklets of his poems were published during his lifetime; I find twelve on my bookshelf but I know there were many more. In any event the first half of his collected poems, entitled *Names and Local Habitations*, has now been published by Jonathan Williams at the Jargon

Society, and the second half is in the works. I recommend these books to everyone.

Unfortunately Joel did not live to see his collected poems. The first copy of the book arrived in Henniker, New Hampshire, where he lived during the last years of his life, the day after his death—at least that is how I remember it. This was in the fall of 1988. I had first met him in about 1980 when he gave a reading at SUNY in Cortland, New York. I went down from Syracuse to hear him because I wanted to meet him after all the years of reading and reviewing his poems. It was a good reading, the audience attentive and responsive, and Joel seemed as glad to meet me as I was to meet him. But he had the worst cough I have ever heard, a deep, croupy cough, and he was smoking those little cigars with plastic mouthpieces attached, inhaling the smoke deeply. Like his other friends I wasn't really surprised when, a year or so later, he was diagnosed with lung cancer. He faced his illness bravely, undertook surgery and repeated courses of chemotherapy, and lived longer than anyone would have predicted; but at last he could hold out no more. I saw him often during the years of his illness, in Henniker and elsewhere. He was always friendly, cheerful, funny, talkative, a great person to hang out with, to talk about baseball with—the game was his passion—and to exchange stories and lies with. At times he could hardly walk, he was so weak from the treatments, but he remained active till the end, teaching, writing, talking, scheming, spending time with family and friends. Theresa Maier, his wife during those last years, was, as he said often, a godsend to him.

I'm sure Oppenheimer is missed by everyone who knew him, including those who knew him only through his poems. He was a member of an important group of American poets in the second half of the twentieth century, namely, those who had been at Black Mountain College in North Carolina during the time when Charles Olson was provost in the late forties— Robert Duncan, Robert Creeley, Jonathan Williams, Edward Dorn, Hilda Morley, Robert Kelly, and others, including those who were Black Mountaineers by association, such as Denise Levertov, Cid Corman, Theodore Enslin, etc. His work is independent and quite different from that of the rest, simpler, less grandiose, not so literary; but certain affinities are evident too, especially the artistic freedom, devotion, integrity, and energy that characterize all these poets, who were and are the true recipients and preservers of the spirit of Pound and Williams in American literature after World War II. I hope Oppenheimer's poems will be remembered and enjoyed for a long time to come. In our present grubby literary situation they are especially needed.

Henry Rago

With vividness I recall a Saturday afternoon in spring, 1947. The South Side was soft and gray; mist, a light rain falling, new leaves on the maples and catalpas. Henry and I sat in one of the 55th Street saloons, probably Harry's, smoking cigarettes, drinking beer, and talking. Henry was excited; he had a new poem, a sequence, in the forthcoming number of *Poetry*, which we knew had been delivered from the printer but not yet distributed. He was quoting from the poem to show me how he had overcome a problem in it, then misquoting and misremembering, until at last in exasperation he jumped from his stool. "Come on, come on." We climbed in my jalopy and drove downtown. The *Poetry* office was closed and locked, the neighborhood empty on a Saturday afternoon. "Give me a boost," Henry said. Standing on my shoulders, he jimmied the window, climbed in, and stole two copies of the magazine, which we took to a cafeteria on Division Street, Willard Motley's hang-out, and there we talked until nightfall.

Two young men burglarizing the magazine they were later to edit, though neither at that time had the least suspicion of what was to come. That was the old *Poetry* office, of course, 212 East Erie, where Harriet Monroe had established it in 1912.

I remember too how Henry talked, how when he was excited he blocked out his words in air with his stonemason's hands. I remember the time at a club on the North Side when he introduced me to "Bottles" Capone, Al's brother, and another time when he introduced me to his old professor at grad school, the philosopher Yves Simon. In the European manner Yves took off his hat to shake hands. I remember Henry's wedding, a big and fashionable occasion, and how Henry was laughing, and how afterward Yves came back to my flat and sat with his crippled leg on the floor, weeping like a peasant mother, though he had eight or ten kids of his own to marry off back in South Bend. I remember a starry summer night when Henry and his girlfriend, and my wife and I, were on a pier sticking out into the lake; we lay on our backs with our heads hanging upside down over the edge, and the million colored lights of the city, reflected on the water, looked like the sky, while the stars looked like the earth, and Henry was enchanted, and kept looking and exclaiming. I remember Henry and I carrying a passed-out girl up three flights to her room on the Near North Side, how we gasped for breath and how Henry cursed when her head struck the banister.

I remember later, when bad luck overtook me and I was forced into seclusion, Henry was the only person in seven years who came to see me. I remember his letters, in which he wrote of his vexations with work at the magazine, his desire to teach and write, his exultation when he could break away to Europe or New Mexico. I remember our meeting again a couple of years ago, after a long time of living at a distance, he in Chicago, I in the East; two old friends surrounded by our families on a hot Chicago night. We had changed, both of us, and we could not help noticing. "So often now we are re-minded of our own deaths," Henry said, quietly. Speaking from his religious knowledge and experience, he called it "a pity." To me it seemed more like a crime.

Henry Rago was my oldest friend in this world. Naturally I remember many things about him. In mentioning some of them I have no desire to violate his privacy, on which he placed a high value, but simply to suggest to general readers what they must already know: that he was of course more than the rescuer of *Poetry*, more than a loved teacher, a valiant and failing poet, a scholar of the great humane, Catholic, and catholic tradition, and a literary arbiter whose authority was widely acknowledged. Many people will write about these pub-lic aspects of the man. I hope that those who write about his poetry will be sensitive to its merits, to its verbal acuity and uncompromising purpose, and that they will recognize its seeming slenderness for what it really was, a failure more creditable than most success. Henry's life as an artist was more intense than any other I have known, but cruelly eroded by conflicts of responsibility, both the obvious and the concealed; yet he bore it without bitterness, as he bore all his burdens of time, and he worked with awesome care. Fidelity was what meant the most to him, I think, fidelity to men, to poetry, and to his knowledge of spiritual reality. He would not be hurried. His criticism was gentle and almost always perceptive. He helped many poets, probably more than will ever be known; scores of my own poems over the years were improved by him, and this was the least of his help to me. He was a poet, capable of joy yet often troubled and discontented, a complex person. But in one respect he was as simple as a child, for always, without thought, he was a true and generous friend.

Henry dead is a sorrow to me still largely unintelligible. Perhaps it always will be, like a part of reality I cannot accept. What is the good of trying to explain? I would not, even if I could.[1]

---

1. This was written not long after Henry Rago's death in 1969. It was first published in a special issue of *Poetry* devoted to his memory. What I would add to it now (1991) is that the decade and a half of Henry's editorship of *Poetry* were, taken altogether, the best years of the magazine by far from its founding to the present.

Reviews

Richard Hugo

Richard Hugo is dead. He died not long ago. Now this new book contains, practically speaking, all his poetry, meaning each of his previous books in full, plus twenty-odd pages of poems written after the last book issued during his lifetime. In such circumstances a reviewer is expected to make some sort of summary. Can it be done? Not well; not within the confines of an ordinary review. Nevertheless one tries to be useful.

First summation: *Making Certain It Goes On* is as tedious a book of poems as anyone could be asked to read, in spite of a few, very few, good and moving poems here and there.

Second summation: it puts me in mind of a time many years ago when I bought the complete poems of Robert Herrick, a poet I admire very much, granting the offensiveness of his cavalier affiliations. Before I had read half the book I was fed to the ears with Herrick. To this day I have not read the second half. For lovers of poetry an anthology is a blessing, even an inferior one.

Third summation: with truly great poets this is not the case; e.g., I can read, seriatim and with pleasure, all of Ben Jonson's lyric poems.

Beyond this I have only inferences, and the easiest way into them is a small segment of personal history. Several years ago I set out to write a book about the generation of American poets roughly ten years ahead of my own: Lowell, Bishop, Berryman, Olson, Schwartz, Rukeyser, etc. It was to be called *Poets of Responsibility*. A publisher offered me a contract and an ad-

---

A review of *Making Certain It Goes On: The Collected Poems of Richard Hugo.*

vance, which, with more sense than I've had sometimes, I turned down. I began with Paul Goodman; eventually I produced an essay that was published separately. Next I went to Theodore Roethke. Because I had, over more than twenty years, reviewed nearly all his books, always favorably and often enthusiastically, I felt quite sure I would find my task easy and enjoyable. For a year I studied Roethke: the poems, the essays, the published notebooks and letters, the works of biographers and critics. At the end I threw up my hands. More and more I was turned off by the man's overweening esthetic and spiritual solipsism. Why? Roethke's anguish was genuine, many readers shared it, and playing cat and mouse with God is after all a long-sanctioned literary schtick. But where other poets had been content to let God play the cat, for Roethke God was the mouse. And for me, an atheist, this was intolerable, all the more as reinforced by his fierceness toward Eliot, Yeats, and every other poet in the life-or-death competitive struggle Roethke took writing to be—clearly revealed in the letters and journals. One effect was an imputed confidential intimacy between the cat-poet and cat-reader on spurious grounds. Roethke was a superbly talented poet, perhaps better equipped than any other of his age, but all his verbal enticements did not overcome his hugely egotistical intention, the comfort of his separate soul. In short he was not a responsible poet at all.

Because I could not write about Roethke with enthusiasm, I gave up my book altogether.

Hugo was born in Seattle, lived there a considerable time, and was, I believe, a student in Roethke's writing class at the University of Washington. His early admiration for Roethke is unmistakable. Many people—not including Hugo, whom I never met—have told me Roethke was a good teacher. Indeed the notion of Roethke's success in the classroom is mythological, used by thousands of teachers of creative writing to encourage themselves in the wastefulness and boredom of their jobs. I am not convinced, however. Roethke was a persuasive teacher—who can doubt it?—but this does not mean he was good. What Hugo got from Roethke, at any rate, the heavy iambic pentameter of "Four for Sir John Davies" and the attitude of poetic megalomania, he was ill-equipped to use: he had neither the verbal talent for the one nor the illusionist metaphysical imagination for the other. Hence what we see in the first hundred or so pages of his book are poems loaded with awkward pentameters—since for whatever reason, apparently a tin ear, Hugo was unable to give his lines the variability and balance that Roethke was master of—and a rapidly deepening decline into pessimism.

But the point is that it was a phony pessimism. Hugo had no god to play the mouse for him, so he substituted what was left, the world and all its creatures, including especially its nonpoetic, non-Hugovian human creatures, with all their thoughts and feelings. A nest of vipers. There was nothing original in this, of course. But inevitably Hugo himself was drawn into the nest; he became a reputable and rewarded de Sade. (Masochism and sexism are very conspicuous and ugly threads through all his work.) Nowhere is Hugo's pessimism sustained by any thoughtful attitude toward causes, such as Roethke—and de Sade—could offer. All is vague, a kind of inverted Darwinism, evolutionary despair.

In the poems of his middle years, which are probably his best, Hugo loosened his prosody, though you can still find plenty of heavy-footed iambs and buried pentameters. The pessimism becomes only grayer and grayer—his favorite color, as *abandoned* is his favorite word. The poems are cryptic, portentous, and above all confidential; they refer us to places we have never heard of as if we had lived there for years, and they tell of people identified only by pronouns, *he* or *you,* as if they were our next-door neighbors. This is not obscurantism, I have come to feel, as much as it is befuddlement. He writes:

> I like bars close to home and home run down,
> a signal to the world, I'm weak. . . .

That's from a poem published in 1975. In fact, many of Hugo's poems occur in barrooms, and the tone is exactly that of the self-pitying drunken stranger who leans on you and erupts his unconnected life and philosophy into your ear. I am reminded of certain popular singers who have cashed in on their ability to sound drunk or stoned.

Fourth summation: Hugo's poetry is not only obviously derivative but degenerative.

Fifth: Hugo's poetry is the dominant influence upon the common American poetic style of recent years, as one may observe it in thousands of books and magazines. Here I know I'm on uncertain ground—if only because at other times I've felt the same thing about other poets. But Hugo's poems are genotypical: the same "free" meter that is nevertheless imbued with a stiffness everywhere recognizable as the mark of academicism, the same pronouns without antecedents, the same present tense (what used to be called the historical present but has now become a nonsensical eternal present), the same unearned sentimental misery, the same specious confidentiality. All this has become the poetic convention of our time.

Finally: if one may relinquish the socio-literary mode demanded of reviewers and take the poems separately as phenomena rather than symptomatologia, then one can—I think almost anyone—choose a good small selection of Hugo's poems for an anthology. This is important. The selection will include some of the few poems in which Hugo speaks from outside his solipsism, poems like "Living Alone," but also some that do not, like "The River Now." Such poems will probably always be among the best of their limited kind in American literature and thoroughly representative as well. We must be leery of the kind, aware of its narrowness and its intellectual and artistic shabbiness—by which I mean that James Wright's poetry, for instance, is of another kind in spite of superficial similarities—but we certainly cannot leave it out in our account of American cultural schizophrenia during the seventies.

Grace Paley

In the *New York Times Book Review* dated June 30 last, Robert Dunn is sharply critical of those whom he calls the writers of "private interest." It's a term from commonplace political theory, which poses a "generational cycle" in American life, periods of intense "public interest" being followed a generation later by periods of "private interest." Mr. Dunn says we are now in a period of "private interest," and that many of our most successful fiction writers are affected by it; they consequently write in a withdrawn, personal way that he calls "minimalist." He names Frederick Barthelme, Bobbie Ann Mason, Mary Robison, and Ray Carver.

He goes on to say that "private interest writers have lost the historical sense," "do not explain our lives," are "in retreat," and "lead to nothing." He calls instead for "fiction of breadth, high ambition, and social, political, and intellectual engagement," fiction that is "expansive," "fiction that connects past, present, and future, shows worlds within worlds, strikes telling tales and images that resonate and endure."

Like almost everything else in the *Times*—and believe me, it's calculated policy—Dunn's piece is simple, adolescent, put together with big words and small meanings. Okay, we're used to it. But what he says is wrong. The idea that we are in a period of public withdrawal from politics could occur only to someone buried in the adolescent culture of the *haute bourgeoisie.* The fact is that today in the United States more people are actively thinking about politics than ever before, and the prospect of what this may lead to, confirmed democrat though I

A review of *Later the Same Day,* by Grace Paley.

am, frankly scares the bejeezus out of me. On the literary side, to impute minimalism to such writers as Ray Carver is absurd.

Every story Carver has written, good or bad, though for my part they are mostly very good, is embedded in a social and cultural fabric that is, while complex, clear and widely representative. If his stories are, as someone has called them, "narrative fragments," nevertheless they are crammed with detail, events, imagery, and insight—the opposite of minimal. As for historical sense, an awareness of the tradition, does Dunn think the cathedral got into Carver's story by that title accidentally? And is he so numb that he cannot apprehend the plain signs of Chekhov, Balzac, Defoe, and—who knows?—Petronius, the plain signs of the whole company of masters behind every paragraph in Carver's books?

What a nasty spectacle it is when the young nobody lashes out at an older writer who has possessed the intelligence, judgment, skill, and grace needed to attain a conspicuous rank in the literary community for four or five years. May not a work be simply there, contained in its limitations, good for what it is and awaiting others to complement it? No story can be complete. I myself do not care equally for fiction of the four writers whom Dunn admonishes, but they have their place, they are needed in the present configuration of the American mind. I do not understand this paucity of spirit that infuses the commerce of art.

Grace Paley is not mentioned in Dunn's essay. Why not? She does all the things he asks for and many more. Maybe Dunn doesn't like stories about petty Jewish shopkeepers and Puerto Rican revolutionaries. Or maybe he is just ignorant. Paley's first collection of stories, *The Little Disturbances of Man,* was published when he was eight years old, and her second, *Enormous Changes at the Last Minute,* when he was twenty-three. (He informs us in his essay that he is now thirty-four.) Myself, I refuse to make allowances for youth. If it can't educate itself—though we know it can—then let it shut up.

Paley's third book, *Later the Same Day,* has just appeared. What remarkable restraint! But then she has been busy with other things, such as raising kids, earning a living, and being very active politically. In its public aspects her life is in many ways, but especially in its reaching out to the common life, superb. And her fiction, quirky and personal though it is, does the same thing.

Political? Yes, decidedly. Thoroughly engaged. I can't think of another writer except Paul Goodman who has put political ideas, explicit political ideas, into fiction so consistently and naturally. The esthetic pattern is not only unrent but undisturbed. No demagoguery whatever; no tractating. Yet most of the people in her stories are political activists, and her own radical concerns and beliefs permeate her authorial presence, which is strong in style, idiom, imagery, external reference, statement, and so on. Nor does her political vision stop at the boundaries of the practical; like all intensely imagined political writing, her stories extend outward to the expectations of the astronaut, backward to the anxieties of Abraham.

Some stories in the new book are slight. I mean literally; they are only two or three pages long, and were not intended, I think, to be more than peeks into New York life. In the whole book they serve a function not unlike interludes on the stage. Moreover I suspect—but we won't know for years— that if it were possible to strike a "mean level of excellence" through all the stories in the new book, it would be a little lower than that of her earlier books. But at least three stories in the new collection are major in Paley's work and in our whole literature of the second half of the century. "Lavinia: An Old Story" is a monologue entirely in black speech. Not undifferentiated or stereotyped black speech either, but precisely that of an intelligent, poor, mature woman in Harlem who has made an effort to acquire at least some of the elegances of literacy—a thoroughly likable person. We have known of Paley's remarkable ear for urban folk idiom before, but this story is so acute in its rhythms and phrasings that it comes near to being a discrete verbal entity, a kind of music. How is it that a white woman can write black speech better than 99 per cent of black authors? Is this another great metaphysical or metapsychical injustice? I wouldn't be surprised.

In "Zagrowsky Tells," another and longer monologue, the speech is Jewish; and though it is one of her most expressly political stories, it is also her funniest. No one knows better than Paley how to use comedy to wrench your heart. Her humor is not simply the one-liner or the pun, as I have heard said, but much more complex, a function of character, situation, and history. She is as like to Mark Twain or Thurber as she is to Singer or Malamud.

The third story, "Friends," almost unbelievably fine, is no more than a series of conversations among a small group of women who have been friends for a long time and are brought together by the terminal illness of one of them. But everything, everything, comes out of these apparently spontaneous exchanges. An extraordinary piece of feminine writing. Not feminist, though it is that too. This story tells us more about women and what and how they feel, and in greater depth, than anything else in English I am aware of. It is a work that Americans must read—and I know exactly how unfashionable my urgency is. So be it. Let the cool bury the cool.

Critics will not find much in Paley's writing to thrash around in, to deconstruct. Ph.D. candidates will keep on hacking at John Barth and Thomas Pynchon. This may be disadvantageous to Paley's reputation in the long run, but never to Paley herself in the individuality of her authorship. Her writing is what it is, very wonderful, lucid and uncategorizable, there on the page—just the thing to present to young Mr. Dunn, may his intelligence sharpen and his manners improve. And obviously what we need now, for everyone who is unacquainted with her earlier work, is a collected edition of all Paley's stories.

David Ignatow

"The soldier is convinced that a certain interval of time, capable of being indefinitely prolonged, will be allowed him before the bullet finds him, the thief before he is caught, men in general before they have to die. This is the amulet which preserves people—and sometimes peoples—not from danger but from the fear of danger, which in certain cases allows them to brave it without actually needing to be brave." This wisdom from the world before apocalypse was written by Marcel Proust.

Poetry is "braving it." One among the many ways. If it has peculiar virtue, this must be its music, by which one does not at all mean its mellifluous syllables but rather its mythifying imagery that orchestrates the complications of existence and concentrates them. Existence as such is grotesque. It is noise. It is alien. George Gershwin, that light-hearted, light-minded man in the best sense, said: "I frequently hear music in the very heart of noise." The last poem in David Ignatow's book is called "The Image":

> The image in the mirror feels nothing
> towards him, though it is his image. He
> weeps, and it weeps with him, but is merely
> the sign of his weeping, yet he knows
> he cannot eat, drink, or make love
> without that image. He is in awe of it.
>
> Though it does not need him,
> he is its servant as he stands there,

A review of *New and Selected Poems, 1970–1985,* by David Ignatow.

doing what is necessary
to keep it in the mirror—humbled
and grateful for its presence,
that which reveals him to himself.
If there is a god, this is he.

Is god the mirror image then? Camus wrote: "God being
dead, there remain only history and power." But the poet,
growing old, knows that history is not merely error but ca-
price, the grotesque of the imagination, while power is useless
because there is nothing against which to exert it. The poet,
growing old, knows that the certain interval allowed him be-
fore his death can be prolonged only in a thought, a noisy
interfabulation of thought, a whimsical technicality. The poet
is "braving it" more and more bravely.

Music is that-which-is-almost-harmonious-but-not-quite.
The music of one's self is always a rondo, obsessions that
overlap but do not coincide, the merry-go-round of psychiat-
ric causality. Notice that the image in the mirror is not exact.
It has no depth. Its color is light, not pigment. It is an image,
not a thing. The music of the looking-glass is unnatural; it
was invented; it was invented long ago by poets, who gave
the idea to smiths and glaziers; it is wonderful music because
it simplifies and generalizes the thing that is imaged. As long
as one does not go too far—that is, as long as one remains
aware of the danger of Plato's narcissistic Ideas—this music
of self-reflectiveness is salutary in its capacity to evoke awe.
Not going too far is another term for braving it.

Oh yes, old age does awesomely compact the music! The
image seems almost evanescent, the sound of falling snow. In
the great grotesque of noise the image becomes a shocking
whisper, smaller and smaller, closer and closer, until the poet
swallows it and for a fraction of a second is conscious of silence.

Not all of Ignatow's hasty readers will respond to the music
of the last poem in his book. They will want something more
conventionally lyrical than this language that contains only
itself. (Yet there is a compelling argument for the poetry of
language that contains only itself.) Fortunately for these read-
ers, this is a big book, in effect the whole second half of Igna-

tow's lifework, the first half having been published in *Poems 1934–1969*—and of course the work is still going on. (Both this earlier collection and the present one are handsome, ample volumes. We owe many thanks to Wesleyan for this, and for the smaller books of Ignatow's poems that have been published along the way.) Plenty of incidental modulations of harmony in Ignatow's writing, as in "One Leaf," a truly splendid modern lyric poem:

> One leaf left on a branch
> and not a sound of sadness
> or despair. One leaf left
> on a branch and no unhappiness.
> One leaf all by itself
> in the air and it does not speak
> of loneliness or death.
> One leaf and it spends itself
> in swaying mildly in the breeze.

So many delicate changes leading up to the high, long vowel in "breeze"; so many just-right rhythmic variations in the interplay of four-, three-, and two-beat lines and in the runover phrasings. Poets will notice these, and will think of a song from one of Dryden's plays or a stanza in the Rubaiyat.

The thing about god is that he—or she—or it—is neither dead nor alive but *in conceptuo.* The black hole is always inverting itself, the molecule of hydrogen is always at the instant prior to the instant of its transformation.

Here is an untitled poem by Ignatow:

> Paint a wall
> cover the weather stains
> and spider webs: who's happy
>
> You who don't exist
> I make you
> out of my great need
> There is no prose for this
> no ordered syntax
> no carefully measured tread
> I am falling beyond depth

into oblivion
I hear breathing
Something must be said
of nothing

I am as queer as the conception of God
I am the god and the heaven
unless I scatter myself
among the animals and furniture of earth.

The breathing heard in oblivion, the cows at night: that's music. Otherwise the world is a disease of the retina. "The birth of the reader must be at the expense of the death of the author," wrote Roland Barthes, which seems to make the book reviewer both executioner and midwife, as he is. How revolting! But at least everyone is humming bits of music. "Without music life would be a mistake," wrote Nietzsche, who was also, like Ignatow, a great redundancer. Without music a mistake would be life.

Musical

The Spun-Off Independent
Dead-End Ten-Star Blast

I am a white artist influenced by and dependent on black American culture, and I want to say something about the place of subsidiarism in the arts in general. Some would call it parasitism, which is okay—often that's what it is, though not always. But first I must for propriety's sake assert the obvious, namely, that black culture itself is subsidiary to, not to say spat on and stomped on by, white American culture, and that an immense though not primary part of its own substance and energy derives from this, which is what we all know. For the present I need to set this aside. Black American culture is also an ethnic and esthetic mainstream in itself, partly because of the energy taken from reacting against oppressions; it is self-generated and self-sustained and now a couple of centuries old; it is a mainstream in the fullest sense. This is what I want to propound, and then against it the much smaller components of serious white culture that go along with it as subsidiary participants. Clearly I don't mean the white grifters and grafters who have profited from stealing black culture and commercializing it, Joel Chandler Harris, Elvis Presley, etc., filmmakers, agents, club-owners and all the rest, to say nothing of white landlords and storekeepers, politicans, etc. I mean the serious participants. And for the sake of simplicity I will exclude myself and all poets. We are dependent on many cultural antecedents in addition to black ones, international, national, and regional. Yet my own position vis-à-vis black culture is what has brought this topic to my mind.

I want to talk about white jazz musicians. We've had a good many great ones, but finding an instance of a white musician dependent on the black tradition who has fed anything back into that tradition is difficult—pretty nearly impossible. Lester Young once said he learned something from Frankie Trumbauer, Miles Davis obviously took certain attitudes from Gil Evans (and he has even said that because he listened to Bobby Hackett a good deal when he was young he has a connection with Bix Beiderbecke), Cecil Taylor has acknowledged a restrained early admiration for Dave Brubeck, for a while in the late thirties and forties almost every clarinetist younger than the original generation of New Orleans reed men, black or white, sounded like Benny Goodman, and one can find a few other such examples. My friend Hank O'Neal, who has listened to more jazz than anyone, thinks Coleman Hawkins may have been influenced early on by Bud Freeman, which is possible; Freeman's first record was made six months before Hawkins's first, in 1926, and three years later Hawkins recorded with the Chicago group, only the second time black and white musicians were recorded together. But has any white musician contributed a major element to the black mainstream? I doubt it. Beiderbecke, who because of his time, place, and personality may have been the greatest white innovator we've had in jazz, and who created a style, technique, and improvisational concept that were genuinely new and expressive in his time, produced almost no effect on black musicians of that time or after. You can listen to black trumpet players from Frankie Newton to Roy Eldridge, for instance, without hearing anything you can ascribe confidently to Beiderbecke. Without question this is true of the other white musicians of the middle west who responded to black jazz from New Orleans in the twenties and went on to make, from the thirties to the sixties, a style which was distinct and powerful, but which at the same time has been ignored, not to say scorned, by critics and has had practically no developmental influence on jazz as a whole. We call it Chicago jazz.

Take the most extreme comparison. The important early recordings in Chicago jazz were made at about the same time, c. 1930, as the important early recordings of Duke Ellington.

On those early records one can hear occasional crossovers of theme and style, but not many. And the progress thereafter of Chicago jazz on one hand and of Ellington on the other was miles apart—musically speaking, that is. Much of the time the two groups were located in the same city, New York. Both were playing jazz, superior jazz, but beyond that they had nothing to do with one another. Yet I would argue, and from our perspective today many would agree, that Pee Wee Russell and Wild Bill Davison ought to have been playing in the Ellington band, and that both they and the band would have benefited if this had been the case. Russell and Davison had exactly the kind of individual stylistic and textural brilliance that Ellington sought and exploited in his sidemen, and they would have added to the band voices unlike those of any other musicians at Ellington's command. Whether Russell or Davison, given their personalities, could have survived in the Ellington band is another question. Probably not. But to me the idea has a wonderful attractiveness.

Gunther Schuller in his *Early Jazz* (1968), which in spite of shortcomings remains the best scholarly book on the subject, gives one subsection to Beiderbecke, but scarcely mentions the other Chicago musicians. Throughout the book, in passing, he mentions—usually, and properly, derogatively—the Original Dixieland Jazz Band and, with mild approbation, the New Orleans Rhythm Kings. One can't complain about this; jazz is a black people's art, and Schuller's analytical history is not intended to be encyclopedic but to explicate the major developments, which are black. But good jazz is good jazz. Often I've said in literary essays that poetry is where you find it, and the same applies to jazz. It is what it is. Yet throughout the literature of jazz the Chicago period is neglected by critics, except by fanatical revivalists like Philip Larkin, who think that second-raters such as Muggsy Spanier, Danny Polo, Phil Napoleon et al., are the greatest. I don't know the whole literature; it has grown so large that no one could; but in fifty years of reading I remember no balanced discussion of Chicago jazz. Not one. Some of the Chicagoans (most of whom did not come from Chicago) were remarkable geniuses. Tastes differ, but everyone would agree on Beiderbecke, most would agree on Teschemacher, Joe Sullivan, Russell, Bunny Berigan, Art Hodes, Davison, Jess Stacey, Gene Krupa, and George Wettling, each of whom was an innovator. (Wettling carried the New Orleans drumming style of Zutty Singleton further than anyone else was ever able to.) Scores of others, musicians like Jack Teagarden, Jimmy McPartland, Bud Freeman, Bobby Hackett, Joe Marsala, and Brad Gowans, had moments of genius, perhaps a good many of them, though not enough to qualify for first rank. And then there were the scores and hundreds of fine musicians who played with spontaneity, urgency, and melodic, harmonic, and rhythmic expressiveness, and who created the *œuvre*, the body of hard-driving Chicago jazz played from 1930 to 1960 and later. Incidentally, some of the latcomers ought to be mentioned too, musicians like Ruby Braff, Bob Wilbur, and Lou McGarity, who were not heard until after 1940 but who contributed a good deal to the final development.

Chicago jazz is not Dixieland. I have written elsewhere about this distinction,[1] and all I'll say now is that jazz is original, spontaneous, authentic, and immediate. Dixieland is antiquarian, nostalgic, and almost always pedantic. Chicago jazz came from white Chicago in the era of Prohibition and the Syndicate. Al Capone was its godfather. A certain hardness and violence is characteristic, much more than in the New Orleans black music that the Chicagoans derived from. What the Chicagoans insisted on from the beginning was Swing. They originated the style and, I think, the term. (At any rate it was not originated by the "swing" musicians and arrangers of the big dance bands, both black and white, of the late thirties and forties, which were called "swing bands" but which took their ideas more from Kansas City black bands like Benny Moten's or East Coast black bands like Duke Ellington's and Fletcher Henderson's than from the white Chicagoans—to the extent that they took their ideas from jazz at all.) From the beginning you can hear a more swinging mode in the Wolver-

---

1. "Eleven Memoranda on the Culture of Jazz," *Conjunctions* 9 (1986); reprinted in *Sitting In: Selected Writings on Jazz, the Blues, and Related Topics* (Iowa City: University of Iowa Press, 1986).

ines, as in "Copenhagen" (1924), and in the early Frankie Trumbauer recordings, such as "Singing the Blues" and "Riverboat Shuffle" (both 1927 and both featuring Beiderbecke), than in the records of the same period made by King Oliver and Louis Armstrong. This was picked up and emphasized by Frank Teschemacher and the "Austin High School gang" (not all of whom attended Austin High) in 1928–30. Teschemacher wanted a sharp, rough-and-ready enthusiasm that drove everything before it. His dynamic and rhythmic inventions—such as the diminuendo chorus, a whispered holding-back, before the final tumultuous ride-out, in which he himself invariably played the clarinet's high notes flat—were all aimed toward this objective. Being in tune didn't matter, relatively speaking; loud and raucous did. And these were the primary elements of most Chicago jazz from that time until it ended, c. 1965 or 1970, whether the piece was something "purty" like "Singin' the Blues," a slow drag like "Sister Kate," a swinging blues like "Friar's Point" or "Tin Roof," or a rag/march like "Panama" or "Fidgety Feet."

A photograph exists of the 1927 Jean Goldkette band, including Beiderbecke and Trumbauer, sitting on top of a small bus operated by the Framingham Taxi Co.—astonishing that such a group could be touring New England at that time, only ten years after the country's first jazz recording by the Original Dixieland Jazz Band from New Orleans—with one of the musicians, bassist Steve Brown, sitting on the hood and flourishing what looks to me like a Colt .38 automatic.

A great deal has been made of the fact that black musicians of that time and earlier worked in brothels, barrelhouses, and other such inconducive *ateliers*. They did. But white jazz musicians worked in gin mills and speaks that weren't much better, many of them owned by the racketeers. The whites had the option if they wanted it—and at one time or another many did—of working with such orchestras as Goldkette's or Paul Whiteman's and playing at good hotels, upper-class clubs, or college proms. They earned money that way, and the money was no doubt good to have. But they did not learn their jazz with Goldkette or Whiteman; they worked it out in the joints, and the literature is full of stories of violence and mayhem among the customers. I expect many of those musicians packed a piece.

Chicago jazz, like any impulse in the arts, split into many modes, dominated by the different personalities of its leading performers. But to my mind the mode I've been describing here, the music of the speaks, expressive—to the extent that any verbal designations can be attached to music—of sex and booze, a hard communal underclass optimism that carried over from the twenties into the Depression, has been epitomized especially by Wild Bill Davison. He was born in 1906 in Ohio, formed his first band when he was in grade school, worked in a commercial dance band when he was an adolescent, played for a while in New York, then went to Chicago in about 1927, where he met Louis Armstrong, Zutty Singleton, and other black musicians from New Orleans, and also Pee Wee Russell, George Wettling, and the young white Chicagoans. Davison played with most of them, though unfortunately not on many recordings. In 1932 he formed a band to work at Guyon's Paradise with Frank Teschemacher on clarinet. Late one night in February, with Davison at the wheel, they ran into a taxi and Teschemacher was killed. (One thinks, inevitably, of what might have been. One thinks of the accident nearly twenty years later on the Pennsylvania Turnpike that killed Clifford Brown and Richie Powell, Bud Powell's younger brother.) Davison, who obviously was not called Wild Bill for nothing, went off to Milwaukee (Siberia) for about ten years. Then he moved to New York in the 1940s and began playing again with his old friends from Chicago. From 1945 until about 1970 his work became stronger and stronger. He died a couple of years ago, working occasionally until the end, though without the wind or the technique of his best years. I've heard he even quit drinking in his old age.

What Davison did for Chicago jazz is easy enough to hear. For example, his recording of "Riverboat Shuffle" for Commodore Records in about 1947. (I'm using the Commodore CD, *Jazz A-Plenty*, 1989, which maddeningly gives none of the original recording numbers or dates, though I bought the original record when it first appeared. It is now in a university library.) The band includes Pee Wee Russell on clarinet,

George Brunis on trombone, and George Wettling on drums. "Riverboat Shuffle" was originally written by Hoagy Carmichael for Bix Beiderbecke and the Wolverines in 1924 and was recorded by them for Gennett in that year; then in 1927 it was recorded for OKeh by the Trumbauer band with Beiderbecke on cornet, and this is the better of the two early recordings. The tune has two themes, minor and major, the second of which has a two-bar break at the end of each eight-bar segment. On the Trumbauer recording these breaks are taken by Eddie Lang on guitar, Irving Riskin on piano, and Don Murray on clarinet—nothing spectacular. Beiderbecke takes the final break of the first chorus and leads immediately into his solo, which is the only reason for listening to the record. He does all the things he was famous for, the upward rips, the hard high notes, the descending softer figures, and he builds his solo with much more complexity and fluidity than was common in that period, using long phrases within the essential eight-bar structure; only Louis Armstrong, from whom Beiderbecke learned, could do as well in 1927; and remember that Beiderbecke had learned from Armstrong in person, before the revolutionary Hot Five recordings of 1926. The rest of "Riverboat Shuffle," until the final chorus, is dismal; even Trumbauer, usually reliable, does poorly. In the final out-chorus Beiderbecke leads the ensemble vigorously, overcoming the ineptitudes of the other musicians.

Davison, who began his professional career only three or four years later than Beiderbecke, learned more from Beiderbecke than from anyone else, and his "Riverboat Shuffle" is an intentional tribute to his teacher. But it is by no means an imitation. Davison takes all the stop-time breaks himself, for instance, but does not give himself a solo chorus. He does many things that resemble Beiderbecke's playing, but he never exactly reproduces them (as so many Dixielanders do), and he intensifies them by a factor of about a hundred. Beiderbecke's held high tones were vigorous but pure in intonation and timbre; Davison's are rough, off-key, seemingly random blasts in the upper register—they are shrieks. Davison's low tones are much more growly than Beiderbecke's, his slurred tones are wider and longer, his pacing more varied and further from the beat. He drives harder. And he has his own maneuvers too, especially the screaming upward glissando that hits its top note like the crack of a whip. His technique is heavy, rough, impudent, yet astonishingly agile. In effect Davison brought the spirit of white Chicago jazz to its peak and did it with musical perfection and the total absorption and enthusiasm that are characteristic of all great artists in every medium. Listen to him, and see.

In the meantime, while Davison was at the top of his form, the bop revolution came and went, the cool revolution as well, and black jazz musicians were into the post-bop experiments and modifications of Charlie Mingus, John Coltrane, Ornette Coleman, Albert Ayler, and others. I don't know what these men thought of Davison. They certainly dismissed him and may have despised him. Although one can find components of their music that might have been taken from him, clearly none were—they came from other and black antecedents. Now, with the deaths of the original Chicagoans, Chicago jazz has long since passed from the scene, without—if you don't count the thousands of people who love it and rely on it in shaping their sensibilities—leaving a trace. And this leads me to three generalizations.

First, the art that leaves no influence is no less an art on that account. It's hard to think of analogues to Chicago jazz vis-à-vis mainstream black jazz. At the beginning of this essay I called it subsidiarism, but spin-offism might be a more descriptive term, the case of a movement in art that evolves naturally enough from the mainstream but then branches off, runs parallel for a while, achieves its own artistic integrity and significance, but finally dies without ever producing an effect on the primary line of development. In fact I have been thinking about this for a week or more, and I cannot come up with a single other example in the history of any art, an example of an appreciable community of artists which attains a significant level of achievement but then departs without leaving a significant influence. Individuals, yes; Ambrose Bierce in American literature, Georgia O'Keefe in American painting. But the only movements I can think of that have followed this pattern have been crack-pot obtrusions achieving nothing. (Yet in religion one can think of many important heresies that died or were wiped out without reentering their parent theologies, but which left meaningful effects in the broader culture.) Nevertheless it is possible; a group can move out, create something fine, and die—right out at the end of the track. And Chicago jazz, so distinct, is the proof. Not that there weren't crossovers and affinities. The jazz associated with Fats Waller and other such small black groups in the thirties was not far from the spirit of Chicago. Waller himself and many other black musicians—from Coleman Hawkins in 1928 to Vic Dickenson in 1980—performed both live and on record with the Chicagoans. But in impulse, attitude, and style the Chicagoans had their own music.

Second, as jazz has evolved toward the present, I expect white influence on black musicians has increased, especially as from individual to individual. It would be surprising if such fine white musicians as Chet Baker, Zoot Sims, Charlie Haden, and Steve Lacy, for example, hadn't been listened to carefully by young musicians of both races. And today if you ask young conservatory-trained black musicians whether or not they've been influenced by white musicians, my guess is they'll say, "Naturally—just as we've been influenced by Asian musicians, Arabic musicians, rock musicians, and all musicians." Of course they'd be talking, with respect to whites, primarily about "classical" musicians, and not Stravinsky and Bartók either, but Adams and Reich. A general rapprochement has occurred; music is music, advanced music is advanced music—refined, as we say, further from the folk roots—and the question of race has become moot. It's interesting—though I am distinctly of two minds about it—that this has happened not as much through social and political processes as through the music itself.

Third, for a long time we've been putting too much emphasis on the new, and we've now reached the point at which the new has run out. We have reached absurdity. In jazz we have run the whole course from primitivism to sophistication to academicism and preciosity in less than a hundred years, thanks to the technology of recording. Records give us the old, meaning what was done last year, in such concrete permanent form that musicians have naturally been impelled to do something different right away. But the course has ended. And the course was perhaps not such a good idea to begin with. Jazz musicians are universally graded by critics on their novelty. A. B. Spellman, in his *Four Lives in the Bebop Business* (1966, 1985), chooses his four biographies, Cecil Taylor, Ornette Coleman, Herbie Nichols, and Jackie McLean, because he believes each of them did something that older bop musicians—not much older—had not yet done. They made "progress." (Some of them called their work "progressive jazz.") Spellman refers to jazz before bop as "social music." Well, I hope all music is social, but that isn't what Spellman means. He means that earlier jazz musicians often had to play in dance bands to make their livings. But is he talking about the likes of Sidney Bechet, Henry Allen, Chu Berry, Joe Venutti, Charlie Christian, Art Tatum? Is he placing these serious artists on the plane of T. Dorsey and G. Lombardo? This is nonsense. In his essay called "The Passing of Jazz's Old Guard," which is reprinted in his *Tuxedo Junction* (1989), Gerald Early writes about Charles Mingus, Thelonious Monk, and Sonny Stitt. Is it only because I was born in 1921, the year in which Mamie Smith recorded "Crazy Blues" and started the whole business of recorded black jazz, that I cannot think of these men as "Jazz's Old Guard"? Jazz did not begin in 1942. Nor did it begin in 1982, as some young people today believe. No one knows exactly when it did begin, as a matter of fact, but it has been going since 1910 or earlier and has always been real jazz—if that isn't a redundancy.

Nowadays when I go down to Sakura's in Syracuse I hear a young guy who can do circular breathing perfectly, he can do it for hours if anyone wants him to, he can play three saxophones at the same time, loudly, and he can play not only the changes on "My Funny Valentine," but the changes on the changes, and the changes on the changes on the changes, a mathematical tizzy. And I ask myself why he doesn't just relax and play some jazz. The truth is he can't; both his training and the pressures exerted on him by current fashion have destroyed his ability to invent a counter-melody worth a damn.

In all the arts I see people struggling, usually in an academic milieu, to discover some novelty of form, structure, concept, or style which will permit them to qualify as the avant-garde, but I do not see them succeeding, except in the most pedantic, uninteresting, feelingless ways. In both reason and practice we know that unending novelty is impossible. No one can foresee what the extended future may bring in jazz, or in painting or literature, but in the shorter view the age of experiment is over. The time demands recapitulation, not innovation. This doesn't mean direct imitativeness of the past—not at all. It means an honest and creative regard for tradition, including recent tradition, it means going back and filling in the gaps that were passed over in the onrush of recorded progress, restoring connections, reviving combinations, as Branford Marsalis does, for example, in his best work. And anyway, hasn't newness in the arts always been essentially a matter, not of calculated or conceptual change, but of personality, both individual and collective? The *dolce stil nuovo* was not engineered in a workshop; it was derived intuitively from the sensibilities of half a dozen northern Italian poets who had certain traditions, old Latin and new Provençal, floating in their heads and sounding in their ears.

It would be great if we could quit listening to so many records and hear live jazz instead. In a city like Syracuse, with a metropolitan population of 750,000, we ought to have six or eight places where we could go regularly to hear different kinds of jazz, not just the one-and-a-half actually here, and we ought to be able to sit comfortably and listen to the music without being deafened by overamplification. I can think of a good many reasons why this may be impossible, why it may never happen again. And I won't give up my records for anything. But I do think in our music—and in our poetry, painting, film, and all the arts—we must, at least for a while, just relax and play some jazz.

Anthems

My friend David Budbill has just sent me (10 September 1989) a copy of the Armstrong recording of Handy's blues, as I had asked him to. I don't know what happened to my copy; I haven't heard it for years. The title is *Louis Armstrong Plays W. C. Handy* (Columbia 591), which I think was originally made in the early fifties. The band included Barney Bigard on clarinet, who was with the Ellington band when I was a kid, c. 1937; Trummy Young on trombone, who was in the Lunceford outfit; Billy Kyle on piano, who played with John Kirby's small band; Arvell Shaw, bass, another relative old-timer; Barrett Deems, drums, whom I don't remember. Vocals are by Velma Middleton and Armstrong, and of course Armstrong plays the trumpet lead.

What a record it is. It should be required listening in every freshman course in the country. These numbers are at the heart of the American tradition, in both substance and manner of performance. Granted, already when I was a boy W. C. Handy was referred to snootily as a poor musician and was accused of "stealing" his compositions from black folk sources and getting rich on them. Well, at least he was black himself, which ought to make it better than what Stephen Foster or Louis Gottschalk did, to say nothing of outright thieves like Sophie Tucker and Al Jolson. As to the former charge, I remember once hearing some very old dim recordings of the Handy band from the late teens or early twenties, and they were awful. Truly. Quite as awful as the Original Dixieland Jazz Band, which was white, from the same period. But what difference does it make? People have said more or less the same things about Armstrong too, as a matter of fact, i.e., that he turned himself into an entertainer at the expense of his musicianship and that he wasn't all that great a trumpet player to begin with. There's enough truth in the business about Armstrong being an entertainer to make it a perennial source of disquiet to all of us, but otherwise this is nonsense. Armstrong was a remarkably talented musician whose early influence was crucial to the development of jazz; the proof is in the listening, especially to the records of the Hot 5 and Hot 7 from the late twenties, and if that's not enough the discussion of Armstrong by Gunther Schuller in his *Early Jazz*, (1968, pp. 89–133 et passim), ought to convince anyone. Armstrong's work in the latter part of his life was perhaps not technically as far advanced beyond his early work as one might wish. But he still was a vigorous, imaginative trumpet player. The others on the recording of Handy's blues were vigorous musicians too, although Bigard was always more of a noodler than a real musician. It's mainline jazz, of course. But these people were not Dixielanders and the music really swings.

What I'm saying is that the time has come to forget all this carping. Young musicians of the fifties, sixties, and seventies had some reason to associate Handy and Armstrong with Uncle Tomism, but we have gone beyond that now. At any rate I believe we should have. My students, black or white, don't know any of the numbers on the recording in question, except perhaps "St. Louis Blues" in some dressed-up version by the Boston Pops. They have never heard of Handy. If they recognize Armstrong's voice at all, it's from hearing "Hello, Dolly" on a tape-loop in the supermarket. Yet these blues—ascribed to Handy, whatever he may or may not have contributed to them; at least he had the gumption to collect and organize them, as Robert Burns collected and organized Scottish folksongs— have more historical and cultural significance in American civilization than all but a very, very few other pieces of music. This is basic. Why can't Handy's blues now be included in the repertoire of contemporary musicians? If John Lewis can do so wonderfully with J. S. Bach, why can't he apply his imagination and sensitivity to W. C. Handy? And I'd love to hear the World Saxophone Quartet do some of Handy's blues and other such numbers from the depth of the tradition. As T. S. Eliot and many others have said about literature, the tradition needs to be added to continually, and we can't do that if we are simply neglecting it.

I know I'd a hell of a lot rather hear "St. Louis Blues"—or "Memphis Blues" or "Yellow Dog Blues" or almost any other blues by W. C. Handy—at the beginning of a ball game than "The Star-Spangled Banner," that rigid musical inanity. Are Handy's lyrics inappropriate for a national anthem? Maybe. Maybe if I were rich I'd offer a fat prize to the poet who could come up with the best alternative lyrics; Handy's lyrics are not as important, and not as well rooted in the folk idiom, as the musical parts of his work. Alas, I'm not rich. But otherwise the idea of having new lyrics seems to me perfectly feasible. Let's bombard Congress with it.

Moreover why must we have only one anthem? Why not five or six? We could have a piece by Foster, one by Joplin, one by Handy, and others by Ellington, Monk, Ives, and Copland. Me, I'd throw in Horace Silver and Cannonball Adderley as well. Let's have a round dozen anthems, all of which are taught to children in grade school, together with something about their importance. If anybody really wants "The Star-Spangled Banner," okay, include that too. But let it take its place in the rotation.

Ben Webster

When I was in high school in 1936, "Lady Be Good" by Count Basie and a small group, the recording that set us all on our ears, was issued. Bill Basie himself was on piano, Lester Young on tenor, Buck Clayton on trumpet, with Walter Page, bass, and Jo Jones, drums. (Freddy Green, who usually played guitar for Basie, was not on this date.) It was the first of a long succession of records by small groups that Basie made over the years, which were—and are—almost invariably more interesting than records by the Basie big band, though it was the big band that paid for the small groups. What interested us the most in 1936 was the two-chorus improvisation by Lester Young, especially the second chorus. This seemed to us remarkably new, different, original, and complex. Compared to what we had been listening to, which had been essentially derived from Armstrong and Beiderbecke of the late twenties, it was. Both rhythmically and melodically, and perhaps even in a few places harmonically, Young did things that had not been done before. We memorized his solo, we even taught it to the eight-year-old brother of one of my friends and had him stand on a glass-topped table in the drug store and sing it. It became a standard for us, against which to measure all jazz performances for a number of years. And of course we paid a lot of attention to Young from that time on, his work with Basie, his playing behind Billie Holiday on her early records, his few recordings on small labels such as Commodore, etc. We studied the Prez, as we called him, with love. We took delight in the way he sat with his legs crossed, holding his horn almost horizontally, the mouthpiece twisted sideways. We smiled knowingly at one another when he hit those blatting low notes in the midst of an up-tempo number, and some of us knew that he probably had taken this idea from Boyce Brown, the alto player (known as the "Mad Monk," because he abandoned his horn and joined a monastery) from Chicago. We were fascinated by stories—which is all we had, since most of us were too poor to hear him in person—of how at the end of the night he took over the Basie band and directed long, wildly swinging sessions on the stand.

We paid so much attention to Young that we scarcely noticed another tenor player from Kansas City who had come to New York earlier than Young with the Bennie Moten band, the outfit which had generated so much of what we used to call the Kansas City or western style, and who then had worked in the Fletcher Henderson band, recorded with small groups led by Teddy Wilson and others, and played on a few of the early Billie Holiday records too. Of course I mean Ben Webster. When I listen to those early Holiday records now, I wonder why I didn't hear at the time that Webster was playing better accompaniment, often, than Young. I didn't. In 1940 Webster joined the Duke Ellington band where he worked with such outstanding musicians as Ray Nance, Johnny Hodges, Harry Carney, Tricky Sam Nanton, Jimmy Blanton, etc., to say nothing of Ellington himself and his collaborator Billy Strayhorn. But many of the most famous recordings Webster made with Ellington, such as "Cottontail" and "Black, Brown, and Beige," were produced during the war, and I didn't hear them until afterward. The same is true of a wonderful record Webster made with a small group under the leadership of James P. Johnson in 1944, a twelve-inch Blue Note with "Joy Mentin'," a medium-tempo blues, on one side, and "After You've Gone" on the other. The rest of the musicians on that date were Sidney de Paris, trumpet; Vic Dickenson, trombone; Jimmy Shirley, guitar; John Simmons, bass; Sid Catlett, drums; and Johnson on piano. All were in good form that day, March 4, 1944, but Webster was superb, especially in the two-chorus improvisation on "After You've Gone." I bought the record in Chicago in 1946, almost forty-five years ago, and have been listening to it ever since. Maybe, from time to time, six months have gone by without my hearing it, but I think never more than that, and I have not tired of it. Thirty years after I first heard the record, when I was writing *The Sleeping Beauty,* I was still so impressed by it that I put a section about it in the poem.

I wrote: "What matters was oneness, the abstract made personal in a tone." I know no other jazz musician of any time who has been as successful as Webster at imbuing his music with feeling, directly, without the interposition of any technique whatever, either instrumental or compositional. Some have come close, but none equals Webster. And most musicians don't even try—they're not interested. Webster had plenty of technique, obviously. He could make his instrument and his sensibility do anything he wanted them to. (What he didn't want wasn't of concern to him.) He played with an enormous dynamic and textural range, from soft purring passages to growls to shrieks; his phrasing was extremely varied, from sequences of staccato blips and bleats to long fluid sentences; his articulation could be lightning fast (listen to the break in the middle of his second chorus of "After You've Gone," which no one has been able to notate for me) or so intensely drawn out that it becomes painful; his rhythmic usage was very flexible, so that he played from far in front of the beat to far behind it; and he was the only jazz musician, as far as I know, who has ever used unvoiced breath-sounds as an integral part of his music. What all this amounts to is not only that no practical distinction existed between his body and his horn—this can be said of many musicians—but that his horn-body was charged to an extraordinary, almost unimaginable degree with feeling—spontaneous, unmediated emotion. And he came just at the right time in the evolution of jazz to turn this into the utmost expressiveness.

He was a big man, proud and irascible. He was unable to keep a job for long, and unlike many of the best musicians who worked for Ellington and stayed in the band nearly all their professional lives, he left after a few years. After 1945 he never worked in a large organization again, but did pick-up gigs, odd record dates, and led small groups for club engagements, usually brief. He was married for a while, but treated his wife and other women badly; yet he lived with his mother and his aunt for some years in California, and faithfully supported and attended them in their old age. When he played, tears would take form on his cheeks. In the ardor of improvisation he normally closed his eyes, but his eyelids would open briefly from time to time, showing his eyes unfocused, turned aside like a blind man's, or sometimes rolled up into his head like a woman's at the height of sexual ecstasy.

He could be a violent man, a wild bar-fighter, known as someone to stay away from when he'd been drinking. Much of the time he was a solitary man. Yet he had close friendships with other musicians, such as Jimmy Blanton and Milt Hinton.

A deep fount of emotion existed inside Webster. No one knows why. It can't be accounted for by the experience of being black in America, which could not have been much worse for him than it was for thousands of other musicians. Something in his early conditioning or genetic makeup, or probably both, made him especially vulnerable. We shall never know what it was. This is what accounts for his anger, occasional ferocity, loyalty, loneliness, awareness of beauty— his passion. And it is all there in the music. I never met Webster, and I never even saw him, except on film. But I feel I know him better than I know people I see every day.

This fusion of emotion and form is what accounts for all success in the arts and what I have striven for in my own poetry. If it is true to say, as we did so confidently thirty years ago, that "form follows function," then what distinguishes artistic form from technological form is the self-evident verity that artistic function is equivalent to feeling. And the more passionate the feeling, the more complex and unified the form.

Webster was a musician's musician. He never enjoyed much popularity with the larger audience, he never made much money, and at times he went without work for longish periods, partly because he refused to work with musicians he didn't respect and partly because he generally wouldn't work for less than he thought he was worth, which was three times union scale. His friend Milt Hinton, the great bassist, who put him up at his home in Brooklyn for months, complained that while he, Hinton, was accepting every gig and recording date offered to him and was going into Manhattan practically every day and night, Webster stayed at home, refused most offers, and brought in little money. Nevertheless Webster was highly respected for his originality and intensity, and worked with the best musicians of his era. He can be heard on many famous recordings, such as the one of Billie Holiday singing "Fine and Mellow" on that live TV show in the fifties. When he needed to put together a group of his own for a record or club date, he always attracted great sidemen. Gerry Mulligan, the prominent baritone sax player from the bop period, asked Webster to join him in one of the series of recorded saxophone duos he originated, and it remains the best in the series—the new reissue of it on CD, which contains several cuts not previously released, is well worth having. We possess, in fact, a pretty good representation of Webster on records, thanks to his friends. One can't say we have enough, but we have records made over forty years in all possible musical environments, reflecting Webster in many moods, many variations of expressiveness.

Nevertheless in 1964, when it became impossible for him to make a living in the United States, he moved to Europe where he remained for the rest of his life, chiefly in Holland and Denmark. He died in September 1973 in relative obscurity.

Webster by his own account learned music from listening to the blues in bars around Kansas City. He played piano before sax, and I have a copy of a homemade tape of him doing a bad stride style on the piano in the basement of Milt Hinton's house, somewhat in the manner of Pete Johnson. Budd Johnson once claimed to have given Webster his first saxophone lessons in Amarillo sometime around 1926 or so, but I don't know if that's reliable. Probably Webster learned much of his technique from Benny Carter (whom he greatly respected all his life) and Coleman Hawkins in the Henderson band during the thirties, and from Johnny Hodges in the Ellington band during the early forties. He is said to have had a special affection for the music of Art Tatum, and I think I can detect in his work some elements of phrasing that he may have picked up, probably unconsciously, from the great pianist. But no musician before him and certainly none after him has played the tenor in a way even remotely resembling Ben Webster's. I think a few later musicians learned something from him perhaps, such musicians as Rahsan Roland Kirk and Albert Ayler, but they learned more from Ornette Coleman and others, and they had the good sense not to try to imitate Webster. He stood alone. He belonged to no school or movement. Even when he played in the Ellington band and was to some extent identified with it, Webster's style was his own, decidedly, as Ellington recognized; using the distinctive styles of his sidemen was part of Ellington's genius. Webster's life extended across the history of jazz from the early thirties to the late sixties, from late New Orleans to Chicago to western to swing to bop to post-bop, and although he worked with musicians in all these sectors, he retained his own way of playing throughout. I say "way of playing" instead of "style" because, I repeat, it is less a matter of musical traits, which many musicians of all kinds develop in their work and which can be notated or oscillographed and studied, than of emotion—emotion concentrated and intensified. Nor am I talking about what we used to call "soul." Soul is a racial quality—I think everyone would agree on that—whereas I am convinced that Webster's music, granted it was jazz and that jazz is in part a social phenomenon and has its roots in African-American consciousness, was personal.

In his book about the cultural underground, *Down and In* (1987), Ronald Sukenick quotes Yoram Kaniuk, who was an Isreali painter and writer living in New York in the fifties and a friend of Charlie Parker's. Sukenick interviewed Kaniuk years later in Tel Aviv:

> "There was a jam session somewhere around Waverly Place in a sort of warehouse," remembers Kaniuk. "We used to have this kind of jam session that lasted two or three days. Ben Webster came, and Miles Davis was very young, and Charlie Parker. And there were others of course, Charlie Mingus, many played, but as it developed something happened. A contest started between Ben Webster, Charlie Parker, and Miles Davis. It was three generations fighting for something. And it was at a time when Charlie Parker was changing his music, he was putting some classical music in it, he was influenced by, I think, Bartók. And Miles was then also trying to break out of Bop. Ben was still playing the old thing. It was a moment in

time when things were changing and we didn't understand it. And it happened without our knowing it. And they were playing, they were angry and loving one another."

This was in the fifties, probably the early fifties, though the event is not dated in Sukenick's book. And maybe it actually happened, this "jam session" in which the musicians were "angry" and "loving," though some aspects of Kaniuk's account seem exaggerated to me. But music does change and people— musicians—are the ones who change it. What pains me about this reminiscence is, first, the implied attribution of an antagonistic relationship between the "old" and the "new" music, aside from the musicians, and second, the assignment of ideological values to music.

These things do happen. They are part of the cultural process. Nobody can do anything about it. But still we must point out, determinedly and repeatedly, that music is music. When the Beat writers, Kerouac, Ginsberg, etc., took to Bop in the fifties as a reinforcement of what they wanted to do in literature, they understood the music no better than most writers understand most music, as Amiri Baraka recognized in his published criticism at the time. The analogue between Bop and Beat was very tenuous. It was a little absurd. I hear some of this same absurdity in Yoram Kaniuk's remembrance of the session with Webster, Parker, and Davis; indeed I hear it throughout Sukenick's book whenever music is mentioned (and painting too, for that matter), and this gives the book a dated quality—which may be appropriate for a memoir. But now the cultural rags and tags of the fifties and sixties have fallen away from Webster, Parker, and Davis, and their musics exist in themselves and on records for us to hear. There is no antagonism among them. We can see that Webster's "old thing" is in some ways more advanced than what Parker and Davis were doing at that time, and in any case they are all contemporary with one another and with great musicians of every time. Means exist, aside from personal taste, by which we can confidently assert that they are all good musics, but none by which we may deem one of them "better" than the others. They stand independently in terms of quality. Does it matter that at one time extraneous cultural value was imputed to them? Perhaps not. But it seems to me that since then this practice has become only more pervasive, all through the many stages and branches of rock and fusion, until in the eighties we came to New Age music, which is ninety-nine per cent cultural and one per cent musical, if that. Meanwhile jazz has been split off from its audience and finds itself in about the same isolation as contemporary "classical" music, including the "minimalist music" of such composers as Reich, Adams, Duckworth, Glass, etc., whose work doubtless influenced Cookie culture and New Age music, though it cannot be blamed for them. A sad outcome.

Of course it's important to recognize cultural procedures and understand them. It's important to know that a connection exists between the music of Handel, the philosophy of Vico, and the French and Indian War. At the moment I am writing this—a frightening moment—it's important to recognize that at least some connection exists between the actions of Saddam Hussein and the treatment of Arabs by Europeans for the past thousand years. But as musicians and listeners we are also entitled to take our music plain, i.e., in and of itself.

Is the intensified feeling I have ascribed to Webster's music a part of the music? I argue that it is, that it is inherent. Earlier I gave it names, "anger," "loneliness," etc., but these were for convenience. Actually it has no literary cognates. Call it what you will—undifferentiated esthetic arousal, for instance—feeling in music is musical feeling, expressed only in music, in pitch, harmony, rhythm, dynamics, and timbre. This was Webster's feeling. I don't say it isn't allied to moral and psychological feeling, but it isn't the same. What Webster did with his horn was music, everything he did with his horn was music, you can't call it anything else. And it was suffused with emotional intensity.

What did Webster actually do? Once a friend and I compared two recordings of "Nancy with the Laughing Face," one by Webster, the other by John Coltrane. Coltrane was a brilliant improviser, but he was also a bop musician; he came out of that movement and retained some of its musical traits. For instance, he frequently interjected rapid little figures, essentially meaningless, between phrases or between major statements, and he often changed registers in the midst of an improvisation, even in the midst of a phrase. I could never see the point in this, though many musicians have done it. What does it mean, beyond a certain virtuosity? Webster played the tune almost straight, without much decoration or melodic deviation. To make the piece moving he relied on phrasing—alterations of lyric timing against the beat—and a whole range of textures and dynamics, through which musical feeling is expressed. Neither of these performances represents Webster or Coltrane at his best, but the contrast between them is instructive.

This is what Webster usually did. He played the melody or, more often, a countermelody invented by himself, many of them very beautiful, and he gave his playing urgency by employing an extraordinary breadth of tonal, textural, and rhythmic expedients. He did not play the changes. In this respect, though they were friends and worked together and doubtless learned from each other, Webster and Coleman Hawkins were at opposite poles. When you analyze a typical solo by Hawkins, you hear a sequence of scales or arpeggios modulated over the basic chord changes. Sometimes I think that when Hawkins discovered, a long time ago, that you can get through the changes of a slow ballad by playing a repeated, chromatically descending figure, he did jazz a disservice from which it has never recovered, but of course if he hadn't, someone else would have. (Years later Parker elaborated it.) Hawkins played with great verve and a wonderfully bold, open tone, and he was popular and influential all his life. But to my ear his work is neither as interesting nor as moving as Webster's, not anywhere near.

If a jazz improvisation is its performer's personality, as Duke Ellington once said, then Ben Webster was one of the greatest personalities in all American art of the twentieth century. I would put him alongside William Carlos Williams, Edward Hopper, and Frank Lloyd Wright. If a jazz improvisation is primarily a phenomenon of black culture, then I would say—if I have a right to, and I think I have—that Ben Webster, beginning with the blues and developing everything implicit in them, gave us the single most expressive articulation of African-American experience and feeling in our civilization. Yes, speaking for myself, I would place him above Bessie Smith, Langston Hughes, Billie Holiday, June Jordan, Toni Morrison, or anyone else. Many people will say, "How absurd!" They will say that such comparative judgments are misleading and invidious. I agree. But at the same time I have been listening to jazz for just short of sixty years, and I believe that an opinion like this one, supported by such reasons as I have given, is worth imparting, for both its general and its particular significance. Listen to Ben Webster. The longer you listen, the more appreciative you will become—I can almost guarantee it, whatever your tastes may be. You will continually discover new subtleties of feeling in his work. They are there, along with many things that aren't subtle at all and require no sophisticated study. Ben Webster was one of the truly great. Everyone needs his music.

UNDER DISCUSSION
Donald Hall, General Editor

Volumes in the Under Discussion series collect reviews and essays about individual poets. The series is concerned with contemporary American and English poets about whom the consensus has not yet been formed and the final vote has not been taken. Titles in the series include:

Elizabeth Bishop and Her Art
edited by Lloyd Schwartz and Sybil P. Estess

Richard Wilbur's Creation
edited and with an Introduction by Wendy Salinger

Reading Adrienne Rich
edited by Jane Roberta Cooper

On the Poetry of Allen Ginsberg
edited by Lewis Hyde

Robert Bly: When Sleepers Awake
edited by Joyce Peseroff

Robert Creeley's Life and Work
edited by John Wilson

On the Poetry of Galway Kinnell
edited by Howard Nelson

On Louis Simpson
edited by Hank Lazer

Anne Sexton
edited by Steven E. Colburn

James Wright
edited by Peter Stitt and Frank Graziano

Frank O'Hara
edited by Jim Elledge

On the Poetry of Philip Levine
edited by Christopher Buckley

Forthcoming volumes will examine the work of Langston Hughes, Muriel Rukeyser, H.D., and Denise Levertov, among others.

Please write for further information on available editions and current prices.

Ann Arbor   **The University of Michigan Press**